Theories and Strategies for Teaching Creative Writing Online

As the online world of creative writing teaching, learning, and collaborating grows in popularity and necessity, this book explores the challenges and unique benefits of teaching creative writing online.

This collection highlights expert voices who have taught creative writing effectively in the online environment, to broaden the conversation regarding online education in the discipline, and to provide clarity for English and writing departments interested in expanding their offerings to include online creative writing courses but doing so in a way that serves students and the discipline appropriately.

Interesting as it is useful, *Theories and Strategies for Teaching Creative Writing Online* offers a contribution to creative writing scholarship and begins a vibrant discussion specifically regarding effectiveness of online education in the discipline.

Tamara Girardi is Assistant Professor of English at HACC, Central Pennsylvania's Community College in their Virtual Learning unit, where she teaches exclusively online. Her primary research interests are creative writing studies, young adult literature, and online education. Dr. Girardi is also an editor for the Digital, Multimodal, and Multimedia section of the *Journal of Creative Writing Studies*. She writes children's literature.

Abigail G. Scheg currently serves as a Styling Team Lead for Stitch Fix. She has taught online and face to face at multiple institutions as well as serving as an administrator in academic and student service roles.

Routledge Studies in Creative Writing

Series Editors: Graeme Harper (Oakland University, USA) and Dianne Donnelly (University of South Florida, USA)

Strategies of Silence
Reflections on the Practice and Pedagogy of Creative Writing
Edited by Moy McCrory and Simon Heywood

Theories and Strategies for Teaching Creative Writing Online
Edited by Tamara Girardi and Abigail G. Scheg

For more information about this series, please visit: https://www.routledge.com/Routledge-Studies-in-Creative-Writing/book-series/RSCW

Theories and Strategies for Teaching Creative Writing Online

Edited by
Tamara Girardi and Abigail G. Scheg

LONDON AND NEW YORK

First published 2021
by Routledge
2 Park Square, Milton Park, Abingdon, Oxon OX14 4RN

and by Routledge
605 Third Avenue, New York, NY 10158

Routledge is an imprint of the Taylor & Francis Group, an informa business

© 2021 selection and editorial matter, Tamara Girardi and Abigail G. Scheg; individual chapters, the contributors

The right of Tamara Girardi and Abigail G. Scheg to be identified as the authors of the editorial material, and of the authors for their individual chapters, has been asserted in accordance with sections 77 and 78 of the Copyright, Designs and Patents Act 1988.

All rights reserved. No part of this book may be reprinted or reproduced or utilised in any form or by any electronic, mechanical, or other means, now known or hereafter invented, including photocopying and recording, or in any information storage or retrieval system, without permission in writing from the publishers.

Trademark notice: Product or corporate names may be trademarks or registered trademarks, and are used only for identification and explanation without intent to infringe.

British Library Cataloguing-in-Publication Data
A catalogue record for this book is available from the British Library

Library of Congress Cataloging-in-Publication Data
Names: Girardi, Tamara, 1981- editor. | Scheg, Abigail G., 1986- editor.
Title: Theories and strategies for teaching creative writing online / edited by Tamara Girardi and Abigail G. Scheg.
Description: London ; New York : Routledge, 2021. |
Series: Routledge studies in creative writing | Includes bibliographical references and index.
Identifiers: LCCN 2020048272 |
Subjects: LCSH: English language–Rhetoric–Study and teaching–Computer-assisted instruction. | Creative writing–Study and teaching–Computer-assisted instruction. | Web-based instruction.
Classification: LCC PE1404 .T4725 2021 | DDC 808/.0420785–dc23
LC record available at https://lccn.loc.gov/2020048272

ISBN: 978-0-367-89526-6 (hbk)
ISBN: 978-0-367-75611-6 (pbk)
ISBN: 978-1-003-01984-8 (ebk)

Typeset in Sabon
by Taylor & Francis Books

Contents

List of illustrations		vii
List of contributors		ix

1 Don't short circuit the muse: Creative writing in the digital age   1
   AMY WITHROW

2 Teaching creative writing online without tears: Discovering the many ways online and creative writing best practices overlap to enhance digital learning   10
   STEPHANIE VANDERSLICE

3 When the way you read is who you are: Developing the teacherly persona for teaching creative writing online   17
   PATRICK BIZZARO AND TAMARA GIRARDI

4 Making the write impression: How to use written materials to boost rapport and connectivity in online creative writing classes   31
   PAUL GLEED

5 Navigating trauma in the online creative writing classroom   41
   LARAINE HERRING

6 Software and hardware tools for teaching creative writing and self-editing online   57
   LEX WILLIFORD

7 Zoom in and Zoom out: Virtual creative writing classroom pedagogy using Zoom   71
   NICOLE ANAE

8 Digital pedagogy in the online creative writing classroom: An integrative, interdisciplinary approach   88
   CYNTHIA PENGILLY

9 Designing peer review: Research and intentional practices for
   effective online creative writing workshops   101
   LORI OSTERGAARD AND MARSHALL KITCHENS

10 Taking the poetry exercise online   119
   CARRIE ETTER

11 A sense of openness: Using individual student blogs in online
   creative writing courses   129
   LUCY BIEDERMAN

12 Motivate, accommodate, and emulate: The 30-Day Writing
   Challenge in an online creative writing classroom   139
   SARAH LAYDEN

13 Using flash fiction as a pedagogical tool in teaching creative writing
   online   149
   ASHLEY JAE CARRANZA

   Index   164

Illustrations

Figures

2.1 Diagram illustrating AWP Hallmarks for undergraduate creative writing   12
6.1 Writing sample   58
7.1 Screen-snip of commentary posted on a weekly forum via the course Moodle site—an open-source Learning Platform (LP) or course management system (CMS)—by a student (Student A) who could not attend a ZoomLive session in real-time (synchronously). Note, in this case, in responding to the feedback of peers, Student A herself alludes to the polyphonic dimensions underlying the online creative writing pedagogy utilized in this course; one having "many voices," and indeed, inspiring various "texts which are not dominated by a single narrative or authorial authority" (Hunt, 2006: 179)   74
7.2 Students could use the "Zoom Tip-Sheet for Collaborative Feedback" to assist them in organizing their peer feedback along conceptual, literary lines. This example is one student's response to a children's fairytale using elements of postmodernism as literary experimentation   76
7.3 Screen-snip of a ZoomLive session with students   77
7.4 In this screen-snip of a ZoomLive session with students, the course coordinator has shared her desktop to display the collaborative feedback document with all participants, including commentary. Note, in this case, the student's (Student C) use of a Newspaper headline generator to add intertextual elements within the piece   81
7.5 In this screen-snip of a ZoomLive session with students, the course coordinator has once again shared her desktop to display the collaborative feedback document with all participants, including commentary. Note, in this case, the student's (C) combined use of a Newspaper headline generator, as well as her use of Word.Art—an online word cloud creator—to add two separate, but interrelated, intertextual elements within the piece: graphic and concrete   82

7.6 Example of the storyboard Student C created to accompany her story 83
8.1 "Desaparecido" written and illustrated by Daniel Craig in ENG 454, Group 1, Spring 2018. Later published in *Manastash: A Journal of Writing and Art*, Volume 29, Spring 2019, page 19 94

Tables

8.1 Listing of required core classes in the PCW program, catalog year 2020–2021 90
8.2 Listing of soundwriting practice exercises and major assignments in ENG 474/574 Writing with Sound, Winter 2020 96
11.1 Grading rubric for course blogs 137

Boxes

Course blog assignment sheet: Blog requirements 134
What should I write about? 136
30/30 Project 142

Contributors

Nicole Anae is Senior Lecturer in Literary and Cultural Studies at Central Queensland University. She graduated from Charles Sturt University with a BEd and DipT before earning her PhD through the Faculty of English, Journalism and European Languages at the University of Tasmania. Her research interests include creative writing, English literature, Shakespeare, theatre history, Australian colonial and postcolonial writing, embodiment and performance, and the interplay between literature, culture, and identity. Her published work appears in a variety of refereed journals and edited collections.

Lucy Biederman is an Assistant Professor of Creative Writing at Heidelberg University in Tiffin, Ohio; in addition to creative writing courses in poetry, fiction, and creative nonfiction, she teaches first-year writing and American literature. She has been teaching online courses since 2014. She is the author of *The Walmart Book of the Dead*, which won the 2017 Vine Leaves Press Vignette Award, was a Finalist for the Foreword Book of the Year in the Fantasy category, and has been adapted for the stage. She has written four chapbooks of poetry, and her short stories, essays, and poems have appeared in *North American Review, Poetry, AGNI, Ploughshares*, and *Pleiades*. Her scholarship, which has been published in *The Henry James Review, Women's Studies, The Emily Dickinson Journal*, and *Studies in the Literary Imagination*, focuses on how contemporary American women writers interpret their literary forebears. She has received creative and scholarly grants from Cleveland Public Theatre, Pennsylvania State University, the Cleveland Jewish Arts and Culture Lab, Case Western Reserve University, and the Tin House Summer Writers Workshop. She holds an MFA in poetry from George Mason University and a PhD in creative writing and American literature from the University of Louisiana-Lafayette.

Patrick Bizzaro has published 12 books and chapbooks of poetry, most recently Against Confusion from Mount Olive College Press and Interruptions from Finishing Line Press; two critical studies of Fred Chappell's poetry and fiction with LSU Press; a book with NCTE on the pedagogy of academic creative writing; four textbooks; and a couple hundred poems, essays, and reviews in magazines. He is on the editorial board of *New Writing* and *Impost* and Contributing Editor of *Asheville Poetry Review*. He has won the Madeline Sadin Award from NYQ and Four Quarters Poetry Prize as well as a Fulbright to South Africa in 2012 to assist in developing an English-language literacy program and writing center at University of the Free State. He is Professor Emeritus of English at East Carolina University and retired in 2015 as Professor of English from Indiana University of Pennsylvania's doctoral program in Composition and TESOL.

Ashley Jae Carranza resides in Las Vegas, Nevada, where she teaches at both the high school and college levels. She has served as an editor for *DASH Literary Journal*, *Helen Literary Magazine*, and *101 Words*. Her fiction appears in numerous online magazines such as *Beautiful Losers*, *Maudlin House*, and more. She recently edited a collection of essays for the book *Our Fears Made Manifest*, published by McFarland, and has academic writing in several collections.

Carrie Etter is originally from Normal, Illinois, but is now Reader in Creative Writing at Bath Spa University, where she has taught since 2004. She has published four collections of poetry, most recently *The Weather in Normal* (UK: Seren; US: Station Hill, 2018), and individual poems in *Boston Review*, *The Iowa Review*, *The New Republic*, *New Statesman*, *The Penguin Book of the Prose Poem*, *Poetry Review*, *The Times Literary Supplement*, and many other journals and anthologies. She edited *Infinite Difference: Other Poetries* by UK Women Poets (Shearsman, 2010) and Linda Lamus's posthumous collection *A Crater the Size of Calcutta* (Mulfran, 2015). She also publishes essays, short fiction, and reviews.

Tamara Girardi is an Associate Professor of English at HACC, Central Pennsylvania's Community College where she teaches creative writing, technical writing, composition, and literature online. She studied fiction at the University of St Andrews in Scotland and writes young adult novels and picture books. Her debut picture book, *Why, Daddy? Why?*, is forthcoming from Familius. She has co-edited the essay collections *Ideology and Identity in Young Adult Literature: Connections to the Composition Classroom* (McFarland) and *Hero or Villain: Essays on Dark Protagonists of Television* (McFarland). Her primary research interests are online pedagogy, student engagement, young adult literature, and creative writing studies. Dr. Girardi also serves as a Digital, Multimodal, and Multimedia section editor for the *Creative Writing Studies Journal* and has published many articles, short stories, and personal essays.

Paul Gleed received a BA in English from Lancaster University, UK, and a PhD from the State University of New York at Buffalo; he now teaches writing at Harrisburg Area Community College, Pennsylvania. He has published academic, fiction, and creative nonfiction writing in numerous publications and authored three volumes of Harold Bloom's How to Write about Literature series. He teaches exclusively online and devotes his professional energy to making his students' virtual learning experiences as engaging and useful as possible.

Laraine Herring holds an MFA in Creative Writing and an MA in Counseling Psychology. Her work includes *Writing Begins with the Breath: Embodying Your Authentic Voice* (Shambhala) and *Lost Fathers: How Women Can Heal from Adolescent Father Loss* (Hazelden). Her latest book, *On Being Stuck: Tapping into the Creative Power of Writer's Block*, was named a top 10 book for writers by Poets & Writers. Her memoir *A Constellation of Ghosts: A Speculative Memoir with Ravens* will be released in 2021 from Regal House. Her fiction has won the Barbara Deming Award for Women and her nonfiction has been nominated for a Pushcart Prize. Her work has appeared in *The New York Times, Tiferet, K'in*, and *The Manifest-Station*, and is widely anthologized. She has taught for 25 years in higher education and has also been on the Arizona Artist Roster, working as a writer-in-the-schools. She has been teaching online classes since 2000 and mentors new faculty in online excellence. She works as a freelance book coach and is a tenured professor of psychology and creative writing at Yavapai College, where she directs the creative writing program. Laraineherring.com

Marshall Kitchens is an Associate Professor in the Department of Writing and Rhetoric and director of the Meadow Brook Writing Project at Oakland University in Rochester, Michigan. He earned a PhD in Rhetoric and Composition from Wayne State University. His research interests include creative nonfiction, prison writing programs, technology and pedagogy, and digital culture. He has been teaching fully online sections of creative nonfiction since 2010.

Sarah Layden is the author of the novel *Trip through Your Wires* and *The Story I Tell Myself about Myself*, winner of the Sonder Press Chapbook Competition. Her short fiction appears in *Boston Review, Blackbird, PANK, Moon City Review, Zone 3, Booth, Best Microfiction 2020*, and elsewhere. A two-time Society of Professional Journalists award winner, her recent essays, interviews, and articles have appeared in *Salon, The Millions, Ladies' Home Journal, The Indianapolis Star, The Writer's Chronicle, NUVO*, and *The Humanist*. She is an Assistant Professor of Creative Writing at Indiana University-Purdue University Indianapolis.

Lori Ostergaard is Professor and the Chair of the Department of Writing and Rhetoric at Oakland University, and co-editor of *WPA: Writing Program Administration*. Her archival research examines the history of writing instruction at Midwestern normal schools and high schools. Her research has appeared in a number of journals, including *College English, Rhetoric Review, Composition Studies*, and *Peitho*. She has also co-edited three collections, including *In the Archives of Composition: Writing and Rhetoric at High Schools and Normal Schools* (2015), which provides accounts of writing instruction within contexts often overlooked by current historical scholarship.

Cynthia Pengilly (PhD, Old Dominion University) is an Assistant Professor of English and Co-Director of the Technical Writing Program at Central Washington University. She teaches courses in composition, technical and professional communication, visual rhetoric, and cultural studies. Her research explores rhetoric, technology, and activism with a particular focus on competing representations and articulations of identity in online spaces and its relationship to/with participatory culture. She also researches digital rhetoric and innovative pedagogical strategies in online writing instruction (OWI) and online tutoring. She has several forthcoming articles and book chapters.

Abigail G. Scheg currently serves as a Styling Team Lead for Stitch Fix. She has taught online and face to face at multiple institutions as well as serving as an administrator in academic and student service roles. She is the author or editor of several texts including *Applied Pedagogies: Strategies for Online Writing Instruction* and *Reforming Teacher Education for Online Pedagogy Development*.

Stephanie Vanderslice is Professor of Creative Writing and Director of the Arkansas Writers MFA Workshop at the University of Central Arkansas. Her most recent book is *The Geek's Guide to the Writing Life: An Instructional Memoir for the Rest of Us* (Bloomsbury), which was listed as a top book for writers by *Poets and Writers* and *The Writer* magazines. Her books on creative writing pedagogy include *Can Creative Writing Really Be Taught? Resisting Lore in Creative Writing* (2nd edition with Rebecca Manery, Bloomsbury) and *Rethinking Creative Writing* (Frontinus). She has published fiction, creative nonfiction, interviews, and creative criticism in such outlets as *Ploughshares Online, Easy Street, Burningword Literary Review, Literary Mama*, and many others. Her column "The Geek's Guide to the Writing Life" appeared regularly in the *Huffington Post* from 2012 to 2017. Her novel *The Lost Son* will be forthcoming from Regal House Publishing.

Lex Williford, a University of Arkansas MFA, has taught in the writing programs at Southern Illinois University at Carbondale and the University of Alabama and has been a distinguished visiting writer at the University of Missouri, St. Louis. His novella *Balsa and Tissue Paper* was published in Fall 2019 as a selection in both the *Ploughshares* Solos longform issue and as a single e-book; his book *Macauley's Thumb* won the 1993 Iowa Short Fiction Award; his chapbook *Superman on the Roof* won the 2016 10th Annual Rose Metal Press Flash Fiction Award. His fiction and nonfiction have appeared in numerous prestigious national journals and anthologies. He has received fellowships from the National Endowment of the Arts, Bread Loaf Writers' Conference, the Blue Mountain Center, the Centrum Foundation, the Djerassi Foundation, the MacDowell Colony, the Millay Colony, the Ragdale Foundation, the Virginia Center for the Creative Arts, Villa Montalvo, the Wurlitzer Foundation, and Yaddo. Co-editor of the popular Scribner Anthology of Contemporary Short Fiction and the Touchstone Anthology of Contemporary Nonfiction, he is the founding director of the online MFA at the University of Texas at El Paso and a former chair of the on-campus bilingual creative writing program, where he currently teaches.

Amy Withrow earned a bachelor's degree in English from the University of Findlay in Findlay, Ohio, in 1992 and a master's degree in English from Bowling Green State University in Bowling Green, Ohio, in 1997. While teaching for the university during her graduate schooling, she developed a passion for education, particularly education at the college level. This passion combined with her previous work experience in database programming resulted in her progression from traditional classroom education to the world of online education. She served as the executive director and associate provost for Virtual Learning at HACC, Central Pennsylvania's Community College, from 2012 to 2018. Under her leadership, the online unit experienced notable enrollment growth while improving the academic success of students taking online classes. She also developed and taught a variety of online English and humanities courses and established Centers for Innovation and Teaching Excellence at various college campuses. She served as the chair of the Online Education Committee of the Pennsylvania Community Colleges from 2014 to 2017 and as a board member for the Sheriff and Deputy Sheriff's Education and Training Program for the state of Pennsylvania from 2014 to 2018.

1 Don't short circuit the muse
Creative writing in the digital age

Amy Withrow

Upon the invention of the printing press, Johannes Trithemius, a German Benedictine abbot, wrote "In Praise of Scribes." In this tract, he declared: "Printed books will never be the equivalent of handwritten codices….The simple reason is that copying by hand involves more diligence and industry" (Odlyzko, 1997: 153). While there is little doubt this statement is true when it comes to the element of diligence and the painstaking work needed to create handwritten texts, the declaration itself becomes quite ironic with the knowledge that Trithemius's "In Praise of Scribes" tract was circulated in manuscript format in 1492; it soon owed its wider readership to this printed edition and later reprints (Odlyzko, 1997).

With each new innovation, there have been those who warned of the corruption or degradation of the standard that came before it. Online education has certainly been a modern source of such debate. The hallowed lessons of history are full of stories about change and the people who effected change in their environments. Often, in hindsight, such change agents are celebrated. However, during the first efforts to effect change, many of those individuals face staunch opposition, sometimes to the level of violence in the worst cases. One stark example is the modern-day work of Malala Yousafzia, who was shot on October 9, 2012, for speaking against the Taliban in defense of a girl's right to be educated. While most change does not escalate into this type of violence, this example demonstrates just how escalated the fear of change can become. Thankfully, Malala Yousafzia survived her wounds and still works as a modern-day change agent for educational and gender equality. History also offers proof that if the change agent persists over time, societal acceptance begins ever slowly to shift. Such shifts in acceptance do not come easily or quickly; yet, the shift, nonetheless, happens. Change is in its truest form a cycle—and a prolonged cycle at that.

Having overseen the operations of a large online unit at a community college in central Pennsylvania for six years, my work and my team's work has been on the forefront of a paradigm shift in higher education. It will come as no surprise that there are supporters and detractors among faculty and administration in regard to the scaling of online educational options, the quality of online courses, and the unique training needed for faculty and the support staff who educate and assist online students. Each year, as face-to-face enrollments decrease and the online enrollments increase, the clashing of two opposing, yet equally well-intended, viewpoints become more evident. The "well-intended" phrase bears repeating. Differing opinions on the scale and quality of online educational offerings does not mean one group is entirely right and one group is entirely wrong. Nor does it mean one group is too rooted in older paradigms of the academy or one group is tearing down the academy of old. Instead, one must understand the psychology of change, the neuroscience of change, to appreciate the prolonged cycle that happens once such change is instigated.

This goal of gaining a deeper understanding into the nuances of change started when I was initially hired as one of the first 100 percent full-time online faculty members at the community college, mentioned above, in 2006. At the first division meeting, myself and two other full-time online faculty hires were sitting in the front row excited to start our tenure-track journey. During the meeting, the topic of the new online faculty hires and the college's plans to increase online offerings arose. At that point, a faculty colleague, whom I grew to respect dearly in the years subsequent to that meeting, stood up and declared the new online faculty were "guns for hire" and expressed deep concern about the college investing in such an endeavor to increase online educational offerings. The excitement of starting a new job quickly shifted into a deep realization of an "us vs. them" paradigm, a bitter criticism that pitted one type of faculty member against another type of faculty member, despite the fact there was full professional equity and commitment in the desire to educate students and to assist them in their educational and career goals.

Why, then, was there such an immediate division? Why was the language used to describe the new online faculty so blunt and fearful? Admittedly, my initial reaction was surprise and a creeping feeling of alienation. However, in the days that progressed, this singular event started a long journey to understanding the "why" answer to those questions.

Higher education has historical roots going back to Plato's Academy founded in Athens in 387 B.C. after "Plato spent 12 years traveling in southern Italy, Sicily, and Egypt, studying with other philosophers including the followers of the mystic mathematician Pythagoras" ("Plato"). Plato's Academy was not structured like the colleges in existence today, but it consisted of scholars and intellectuals sharing the educational pursuits of philosophy, mathematics, and astronomy. These intellectuals would meet in a public grove near the ancient city of Athens.

> According to tradition, a dozen olive trees, scions of the Sacred Tree of Athena on the Acropolis, formed a Sacred Grove at the Academy. In the sixth century BC, one of the three public gymnasia at Athens was founded at the Academy. At the end of the same century, Hipparchus built a wall around the Academy.
>
> (Kalligas et al., 2020: 35)

Plato lectured to students who gathered from around the Greek world, many of whom came from outside Athens. With this advancement in educational delivery, Plato challenged the philosophy of his own teacher, Socrates, who questioned the ability of a learned scholar to impart knowledge. Yes, Plato in this regard was a change agent. "The abolishment of Plato's Academy (attributed to Emperor Justinian in 529) imposed silence on a school which for more than nine centuries produced ideas that influenced and, to some extent, determined the natural sciences and philosophical and political thought" (Kalligas et al., 2020: 28). However, the foundational philosophy of a scholar physically standing before his students, orally lecturing in a given space at a given time, had taken root.

It is little wonder that the technological advances of the past 50 years, with the invention of the Internet and reality of Moore's Law allowing for more affordable, more functional, and smaller personal computers and smartphones, would send something akin to an earthquake through the 2000-year-old foundation of higher education. Space and time no longer mattered as scholars recording audio podcasts and, eventually, video lectures reached vast amounts of students across the globe. Access to such education used to be available only to people of certain social classes, races, gender, and geography. However, within a mere few decades, all that is needed to access the educational content of massive open online courses (MOOCs) and iTunes U courses and collections is an Internet connection and a compatible technological device. Accredited colleges and universities are now being forced to face this new reality in the briefest of timeframes, considering the long history of academia.

This change to the well-known lecturer model of academia became a threat. It became a threat to the survival of skillful lecturers, some of whom, understandably, have little interest in learning how to teach online. It became a threat to educators who doubted the effectiveness of a student's ability to reach key learning outcomes in an online setting. It became a threat to educational innovators who wanted to embrace online delivery and feared falling behind the curve if their institution did not put enough resources toward creating effective online courses. It became a threat as faculty saw templated online courses rolled out by publishers, taking away one of the greatest joys of teaching: selecting texts, creating assignments, designing materials, and drafting discussions to ensure students achieve the learning outcomes for each course they teach. Thus came into being the collision of those new online faculty hires sitting in the front row of their first division meeting, those who viewed them as "guns for hire," and the many other faculty whose viewpoints rested somewhere between those two diverse views.

One may think such a gap in teaching philosophy is too wide to overcome. However, there is common ground, and that common ground lies with increased understanding of the human brain and the innate reaction to behavior change. Elliot T. Berkman, author of "The Neuroscience of Goal and Behavior Change," states the following:

> To understand why new behavior is so hard, it's useful to think about two dimensions that give rise to behaviors. The first dimension captures the

skills, capacities, and knowledge required to engage in a behavior. This includes mapping out the steps to take and having the skill to execute an action, as well as related cognitive processes such as attentional focus, inhibitory control, and working memory capacity. Because it reflects the means used to achieve a goal, I refer to the first dimension as the *way*. The second dimension captures the desire for and importance of a behavior. This includes wanting to achieve a goal and prioritizing it over other goals, as well as related motivational processes such as volition, intention, and the nature and strength of the drive for achievement. Because it relates to the motivation to engage in a behavior, I refer to the second dimension as the *will*.

As shown in [Figure 1.1], these two dimensions give rise to four broad types of action.

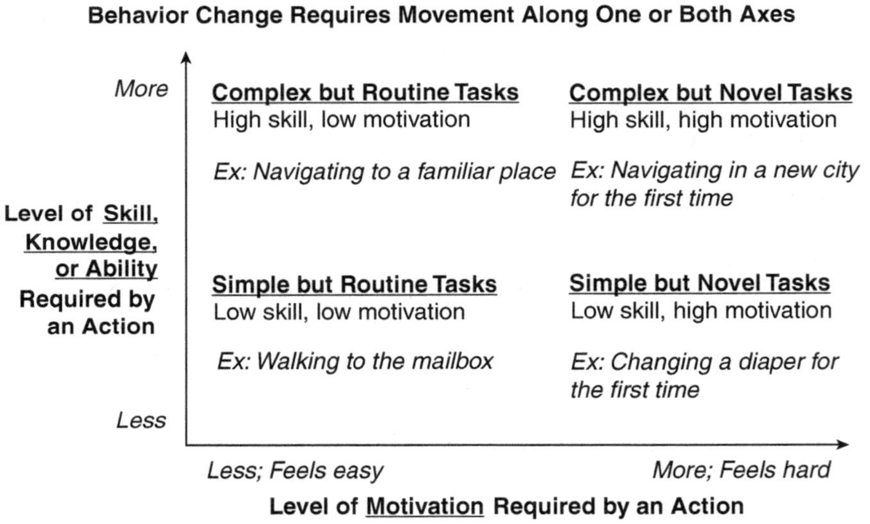

Behavior Change Requires Movement Along One or Both Axes

	Complex but Routine Tasks High skill, low motivation Ex: Navigating to a familiar place	**Complex but Novel Tasks** High skill, high motivation Ex: Navigating in a new city for the first time
	Simple but Routine Tasks Low skill, low motivation Ex: Walking to the mailbox	**Simple but Novel Tasks** Low skill, high motivation Ex: Changing a diaper for the first time

Vertical axis: Level of **Skill, Knowledge, or Ability** Required by an Action (Less to More)

Horizontal axis: Level of **Motivation** Required by an Action (Less; Feels easy to More; Feels hard)

Figure 1.1

(Berkman 2018: 29)

It is important to stop and deeply consider the complexity of behavior change one is asking faculty to make in order to embrace online education. If faculty lack the technological skills of teaching online and the understanding of online pedagogy, and, in addition, they are not motivated to assist in ushering in the paradigm shift toward online education, trying to effect behavior change without actively addressing those areas will result in tension and disagreement. Furthermore, if there are skills yet no motivation, trying to effect behavior change without addressing the lack of motivation will also result in failure. Conversely, if there is motivation but limited skills, trying to effect behavior change without creating a solid, supportive environment to develop those skills will result in failure yet again. Any move to the top or right of the diagram shown in Figure 1.1, without proper conversation and administrative support, will "feel hard." It will feel like a threat. For faculty who are already confident in their technological skills, are highly motivated, and support such a paradigm shift in online education, that transition will "feel eas[ier]"; their confidence and commitment to produce successful online courses should, likewise, be supported and respected.

This example demonstrates that the fundamental issue is far more complex than a rush-to-judgment "us vs. them" classification. It is vitally important that we do not debase this differing of philosophies about online education and what can be taught successfully online and, instead, embrace frank conversations and address the core reasons why such change is challenging. It is equally important to cultivate a culture that encourages motivation and skill building in regard to online education.

This anthology is filled with excellent advice on how best to teach creative writing online. These best practices will serve any online educator in planning, constructing, and teaching a successful creative writing course that is filled with all the faculty-to-student, student-to-student, and student-to-content interactivity needed to develop the core knowledge, skills, and constructive inspiration needed for such creative pursuits. The goal of this essay, however, is to provide key steps to engage faculty and administration in conversations about how to support new online offerings, including creative writing.

Let's first address motivation:

1 Create time for faculty to discuss, without judgment or rush, concerns and solutions for developing online classes

Faculty should engage in thoughtful discussions on how best to construct online courses with the existing learning outcomes established for face-to-face offerings. The conversation should be focused on "how we might accomplish" given learning outcomes instead of broader, more fearful statements immediately proclaiming that certain learning outcomes cannot be accomplished online. This requires a fair facilitator who will ensure honest, open conversations that will determine what can be accomplished online and what cannot.

Present Think Tank Days: Think Tank Days are designed to promote discussions about possibilities in online course delivery. Clear the faculty members' morning or afternoon schedule, if possible. At minimum, try to allow for limited interruptions and ensure the discussions last for more than an hour. It takes time for individuals to shed the pressures of the day and immerse themselves in deeper critical thinking. There should be no specific agenda or outcomes. Instead, the facilitator should come prepared with a list of questions for faculty to discuss. Additionally, he or she should come prepared with a list of new technologies that could be made available to faculty. All questions should be open-ended. For example, ask a question like: how do you ensure student creativity in the classroom? Share one assignment you are particularly pleased with or that works particularly well. How might that assignment look in an online setting? Let the faculty talk with each other. The facilitator is vital in knowing when to get out of the way in the discussion and when to refocus the discussion. The facilitator can also mention new technologies. For example, ask a question like: what one might be able to do if students could mark up pictures directly in the online class setting? The technology does not need to be named. Just focus on what the technology can do, and let the faculty discuss how it could be used ... or not. Think Tank Days allow faculty to tap into deeper aspects of creative thinking than is typically allowed in a regular workday. Think Tank Days should be held once a semester and advertised well in advance of the day to ensure calendars are cleared as much as possible.

Present Online Strategic Retreats: Strategic retreats are more inclusive and more structured than Think Tank Days. Typically, there are key goals for the retreat: increased student retention or improved student success are examples. In addition to sharing key data, which will be discussed in more detail in the next section, small group discussions should involve both faculty and academic or student support staff. Each small group table should have a specific question or goal to improve upon or resolve. There should be a note-taker capturing key points or issues to follow up on, and faculty and staff should discuss concerns, successes, and needs for their classrooms or for student support. It is the administration's responsibility to determine from these discussions what needs are not being fulfilled in the classroom, what training gaps need to be addressed, and/or what technological needs, software or hardware, need to be provided or reconsidered. If administration demonstrates an investment of time and support of faculty and staff, motivation will improve.

2 Discuss the elephant in the room: scheduling and how online enrollments may affect face-to-face enrollment

The discussion few seem to want to have is how increased online enrollments affect on-campus enrollments. This enrollment shift, again, is a threat to the status quo of the past; yet, it does little good for the college and the students it serves not to have conversations about what that shift does to student schedules and faculty workload and needs. Proactive discussions about scheduling results in collegial decisions that are far better than emotional reactions to the shifting enrollments had after they have happened. Do not hide data. Share the good, the bad, and the ugly. When people lack information, rumors and misunderstandings can run rampant. This, in turn, will hinder motivation.

Consistent Presentation of Data: Whether through monthly meetings or email, make sure faculty are aware of the enrollments for both online and on-campus classes. Ensure they have consistent access to the trends over time too. A snapshot of one semester is not enough to present the picture of what changes are happening in academia. While some faculty may not be interested, I have found that most are, indeed, quite interested. Seeing the numbers instead of being told more students are taking online classes, allows faculty to be a part of the change and the decision making to address the change. Share any student survey data that might have been gathered that semester. Telling faculty about the changes in higher education creates division and hierarchy. Showing faculty the data and trends facing higher education and asking them for their thoughts and solutions creates a team environment and encourages motivation. As noted previously, increased motivation will allow for a greater acceptance of change.

Online Students Have Unique Needs: Scheduling new online classes for the first time will typically affect on-campus enrollments in a negative manner. This point is glossed over too often as online administrators sometimes try to argue that online enrollments are not hindering on-campus enrollments. That simply is not accurate. Offering more online classes will draw from on-campus enrollments. However, in surveys, many online students, the majority in my experience, will state they can only take online courses for a variety of reasons, ranging from transportation issues, work schedule conflicts, scheduling issues with their children's activities, or even preference. These are students that would not be served if the courses were not offered online. First and foremost, the students' needs should be met, but that does not negate the need for thoughtful scheduling of rollouts of new online courses and open, transparent communication about how that will affect on-campus faculty workloads. Allowing for frank, honest discussions about scheduling and student needs will, albeit challenging at times, create a greater sense of motivation to meet students' needs.

Now let's address skills, knowledge, and ability:

3 Create clear and robust training opportunities for faculty interested in learning more about teaching online

Too often, it is perceived that administration's focus on expanding online educational opportunities rests solely in the desire for greater geographical reach and increased revenues. When college strategic plans include expanding online education without evidence of creating support structures within the college that effectively address skills, knowledge, and ability, friction between faculty and administration occurs. Therefore, this is a vital collaboration needed between faculty and administration. Administrators have the responsibility to put in place systems that promote strong support systems within the college instead of selecting the easy option of outsourcing training and resources needed for the effective creation and delivery of online classes. To expect faculty to embrace online education when they are forced to use templated online courses created by someone else is an unreasonable expectation. Allowing faculty, who are willing, to partner with skilled instructional designers or other online faculty to discuss pedagogical vision in online courses and to improve their technological skills helps to transform the conversation from fear and threats to logical step-by-step actions.

Offer Robust Internal Training: A great success at our community college was the implementation of an eAcademy training for faculty interested in learning how to teach online. This training was created by a skilled online faculty member and a team of instructional designers. It consisted of two parts: 1) a full exploration of online pedagogy; and 2) technological "how to" training about the creation, uploading, and modification of online content, along with the technical aspects of operating within the learning management system (LMS). The discussion of online pedagogy and visualization of how an online course might be created was vital as the first step. Too often, once technology gets placed before the faculty member, he or she will be drawn to that first. This two-step model allowed faculty, with the strong support of instructional designers, to envision their course first and foremost. The natural evolution is to ask what tools are available to make that vision happen. This leads to the second part of the training, the "how to" part of online course design and operations. It is far too easy for administrators to want to cut costs, reduce instructional design staff, or to outsource online course creation to publishers. These are often shortsighted, however, and will lead to conflict and resistance to change. Again, the keys to change involve motivation and the support of skills, knowledge, and ability. One without the other, or even worse, none of the two will result in painful conflicts between faculty and administration. Offering both, equally, will lead to improved motivation and acceptance of change.

Offer Frequent Technological and Pedagogical Trainings throughout the Academic Year: Once the foundational training is completed, shorter and more frequent opportunities for targeted training should be offered. Our community college offered 30-minute to 60-minute faculty-led trainings through what was called the Centers for Innovation and Teaching Excellence (CITE). The technical training was offered by the college's instructional designers. This combination of internal and continuing professional development addressed both online pedagogy and technological skills. This provided consistent access for improved skills, knowledge, and ability. All professional development sessions were recorded and offered for asynchronous viewing should synchronous attendance not be possible. Faculty will notice if administration is supporting their needs in a tangible, effective manner; doing so is a key part of encouraging acceptance to change.

4 Engage online students in an advisory council and solicit feedback

No one knows the online learning experience as well as the students who learn in the online setting. Create consistent student surveys that go beyond the individual classroom experience and allow students to provide feedback about their online learning experience in its totality. Explore why students are taking online courses. Ask about ease of navigation, their sense of community as online students, the courses they need to have converted to online delivery, what they would most like to see changed, and what they liked the most. There should be full transparency, except for the redaction of specific faculty, staff, and student names, in presenting the survey results. Future faculty trainings should address key revelations from the surveys, and measurable outcomes should be set in place to determine if any changes implemented are successful. Asking online faculty to make changes without training or technology supports will create resistance. Sharing key data, discussing that data, and then implementing appropriate training and/or technological supports and solutions will result, once again, in a greater acceptance of change.

Online education has come a long way since the 1980s, but national data have shown lagging online student success rates compared to face-to-face student success rates. Faculty are well aware of this fact. There are ways to address this and to narrow the gap, which go beyond the scope of this essay. However, online course improvements should be driven, in good part, by data collection and assessment including comparable retention rates, grade distribution, degree completion, course evaluations, and student surveys. The administration of the college needs to commit to such transparency and dedication of resources to ensure this happens on a consistent basis. Faculty, regardless of where they ultimately stand on the topic of online education, care about student success. A full shift toward acceptance of online education will not happen without the knowledge that students are receiving the quality education they deserve. Like the invention of the printing press, access to education, and, perhaps even more importantly, greater equity in how students can access education has taken another leap forward. There is no going back. Such shifts in acceptance do not come easily or quickly; yet, the shift, nonetheless, happens.

This brings us to the more specific topic of this anthology: teaching creative writing online. Having the benefit of an MFA degree in creative writing/poetry and over 15 years as an online education expert, I can attest creative writing can be taught, and taught well, online. Online classes can offer greater equity in students' participation and feedback. Additionally, students can reflect a bit longer on a reading or a peer review in comparison to a face-to-face course offered in a specific 50-minute or 75-minute class period. Skilled online faculty will likewise find ways to promote a close community in online creative writing courses, including synchronous online drafting times. Online creative writing classes can be every bit the community-driven, collaborative experience students have come to know and appreciate in the face-to-face classroom.

May the following essays provide the reader with the motivation and the skills, knowledge, and ability needed to open a new world of online creative writing education to students across the globe.

Works cited

Berkman, Elliot T. "The Neuroscience of Goals and Behavior Change." *Consulting Psychology Journal: Practice and Research*, vol. 70, no. 1, Mar. 2018, pp. 28–44. EBSCOhost, doi:10.1037/cpb0000094..

Kalligas, Paul, et al., eds. *Plato's Academy: Its Workings and Its History*. Cambridge: Cambridge University Press, 2020.

Odlyzko, Andrew. "Silicon Dreams and Silicon Bricks: The Continuing Evolution of Libraries." *Library Trends*, vol. 46, no. 1, 1997, pp. 152–167. ProQuest, http://search.proquest.com.ezproxy.hacc.edu/docview/220451053?accountid=11302.

"Plato." *History*, 23 Aug. 2019, https://www.history.com/topics/ancient-history/plato. Accessed 27 April 2020.

2 Teaching creative writing online without tears

Discovering the many ways online and creative writing best practices overlap to enhance digital learning

Stephanie Vanderslice

In the last ten years, my experience with teaching online has been one of approach and avoidance. I am neither a digital native nor an early adopter, but I am no Luddite either. I had unofficially been teaching creative writing online in the summer for a few years before our university recently asked each program to "officially" convert a lower division course to online delivery. When I say unofficially, I mean that I used my own learning management system, writing@coloradostate (sadly now discontinued), in my opinion a much more user-friendly and intuitive platform than Blackboard, our university's LMS. In addition, I had also developed my course completely on my own, without the assistance of one of our instructional designers. Both of these were required to officially convert the course, however, and, importantly, to receive the small stipend that came with doing so, which had been one of my motivations to volunteer when no one else raised their hand. To make the course "official" it was also necessary to take three online courses from the Online Learning Consortium—something which I, a perennial student, actually enjoyed and found the easiest part of the process.

Since I already had some experience teaching hybrid/online courses, I initially delved into the project with a kind of naïve enthusiasm, believing all that was required was tweaking my courses and organizing them more clearly into modules; that is, transitioning from the "syllabus" mindset into the "module" mindset that, according to the instructional designer (ID), better represented the online experience for students. Even after our first meeting, when the ID gave me an extensive course "grid" to facilitate the conversion of the introductory creative writing course I had been teaching for more than 20 years to an online format, I remained undaunted. Before the next meeting, I dutifully filled out the course grid, enumerating the goals and objectives for each week of the course, and took the online pedagogy courses, filling half a composition book with notes on optimal online course delivery and enjoying really sinking my teeth into something new. Based on the online classes I was experiencing, online teaching didn't seem that different from what I already did in the classroom: leading students in weekly discussions of readings from my go-to Intro Creative

Writing books, Elizabeth Gilbert's *Big Magic* (2016) and Heather Sellers' *The Practice of Creative Writing* (2007), numerous in-class exercises to give students plenty of material to draw from in their writing projects, responding to student writing, and online workshops and discussions. In fact, the online courses I took from the consortium had much the same format: in addition to initial community building exercises, they revolved around a familiar constellation of reading, discussion, writing, peer and instructor review. As I designed my own course, I introduced links to additional resources for students wherever I could, in case they wanted to go above and beyond what they were doing in class, including author interviews and other further reading but, for the most part, I stuck to the reading, student writing, and online discussion.

My enthusiasm began to dim when, after about six months of work, when I thought I was almost finished, the ID informed me this would not be enough. In addition to core content, each module had to have a welcome and introduction, then an explanation of the content, the content itself, and additional illustrations and videos to enhance the content. A module without illustrations and videos, I discovered during this experience, was no module at all. Despite the fact that most of the online courses I had already taken were *sans* illustrations and videos, I was sent back to the blackboard (pun intended), actually to YouTube, to find videos to correspond to every module I taught, including scripting and filming four videos of myself explaining aspects of craft. I'm not going to lie; I was beginning to get frustrated. Finding, vetting, and including all of this video was challenging and then figuring out, via online tutorials, how to upload it into the module where the ID wanted them was pushing me to the breaking point. The inscrutable idiosyncrasies of Blackboard were also driving me to distraction—if I heard the ID tell me one more time, "Yeah, Blackboard is really weird that way," I was going to scream outwardly instead of just inwardly.

The tipping point might have been when, over a year and a half into the process and with less than a month before the class was set to start, the ID got a faraway look in her eyes and said, "What if ... you create a fictional student for the course and write a story about them navigating each module."

"I don't think I can do that at this late date," I said as honestly and evenly as I could without crying, though in retrospect, I did blink a lot. To her credit, that was when the ID backed off. I wasn't her personal pedagogical guinea pig, after all. The summer was running out and I had a course to teach.

Since then, I've thought a lot about this experience and I've continued to research best practice in online pedagogy—research that has admittedly revolved around determining whether I'm really required to include videos and pictures with every single module and other best practices for teaching online. This was in part because every time I met with my ID the finish line for creating a quality online course moved further away. Fortunately, the more research I read the more I believe my, ahem, enthusiastic ID and I were operating from a somewhat different understanding of the foundational pedagogy of an undergraduate creative writing course. She was used to assisting faculty in converting *lecture-based*, traditional courses to an online format that necessitated more student engagement and instructor facilitation, online courses where according to Casey, Shaw, Whittingham, and Gallavan (2018), "the learning is more active than passive in nature," allowing the "instructor to serve as a facilitator to provide scaffolding of content for the learners, but the learning is actively enhanced through an in-depth exploration by the learner." But, as a teacher of creative writing whose courses were not generally lecture-based, my courses were already designed that way. My face-to-face classroom, like most creative writing classrooms, relied not on the lecture but on "well-conceived discussion prompts that invite discourse," "cooperative group work," and "performance-based adaptive assessments that allow the learner to demonstrate understanding of content," all elements that were also features of online best practice (Casey, Shaw, Whittingham, and Gallavan, 2018). Whether online or face to face, my students learned by discussing what they were reading and putting it into practice in writing exercises I responded to along with their peers. They learned by doing, not by listening and watching.

So what started out—and perhaps continues to be—an investigation to defend my own teaching practices against a particularly energetic ID has evolved into an exploration of the ways in which the face-to-face undergraduate creative writing classroom pedagogy may *already* mirror best practices in online education and be thus relatively easily translated to a virtual format. Perhaps an illustration—yes, even I think illustrations have their place—may optimally demonstrate this theory. Let me draw your attention to the Venn diagram I've created to show how the two pedagogies, online pedagogy and creative writing pedagogy, overlap (see Figure 2.1).

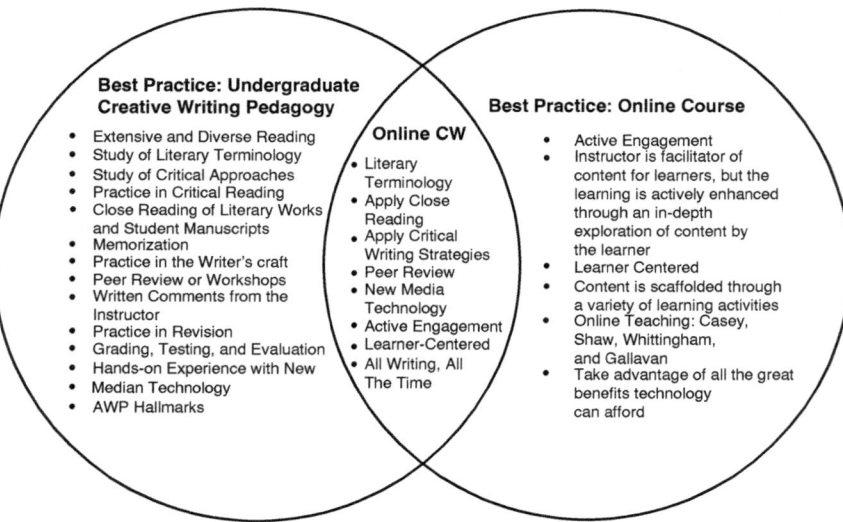

Figure 2.1 Diagram illustrating AWP Hallmarks for undergraduate creative writing.

As you can see, the online creative writing course has the opportunity to combine the best of both worlds. Students must necessarily engage with each other and, importantly, with the content, in online discussions, and they must actively apply literary terms they're learning. Moreover, they interact directly with any number of digital technologies, including the technology of the learning management system itself. Online discussions and workshops, moreover, mean that everyone in the class participates in the peer review and critiques, not just the particularly vocal students. Finally, and perhaps most obvious, all of this engagement happens in the form of writing itself, which only serves to enhance student's metacognition and fluency.

At least this meeting of both worlds looked promising on paper, anyway. But as the months progressed in this, my first "official" online creative writing course, I couldn't help but start to worry. What would the students think of a class where they were really on their own to discuss the content, where I only chimed in, as per the professional development I'd received, periodically to summarize the discussions rather than leading them. Where I observed peer review/workshops from the sidelines like a coach rather than directing them like a conductor.

So maybe my evaluations might not be so hot this semester, I rationalized. Even veteran teachers make mistakes, right? How else can a teacher take risks, find out what works and what doesn't? It's all part of the learning curve.

To my surprise, I didn't even get to the student evaluations before the feedback started coming in. For years, my Introduction to Creative Writing course has ended the semester with a final portfolio of "best, revised" work as well as a critical introduction describing their development as writers over the course of the semester—fairly typical for that kind of class. What was surprising was the introductions themselves, which were, on the whole, *far* more substantive than introductions I had received in the past, where introductions seemed to range from superficial to reflective and considered. These students seemed to have become very familiar with the act of *writing about writing* itself because the online, writing-intensive nature of course required that they do it *all the time*. I have since taught this course a second time with virtually the same result. Moreover, as I heard myself telling my partner this past fall, "These online students are really strong; their portfolio introductions are almost all incredibly detailed and articulate, compared to the introductions in face-to-face courses, which tend to range from weak to average to very strong," I caught myself as I remembered telling him the same thing the year before, about the students in the first online course I ever taught.

What was even better was that in their articulate, considered descriptions of their own development as writers they often tied their progression directly to the online class workshop. Several students reported, in fact, that they found online discussions of their work and that of their peers to be fertile opportunities to really think about what makes a piece of writing work for a reader, opportunities that helped them develop far beyond the "writer-based" stage where many of them had begun the semester. Upon consideration, this outcome isn't surprising either—students have been writing to make themselves understood to their peers in the course all semester, every time they engage online, not just in their first creative attempts: writing is their sole form of communication. Naturally, this kind of engagement might have the effect of speeding up their development as writers of reader-based prose.[1]

I spent five years early in my career as the Writing-Across-the-Curriculum (WAC) coordinator at my university, which involved not only knowing WAC theory but also presenting it to my colleagues across the university in workshops and seminars, often extolling the value of expressive writing-to-learn activities—activities that involved students not in writing for a grade, but in writing to explore their own knowledge and learning, such as journal entries and informal, ungraded responses. Such low-stakes writing-to-learn activities can, as seminal WAC research such as Janet Emig's landmark essay "Writing as a Mode of Learning" articulates, supercharge learning because writing is at their heart. Writing is an effective mode of learning because it engages the learner in thinking and doing (Emig, 1977). Consequently, the online creative writing course enhances student learning because it involves many more of these writing-to-learn activities. Students must actively engage in the course *in writing* in an online creative writing journal and in literally dozens of written peer responses and responses to texts and literary readings. No wonder their final portfolios seem to indicate that they have learned more.

The AWP Hallmarks of effective creative writing pedagogy also emphasize close reading, something that the online creative writing course features in abundance. In both my face-to-face and online classes, students read dozens of examples of the craft elements described in Sellers' *The Practice of Creative Writing* in the creative works sections at the back of each chapter—short stories, poems, essays, graphic novel and script excerpts. But the students in the online class must write responses to these creative works and read the responses their classmates have posted, in order to respond to them in the online discussion as part of their grade. If the online creative writing course's primary focus, then, is writing, writing, writing, the secondary focus is reading, reading, reading. Reading the texts, reading the examples of craft, reading their peer's creative work, reading their peer's responses to their work and that of others, and reading to their peer's responses to the reading. Students in an online creative writing course write more and read more than their face-to-face counterparts, both essential elements of any effective pedagogy.

Certainly, these observations are not scientific but based on the anecdotal observations of one particular online class that may be unique. But they give me hope and they bear out preliminary research that tells me that there is a great deal already working in the online creative writing classroom, without the bells and whistles, without images and videos or writing a student-centered novel to illustrate the course. Indeed, in some ways the online creative writing classroom is the face-to-face creative writing classroom on steroids. This epiphany doesn't mean that I'll turn away from online innovations—this semester, for example, I'm trying out, on the suggestion of the ID, Answergarden, a new classroom feedback and brainstorming tool along the lines of Wordle that helps aggregate and highlight trends in online conversations that can lead students to thinking even more reflectively about group discussions. But at heart, I feel more confident in all the ways the nuts and bolts online creative writing class actually delivers the optimum in creative writing pedagogy and online pedagogy. It is this confidence, in fact, that allows me to take risks and try future innovations like Answergarden, without tears. If such innovations fall flat, I know that as long as I'm engaging students in core creative writing and online best practice—extensive content discussion and peer review—they will get what they need to develop as writers and to be ready for the next level of coursework our undergraduate major demands of them: forms and workshop courses. After all, preparing them as students and as writers for the next level of our curriculum is really what matters. In fact, it's likely online students will get more than what they need from this prerequisite to every other course in our curriculum, that they will be better prepared, with more experience in writing and reading and more experience in participating in their online classroom community independent of their instructor, than their face-to-face counterparts.

Of course, at this point, these findings are still anecdotal. The next step would be to compare the learning rates of students in online introductory creative writing courses against the learning rates of students in a face-to-face course. It would be interesting, as well, to compare student metacognition *about* their learning in both courses as well as what they remember learning in both courses. Moreover, it would also be interesting to follow a cohort of students in both kinds of courses throughout our creative writing program, examining their comparative performance on our outgoing portfolio assessment.

Creative writing pedagogy is so deeply embedded in the signature pedagogy of the face-to-face workshop that those who have not experienced the online workshop—instructors or students—might find it difficult to imagine that such a workshop, absent the physical classroom community, could be effective at all. Initial results suggest the opposite, that the online creative writing workshop is not only an effective pedagogy; it may even be *more* effective. Regardless, an exciting area of research has emerged to determine if this is true.

Note

1 Linda Flower's distinctions between writer-based and reader-based prose, developed in understanding cognitive-based theories of writing acquisition, also shed important light on creative writing development. Reader-based prose, as Flower (2018) describes it, takes the reader into account, while writer-based prose consists of the writer talking to himself. The transition from writer-based to reader-based writing is of critical importance to the progress of the nascent creative writer, a transition that often begins to happen in introductory creative writing classes when students first encounter readers outside themselves.

Works cited

"AWP Recommendations on the Teaching of Writing to Undergraduates." *AWP: Writer's Chronicle Features Archive*, Jan. 2019, www.awpwriter.org/guide/directors_handbook_recommendations_on_the_teaching_of_creative_writing_to_undergraduates.

Casey, K. Michael, et al. *Online Teaching: Tools and Techniques to Achieve Success with Learners*. Lanham, MD: Rowman & Littlefield, 2018.

Emig, Janet. "Writing as a Mode of Learning." *College Composition and Communication*. Vol. 28, No. 2 (May, 1977), pp. 122–128.

Flower, Linda. "Revising Writer-Based Prose." Wac.colostate.edu, January 2019, wac.colostate.edu/jbw/v3n3/flower.pdf.

Gilbert, Elizabeth. *Big Magic: Creative Living Beyond Fear*. London: Penguin, 2016.

3 When the way you read is who you are
Developing the teacherly persona for teaching creative writing online

Patrick Bizzaro and Tamara Girardi

> "meaning cannot ever be other or more than meaning for myself"
>
> (Kress, 2003: 39)

Of necessity in an essay that focuses ultimately on ways to develop the teacherly persona of writing teachers teaching online, we must begin in critique mode. While we agree with the assertion Gunther Kress makes in the above statement from his well-known *Literacy in the New Media Age*—that is, that meaning is what *we* make it to be—Kress goes on to confusingly argue for the meaning-making power of the author independent of a reader. But for a theory of reading to be helpful in assisting online teachers in their efforts to project their personae as teachers, the question of meaning must be resolved by ultimately determining where it might be found, who makes the meaning of a text. Kress brings to mind, at least at first, the text and the reader as reception theorist Wolfgang Iser posits them when he argues, on the basis of social interaction theories, that each text has gaps in it that readers fill (to make meaning) "by filling the blanks with projections" (1676). More specifically, the confusion over who holds authority for the meaning of the text is further obscured when Kress adds, "the reader 'fills' the form with her or his meaning, hence the form as interpreted by the reader is always a *transformation* of the maker's meaning" (39). In the quote that introduces this section, the meaning is ostensibly located in the reader who receives the text. In Kress's comment on "transformation," however, it seems the meaning is located in a person Kress calls "the maker." The maker to whom Kress refers, in this context, can be none other than the author. Kress, then, has not worked out the dilemma of meaning as situated, a dilemma important to the case we make here for the necessity that online teachers have a personality that can be developed through language in a writer–text–reader relationship of the sort developed by Wolfgang Iser.

In "Interaction between Text and Reader," Iser addresses the conundrum of where meaning is situated by arguing that the location of meaning "should concern not only the actual text but also, and in equal measure, the actions involved in responding to that text" (1673). By this, Iser asserts the belief that the maker, to use Kress's term for the author, makes a text which "simply offers 'schematized aspects' through which the aesthetic object of the work can be produced" (1674). One such aesthetic object, we assert here, is the teacherly persona. Persona of teachers in online classes has simply not been adequately studied; persona has been an element of the rhetorical situation of teaching online nonetheless. The actor involved is the reader, of course, which permits Iser to situate meaning when he concludes that there must be two "poles" of the encounter between reader and writer that we might call meaning-making. One, the "artistic pole," is described as "the author's text." The other, "the aesthetic," he describes as "the realization accomplished by the reader" (1674), which we construe to be assertion of all rhetorical elements of a text, including the understudied persona. Iser's view seems compatible with Kress's until Iser states his all-important corollary to this view: "the work itself cannot be identical with the text or with its actualization but must be situated somewhere between the two. It must inevitably be virtual in character, as it cannot be reduced to the reality of the text or to the subjectivity of the reader ..." (1674).

Important to our effort to understand how language may be used to assist a teacher in projecting a teacherly persona in teaching online, Iser solves this complex dilemma of situatedness by employing the then-current thinking on "interpersonal relationships" done by R. D. Laing in his co-authored book *Interpersonal Perceptions: A Theory and a Method of Research* (1972). Iser's thinking does the important work of connecting the development of textual meaning with the establishment of relationships, such as the one between student and teacher. Laing opens a line of inquiry relevant to this essay: Who is the person we see in front of us? How do we come to "see" her or him? Laing addresses these questions when he writes in his subsequent book *The Politics of Experience* that "I may not actually be able to see myself as others see me, but I am constantly supposing them to be seeing me in particular ways, and I am constantly acting in the light of the actual or supposed attitudes, opinions, needs, and so on the other has in respect of me" (qtd. in Iser 1674). The logical consequence of Laing's view is that meaning is situated somewhere between the author and the reader, as an object Laing describes as "no-thing," not the writer's perception of the meaning and not the reader's, but something virtual, shared, and in-between. If this is true, what, exactly, does it tell us about our interpersonal relationships online? Iser interprets Laing on this point to make Laing relevant to a theory of reading: "In all our interpersonal relations we build upon this 'no-thing,' for we react as if we knew how our partners experienced us; we continually form views of their views, and then act as if our view of their views were realities" (1675). Online teachers are no doubt being constructed as real persons by their students who use the exchange of language between the teacher and student as the basis for that characterization. This is a use of language teachers might use to their own benefit if they use language in a systematic effort to assert a level of authority that both reflects their view of themselves as teachers and projects that view to students they are teaching online.

This theory of interpersonal relations has considerable bearing on any evolving theory for developing the teacherly persona of teachers online. Students taking writing courses (and other courses as well) online come to know their teachers in this virtual middle state where realities and meanings are understood, and this "no-thing" is simultaneously the teacher and the teacher's methodology, at least as the student comes to understand it. Is it the "real" teacher? Probably not. Is it the "real" methodology? Probably not, especially in that the meaning is unlikely to be consistent among students as most student evaluations demonstrate. Students do not develop identical perceptions of a teacher's persona. Furthermore, teachers may wish to be viewed in a way not actually identical to students' views. In other words, the teacher persona is an incredibly complicated concept. However, theories of interpersonal relations give us a glimpse of what happens to the teacherly persona when we teach courses online. The teacher offers language in the form of syllabus, assignment descriptions, evaluations, and responses to student questions. From that language, students construct the teacher as a "person." The task of persona-making is complicated as well by the fact that a creative writing teacher's persona must also be writerly.

Why is this important? This too is a complicated question and one seldom addressed. The history of rhetoric, like the history of our studies of interpersonal relations, is mostly understudied as it affects our thinking about teaching creative writing, not to mention our study of problems only now becoming relevant in the world of technology: "one of our problems is not just change itself, but the fact that we are forced to confront this world of change with theories which were shaped to account for a world of stability" (Kress, 2003: 11). While Kress is well known for this belief—the belief that by moving our teaching online we must develop entirely new theories for teaching and writing and reading—we argue that the development of persona, teacherly and writerly, is sustained by existing theories, that persona is stable in its intent and in our understanding of it, online or face-to-face. It is rhetorical. So, not every theory we employ to understand online teaching must be new. It is prudent to test all of our theories against our emerging technologies.

It seems self-evident that identity formation for online teachers is a complicated matter. We assert as well that because the credibility of creative writing teachers has historically come from their history as published creative writers the persona of the creative writing teacher is, perhaps, an even more complicated one to understand. A pedagogy that honors individual voice and literariness of texts requires a teacher who is willing to become the reader the text creates. From this perspective, then, we argue that the student-writer not only makes a text. She also makes a reader. A strong, writerly teacher must be willing to become the reader the text summons her to be.

Because Aristotle separated his lectures on the rhetoric from his lectures on the poetic, we as a profession have allowed this neat categorization to stand in such a way that we have not studied how the growth of the rhetor might parallel the growth of the poet. Though it would take a much larger platform than a short essay to comprehensively study this parallel, suffice it to say that there are numerous points of contact between the two. Here is just one that we think is especially relevant to projecting a teacherly persona. Poet Galway Kinnell (1978) advocates for the view that what readers want in a poet is someone who is trustworthy in her interpretations of life experiences readers are likewise apt to have. This view of the poet brings to mind Quintilian's view of the rhetorician as "a good man speaking well" (Bizzell and Herzberg, 2001: 389). How do we convince our students that we too, as teachers of creative writing, are trustworthy and "good"? We present ourselves that way through our language encounters with readers. We cannot control how a student constructs us as teachers, but we can certainly gain some insight into the teacher/student relationship as "interpersonal" by understanding Iser, Laing, and Kress, and then by developing an attitude we want to convey to readers and a way to actually convey that attitude consistently through language.

What, then, do we mean in this essay by "an attitude"? In a creative writing course, as Bizzaro argued nearly 25 years ago in *Responding to Student Poems: Applications of Critical Theory* (1993), "attitude" of the teacher as a reader is aligned with critical theory—that is, with methods of reading. Bizzaro studied New Criticism, reader-response criticism, feminism, and poststructural theories to demonstrate how each projects a different teacherly self into the teacher–student relationship by valuing certain aspects of the text and by employing varying degrees of authority. Let's look at just one of these approaches that Bizzaro advocated, reader-response criticism, and assess its value in developing an interpersonal relationship with students and a teacherly persona.

We choose reader-response criticism for this essay, though any of the approaches might work because they demonstrate a range of authority relationships of teachers with their students. reader-response seems to us most interactive or, in the parlance of relationship-building, most interpersonal, which is a major reason for advocating for it here. The appeal of reader-response, generally, comes from its moderate authority agenda. The reader needs the author as the author needs the reader. This is a view parallel to the self-evident premise of all teaching, that the student needs the teacher as the teacher needs the student. The reader using reader-response methods recreates the text's meaning and, unlike the teacher–student relationship that accompanies New Critical, text-based responses, does not require the students to rewrite the text exactly as the teacher would have written it. To the end of engaging the student as author, the teacher developing a teacherly persona might simply ask questions about the text, itself, or about how the text has invited the reader to participate in the construction of its meaning. From this perspective, the author, through her text, gives the reader instructions in how the text should be read. In short, how is the teacher invoked as a reader by the text under scrutiny? If the job the student-writer has undertaken is not only to make a text, but also to make a reader, has the teacher who has accepted the role of the reader the text evokes become that reader? If not, what has gone wrong that the writer ought to know about?

More to the point, after his analysis of the use of reader-response criticism in reading a student poem, Bizzaro reaches this conclusion:

> I have been less a judgmental and authoritarian evaluator than a writerly reader who participates in the making of the poem and who, through questioning [rather than offering directives for revision], shares observations that make it essential for the author to consider both how the poem has been read as well as how she would like it to be read (perhaps heretofore unknown).
>
> (1993: 78)

In making this assessment, Bizzaro makes a case for using reading theory in remarks on student poems and stories as a way of asserting the teacherly persona of one who seeks to return authority for the text to the student who wrote it. Without making an overt argument at the time (1992, when he wrote the book), Bizzaro makes a case as well for using language to assert the persona of a teacher who, in all cases, wants to share authority with the students. This is a use of language similar in many ways to what Janelle Adsit calls "code-switching" in her essay "Giving an Account of Ourselves: Teaching identity Construction and Authorship in Creative Nonfiction and Social Media," (2015) with reference to student voices. It might be argued that the subtle difference in language use by the reader-response-influenced teacher and the large majority who continue to make text-based commentary driven by New Critical values is too subtle for students to ascertain. But students studied in the *responding* book attest to knowing the difference when they sat down to revise their work and comment on each other's writing. It is true, some wanted more directives and fewer questions. But they soon came to understand that they had to make decisions on their own based on the answers to those questions.

In a situation, like the teaching of writing online, where language determines how students construct their teachers' identities, teachers can use language and classroom activities and structure to affect how their students view them. But how do online creative writing teachers specifically, or any online teachers for that matter, present themselves as approachable? How can teachers, such as ourselves, who believe creative writing students should possess and wield the autonomy to create their own meaning and their own readers, embody an online teaching persona that fosters such a learning environment? Those questions are at the heart of this essay.

The conversation of teacher persona in the online creative writing classroom is a complex one as it incorporates scholarship from several perspectives and realms. For instance, research in the writer-teacher persona of writing teachers is relevant as is scholarship regarding the online teacher persona. Within creative writing studies, arguments have been made against the "star professor" persona that encourages creative writing student writers to model their teachers' writing styles and processes rather than developing their own. Debates have also occurred within the creative writing studies discipline regarding the role of the teacher-writer in the classroom, especially regarding authority and appropriation of student texts.

As we move into this uncharted discussion of teacher persona specifically in *online* creative writing classes, let us first consider scholarship that addresses practices of successful teachers in the online environment. In their research, Baran and Correia (2013) "revealed seven exemplary practices that successful online teachers follow: (1) knowing and creating course content; (2) designing and structuring the online course; (3) knowing the students; (4) enhancing teacher–student relationships; (5) guiding student learning; (6) evaluating online courses; and (7) maintaining teacher presence." Of the seven exemplary practices, teacher persona can be connected to several, most prominently "enhancing teacher–student relationships," "guiding student learning," and "maintaining teacher presence."

However, as previously demonstrated, the concept of persona is an interdisciplinary one. Dennen (2007) argues that positioning theory, which developed from the field of social psychology, provides a foundation for how faculty might consider both their role and their positioning in achieving the exemplary practices Baran and Correia advocated for in their research, first of all determining the value overall of teacher persona. "How students perceive their teacher influences the overall learning experience, affecting motivation, communication, and perhaps effort" (95).

Dennen's study analyzed the discussion board practices of three teachers, specifically evaluating the frequency of teacher interactions with students, but also the content of those interactions such as their positioning (as teacher as expert or facilitator, for instance) and their intentionality. In other words, some posts encouraged students to share their ideas while others identified the teacher as the expert voice with posts such as "I've taught this class for the past ten years" (100).

Therefore, Dennen found one teacher did not participate frequently enough to maintain a strong teacher persona and one teacher interjected their voice as expert too frequently to maintain an effective persona. The third teacher both responded frequently and also positioned their voice appropriately to maintain a balance that suited students. If that is the case, then, Dennen's research shows it is the content of what teachers say, how they say it, and how frequently they say it that defines the teacher persona they present to student-writers.

It is the work of the many scholars discussed in this essay that help us shape our vision of developing a teacherly persona for teaching creative writing online. To help focus the many relevant ideas, we've chosen to advocate for developing a teacherly persona that engages and empowers student-writers, with the following specific points in mind: 1) demonstrate the teacherly persona from the initial student contacts early in the semester; 2) develop strategies for feedback and response that further support the teacherly persona; 3) interact with students frequently to demonstrate presence, but not so frequently that student-writer voices are silenced.

Demonstrate the teacherly persona from the initial student contact

Students enter a new classroom with all of their apprehensions and vulnerabilities; for students entering an online classroom for the first time, additional concerns are present. They often self-identify with comments such as, "This is my first online class, so I'm not sure what to expect." Or, "I've never taken an online class before ...," a statement that leaves much unsaid, and as online teachers sensitive to how our interactions demonstrate our teacherly persona to students, we must read these initial student contacts with acknowledgment that the true "meaning" may lie somewhere between the students' expectations and apprehensions of an online learning environment and the teacher's prejudgments regarding potential responses and outcomes for student-writers new to the online environment. Thus, teachers must "make meaning" with the students through these initial contacts by asking questions to gain a clearer reading: Do you have any questions about the online environment? Do you have any questions about the technologies we use in the class? Would you like to set up a time for us to talk?

The desire to bridge the gap between the student-writer's meaning and the teacher's meaning demonstrates the teacherly persona the teacher wishes to convey. Some teachers argue these interactions should be private to create opportunity for the "new" students to feel comfort in sharing apprehensions; however, a better approach is two-fold. If a student self-identifies as new to the environment via a public forum such as the discussion board, then the teacher must also publicly welcome discussion or questions regarding the environment in the public forum. As a result, other students who may not self-identify as new or even those students who have online learning experience may then feel emboldened to ask questions. They may also identify the teacher's teacherly persona as one being open to student questions and concerns. Finally, the teacher may always follow up with the student who made the original post privately to demonstrate further consideration of the student's needs.

Initial student contacts create multiple opportunities to build teacherly persona; one of the criticisms of the online environment especially in the creative writing class is that it cannot sustain the same kinds of community-building opportunities that the onsite classroom offers. However, through creativity and effective use of technology, community-building opportunities abound online. Take, for instance, the traditional introductions. Many online classes call for an introduction discussion area where students, well, introduce themselves. One semester of these relatively nondescript, less-than-captivating text introductions may drive online teachers to more creative approaches, and what better context than in creative writing class. Teachers may call for students to include photos, videos, GIFs, memes, emojis, etc. to demonstrate their identities through creative means, but why not develop even more opportunities for creativity? Students may be invited to share a poem in their introduction that speaks to them. They may share a brief creative nonfiction piece or quotation that they've felt personally connected to. These introductions then become opportunities to develop community and for the student-writers to bond with each other and with their teacher.

Here's the crucial point, though: it's in the teacher's *reading* of these introductions that further demonstrates their teacherly persona to students. One simple recommendation is to respond to every introduction. This may seem an overwhelming task. Online discussion forums can become unwieldy, especially if teachers structure them effectively. In a given day, online teachers may open their learning management system to find hundreds of unread discussion posts; it's not feasible to respond to every post. However, the introduction posts are different. They represent the first times the student-writers have stepped out into the virtual space, extending their vulnerability into the void of strangers; to develop a welcoming teacherly persona, teachers should absolutely respond to every student in a meaningful way. In other words, the responses should identify a specific detail of each introduction or multiple details as points of community-building.

For instance, in a recent introduction, the student-writer noted, "This was out of my comfort zone … Also, my nephew says, 'Hi guys!' and he's fine. He just needed help carrying all of his superheroes." To which the response was, "No worries, [student name]. Being out of your comfort zone is a good thing! And my kids try to come in and say hello every video chat they can, so you will probably see them during one of our write-ins :) You did great here! You did not ramble! I hope you feel good after having completed the video. So glad to have you in the class." As you can see the response includes several exclamation points and an emoticon. It also offers a bonding opportunity by identifying that children in the student's life are welcome as they are in the teacher's life as well. Each response also includes notes of encouragement and welcome. The aim is to demonstrate a teacherly persona that is welcoming and encouraging; it values the students' voices and contributions to the course. To ensure authenticity of the teacherly persona, the teacher must strive to demonstrate it in all readings and writings in the course.

That said, while this chapter focuses primarily on the teachers' readings as defining who they are, we urge creative writing faculty to think more broadly about reading. Reading students' creative assignments, discussion posts, and other texts, of course, but also consider student-writers feedback in the course overall, and ensure that in the initial contacts at the start of the course, the teacherly persona is appropriately demonstrated in all contexts, including the syllabus. An entire chapter could be dedicated to the development of a syllabus that represents the teacherly persona, but as you "read" students' perspectives and validate their voices throughout the semester, evaluate the ways you may revise your syllabus to ensure it reads the way you intend it to, so that your teacherly persona is intact from day one of the course.

Develop strategies for feedback and response that further support the teacherly persona

As a significant aspect of our pedagogy, we advocate for student-writer autonomy in creative writing classes (in all writing classes, actually) as demonstrated by referencing Bizzaro's reader-response approach to responding to student writing earlier in this essay. The choice by an online writing teacher to limit her authority is an interesting and understudied one, but it also represents a shift in the direction of developing a teacherly persona of the sort we have thus far advocated. But it is important to maintain this persona by employing it consistently in the various interactions involving language exchange, including response. As Girardi argued, "an individualized approach grounded in learner-centeredness in the creative writing classroom is imperative" (2014: 28) in facilitating student learning in a non-threatening environment. By individualized, we once again consider the student-writer as maker of meaning, as, truly, the first reader of his or her text. A student-writer authoring science-fiction stories, for instance, might require a different set of responses to her story than a student-writer whose focus is chiefly on the writing of poetry. If we are teachers who aim to develop a persona that fosters student-writer autonomy, we must establish consistent feedback methods and response strategies within our online classes that demonstrate that pedagogy. We must consider the content of what we say, how we say what we say, and how frequently we say what we say to ensure that student-writers avoid what Minot cautioned creative writing teachers against decades ago: "When we fail [to consider students' motives,] we begin to reward those whose approach to writing mirrors our own and unconsciously punish the rest" (qtd. in Royster, 2005: 35). How does parallel text response based on reader-response theories remedy the problem of social equity to which Royster refers and share meaning-making with the student/writer?

Parallel text response is a method for responding to drafts of student writing, which, instead of focusing on analysis of the text's features, gives teachers an opportunity to demonstrate to students how the text was read—that is, how the reader (who is implied by the text) comes to construe meaning there. In making a parallel text response, teachers employ a double-entry format reminiscent of Berthoff's (1981) double-entry journal. This strategy, as modeled in greater detail in *Responding to Student Poems*, enables teachers to carry on a written dialogue with an author in an effort to reveal to the author how the essay was read. This also allows the teacher to continue to develop her persona, hopefully consistent with the personae developed through other interactions that involve the exchange of language.

Rather than acting out the role of "expert reader" by making comments that give students directions as to how to write on a specific subject to a particular audience, a teacher employing Parallel text response reflects to student/authors how one willing and receptive reader—the reader invoked by the author, the implied reader—constructs the text's meaning. Since the reader's text is alongside rather than on top of the author's, teachers can reveal to their students how the student text was read by responding to various textual cues as the reader encounters them. By doing so, teachers can offer comments that either predict what will come next in the student essay or indicate to the student what additional information the reader needs if the teacher is to become the reader the student hopes to create.

As should be clear, parallel text response requires that teachers read differently. Rather than reading *every* text in the same way—that is, reading to evaluate certain features despite differences in the text's intended audience, genre, and purposes in those particular writings—the teacher employing parallel text response must make every effort to accept the text on the text's terms—that is, to read with the same purpose in mind as she supposes the author had in writing it.

To effectively use parallel text response, teachers need to approach in-process evaluation of student texts with the following tenets in mind:

1. Ask questions rather than offer directives about changing the features of the text.
2. Receive the text as readers reading with the same purpose in mind as the authors had in writing the text by reading as the implied reader would read.
3. Suspend the "error hunt" until late in the writing process when it might be more advantageous to read the newly completed text from a more traditional perspective.
4. Pay attention to *how* the student text is read, not exclusively or even primarily to *what* has been read.
5. Remember that reading is a process of responding to cues writers place in the text and, thereby, a process of reconstructing the text.

Some of these comments appropriate for use in the parallel text format, especially the questions, might be described as *participatory comments*, the goal of which is to reflect to the student/author what in the process of reconstructing the text the reader seeking an understanding of the text needs to know to become the reader the text seems to summons. Comments concerning the use of metaphor and comparison model these kinds of comments. Other comments might be termed *protocol identifiers* because they hypothesize, on the basis of cues in the text, how readers are apt to respond to the decisions the author has made. These kinds of comments may also signal to the author what additional information a reader needs to become the reader the author hopes to summon through his language choices.

More important to the purposes of this essay, by avoiding directives intended to control the direction of a student text, the reader using the parallel text has simply responded as a reader receiving a text. We believe this method of response strongly signals a teacher's persona. Numerous examples of parallel text responses to student poems may be found in Chapter 4 of *Responding to Student Poems*, "Interaction and Assessment: Some Applications of Reader-Response Criticism."

Interact with students frequently to demonstrate presence, but not so frequently that student-writer voices are silenced

Faculty familiar with the face-to-face classroom understand that there are moments when the teacher steps away, allowing the students to grapple with concepts and ideas amongst themselves. Likewise, moments exist when faculty step closer to students, listening intently to ideas, perhaps without interjecting their own beliefs or considerations. Finally, faculty embrace opportunities or teacherly moments when they should and do speak up, sharing their depth of expertise and knowledge or demonstrating their refined skill of furthering thought and conversation with the appropriate interjection of ideas or interrogatives. Faculty learn the appropriate balance of these actions through practice and often as well through the nonverbal communication of the students in the classroom, who often demonstrate fairly obviously which of the three aforementioned approaches are needed in the moment.

Similarly, teacherly presence is a delicate concept in the online creative writing classroom. Scholars in the creative writing discipline have argued for a more democratic pedagogy that values student-writers' voices and agency as preferred to the star-writer-as-teacher pedagogy prevalent in decades past (Bizzaro and McClanahan, 2007; Mayers, 2005; Vanderslice, 2008). Nevertheless, creative writing teachers must be sensitive to the fact that because of the power structure in academia, student-writers may naturally value the teacher voice more than the voices of their peers in online discussions. As a result, when developing a teacherly persona for teaching creative writing online, teachers should strive for that balance of frequent interaction to demonstrate presence, but not such an overwhelming presence that student-writers in the course feel that their own voices are less than, or worse that their contributions to the class discussion are not welcomed. Recalling Iser's assertion that meaning is found in "not only the actual text but also, and in equal measure, the actions involved in responding to that text" (1673), teachers must be aware that their responses to student posts, which we are referring to as texts in this context, assign meaning to the texts and the discussions overall.

The above recommendation to aim for a delicate balance regarding teacher presence, though, is vague and difficult to measure, which further demonstrates the complexity of the task. To identify that delicate balance, online creative writing teachers can do several things:

1   Strive for it

This may seem obvious, but faculty who have identified the need to reach a balance are much more likely to do so. While this chapter aims to contribute concrete examples to assist faculty in developing teacherly personas in the online classroom, our primary intention in writing this text is to ensure that faculty are aware of the need to do so. In that same vein, awareness of the delicate balance regarding teacher presence in online learning environments will further teachers' development of their personas.

2   Talk with colleagues

Talk with colleagues about how student-writers in their courses react to teacherly presence in the classroom. If the teacherly presence is too prominent, thus it is the primary response that makes meaning of student work, students may respond to a peer's question or comment by sitting back in silence and waiting for the teacher to respond. If the teacherly presence is lacking, student-writers may actually request in their posts that the teacher weigh in by posting comments such as, "I wonder what the professor thinks about this," or "Maybe the professor can clarify if we're on the right track here." Conversations with colleagues about these topics can lead to greater clarity in attaining the appropriate balance of teacher presence.

3   Respond second

By this, we suggest that faculty can foster stronger interactions within the online classroom by waiting to respond until after other students have done so. For instance, in the case of the writing workshop in which all student-writers are reading their classmates' works and offering feedback, feedback may be heavily influenced if the teacher posts before the classmates do. By responding second, teachers make space for student-writers to read each other. For instance, if a student-writer posts in the discussions and the teacher responds first, then it's the teacher's response that makes the meaning. Every interjection of the teacher voice in the course makes meaning for student-writers, a realization that further demonstrates the need to respond second, allowing student-writers to first make meaning of their own in the online space.

4   Time responses

There is some inherent contradiction in this suggestion; when teachers time their responses to be spaced out throughout the unit, week, etc., doing so creates space for students to enter the conversation and contribute to the meaning of ideas. For instance, if the unit begins on Monday and ends on Sunday as so many do in the online learning environment, teachers might post once or twice on Tuesday to fuel deeper critical thinking, but then not post again until Friday, which allows students to engage in those days between. To be clear, those first posts on Tuesday demonstrate to students that teacherly presence exists; the teacher is present by reading and responding to students, which helps other students feel investment in their thoughts and ideas, but the teacher then steps back and makes space for students to contribute over multiple days. Finally, the teacher may step forward again, making their presence known near the Sunday deadline or even the following Monday after all student-writers have contributed to the discussion or workshop.

5   Consider language

Earlier in the chapter, we asserted that a teacher must be willing to become the reader the text creates; doing so is a complicated endeavor as student-writers' intentions are not always clear or interpreted accurately (as could be said about all writers). That said, teacher language should first demonstrate the interest to understand student texts rather than interject a teacher's meaning upon them. Often interrogative statements work more effectively than declarative ones to better understanding student-writers' intended meaning and audience. Nevertheless, the meaning for any text will always be found at the intersection of reader and writer; teachers should ask themselves whether their language choices aim to get closer to that meaning or instead shift the meaning to be what the teacher as reader intends rather than what the student as writer intended.

6   Survey students

There is much to be said about actually asking students how something is working. Faculty may ask students directly with questions such as "Did you feel your teacher was present in class discussions/writing workshops/etc.?" "Did you feel your voice was valued and welcomed in the discussions/writing workshops/etc.?" "Would you like your teacher to participate in class discussions more frequently/less frequently?" As we know from student evaluations, responses will always vary, but over time, a teacher could positively evolve their teacherly presence based on the feedback from student-writers.

As previously mentioned, faculty should develop their teacherly persona as one that makes space for all voices in the classroom.

While these concepts are ideal in the creative writing classroom, we must also note the online environment creates challenges perhaps not present in the onsite classroom, and those challenges must be addressed. Namely, online students who are not compelled to meet on a regular day and time report difficulty in motivation and potentially falling behind in classes. As a result, online creative writing teachers, despite their best intentions to support a writer-centered environment that balances the authority of both the student and the teacher as meaning-makers, may be forced to engage their authority to ensure online student-writers meet basic expectations of the courses.

In doing so, they may contradict the persona they have worked so hard, and in so many ways, to develop. And throughout our theoretical and practical writings regarding teacherly persona, one point remains true: developing a teacherly persona that honors the true intentions of a teacher and also maintains those intentions over time with consistency is a difficult task. This chapter has demonstrated that the way teachers read and respond to student texts and contributions in the online environment, and especially in the creative writing classroom, reflect and influence their teacherly persona. Thoughtful conversations and research remain necessary on this topic. As we began in critique mode, so, too, we conclude: how would you identify your teacherly persona? Do your actions and responses in your online creative course uphold that persona? What changes, if any, might be appropriate to ensure the consistency and clarity of your teacherly persona in the future?

Works cited

Adsit, Janelle. "Giving an Account of Oneself: Teaching Identity Construction and Authorship in Creative Nonfiction and Social Media." *Creative Writing in the Digital Age: Theory, Practice, and Pedagogy*. Michael Dean Clark, Trent Hergenrader, and Joseph Rein, eds. London: Bloomsbury Academic, 2015.

Baran, Evrim & Correia, Ana-Paula. "Tracing Successful Online Teaching in Higher Education: Voices of Exemplary Online Teachers." *Teachers College Record*, vol. 115, 2013, pp. 1–41.

Berthoff, Ann E. *The Making of Meaning*. Montclair, NJ: Boyton, 1981.

Bizzaro, Patrick. *Responding to Student Poems: Applications of Critical Theory*. Urbana, IL: NCTE, 1993.

Bizzaro, Patrick and Michael McClanahan. "Putting Wings on the Invisible: Voice, Authorship and the Authentic Self." *Can It Really Be Taught: Resisting Lore in Creative Writing Pedagogy*. Kelly Ritter and Stephanie Vanderslice, eds. Portsmouth, NH: Boynton/Cook, 2007: 77–90.

Dennen, Vanessa Paz. "Presence and Positioning as Components of Online Instructor Persona." *Journal of Research on Technology in Education*, vol. 40, no. 1, 2007, pp. 95–108.

Girardi, Tamara. It Can Be Acquired and Learned: Building a Writer-Centered Approach to Creative Writing. Indiana University of Pennsylvania, PhD dissertation, 2014.

Iser, Wolfgang. "Interaction between Text and Reader." Vincent B. Leitch, ed. *Norton Anthology of Theory and Criticism*. New York: Norton, 2001: 1673–1681.

Kinnell, Galway. *Walking Down the Stairs*. Ann Arbor, MI: University of Michigan Press, 1978.

Kress, Gunther. *Literacy in the New Media Age*. New York: Routledge, 2003.

Laing, R. D., H. Philipson, and A. R. Lee. *Interpersonal Perception: A Theory and a Method of Research*. New York: Harper, 1972.

Mayers, Tim. *(Re)Writing Craft: Composition, Creative Writing, and the Future of English Studies*. Pittsburgh, PA: University of Pittsburgh Press, 2005.

Minot, Stephen. "Creative Writing: Start with the Students' Motive." *College Composition and Communication*, vol. 27, no. 4, 1976, pp. 392–394.

Quintilian. Institutes of Oratory II. 15. Patricia Bizzell and Bruce Herzberg, Eds. *The Rhetorical Tradition: Readings from Classical Times to the Present*. 2nd edition. Boston: Bedford/St. Martin's, 2001: 385–389.

Royster, Brent. "Inspiration, Creativity, and Crisis: The Romantic Myrtle of the Writer Meets the Contemporary Classroom." *Power and Identity in the Creative Writing Classroom: The Authority Project*, Anna Leahy, ed. Bristol, UK:Multilingual Matters, 2005, 26–38.

Vanderslice, Stephanie. "Sleeping with Proust vs. Tinkering under the Bonnet: The Origins and Consequences of the American and British Approaches to Creative Writing in Higher Education." *Creative Writing Studies: Practice, Research, and Pedagogy*, Graeme Harper and Jeri Kroll, eds. Bristol, UK: Multilingual Matters, 2008, 66–74.

4 Making the write impression

How to use written materials to boost rapport and connectivity in online creative writing classes

Paul Gleed

I remember chatting with an acquaintance some years ago, soon after I had transitioned into online teaching following more than a decade working in the bricks-and-mortar classroom. "Oh no," my interlocutor protested, "I wouldn't want to take an online course. I'd need to be taught by a human being." His remark was off-the-cuff and not intended as an insult, but it nonetheless encapsulates one of the central challenges of online pedagogy: how to remind students that there is a human being behind that mechanical curtain of the learning management system (LMS). After all, student learning and interest are enhanced when productive, positive relationships develop between an instructor and her students. So the art of building rapport with students in the online classroom should be of paramount importance to all online teachers; without good instructor/student rapport, desirable metrics from student learning to retention inevitably suffer.

As Means, Bakia, and Murphy report, research suggests that a student's sense that an "instructor is present online and interacting with students is even more important than interactions [between peers in class]" for building community (2014: 157). Citing a study by Boston et al., they add that the primary indicator of student success is "instructor behaviors such as clear communication of course goals, objectives, and instructions; guiding the class toward understanding; and helping to keep participants engaged and on task" (157). We all have a good sense, then, of the types of instructor behavior that fosters good rapport, but building it actively and successfully into the online learning environment is neither easy nor intuitive.

Creative writing, the field at the heart of this essay, offers a particularly interesting example of a discipline that really demands and trades on rapport and community within the classroom. After all, the identity of creative writing as an academic discipline is traditionally intertwined with immediate, face-to-face interaction around the ubiquitous seminar table (though increasing numbers of online instructors have sought to challenge this preconception over the years). Uniquely, both in the popular imagination and some quarters of the Ivory Tower, the discipline of creative writing is in large part identified through the style and materiality of its teaching space: the creative writing workshop. So, perhaps as much as any other discipline, creative writing has witnessed resistance within its ranks to the advancement of online learning. Those critics fear that the dynamic, engaging, and productive model of workshop learning cannot be replicated online, and that, further, the revered interactions and relationships fostered in traditional creative writing classes will only be diminished when transplanted into an online platform. If solid rapport-building strategies are essential for all online instructors, then, they seem a particularly—even existentially—urgent matter for online creative writing instructors.

The aim of this short piece is to highlight the need for rapport-building strategies when crafting written course materials, communications, and feedback in online creative writing courses (though many of the techniques and strategies presented in this chapter might be modified for use in writing classes more broadly). By focusing on the use of written materials as rapport-building tools, this essay appears out of step with the widely endorsed idea that written materials in online courses are not particularly helpful to good classroom rapport-building. While I strongly agree with the idea that online courses should and must embrace multimodal technologies in order to fully nurture rapport between instructors and students and between classmates themselves, as we shall see, it remains true that written materials do and will continue to play a key role in online courses

Nonetheless, the movement in online class design has been to *reduce* dependence on the written word in course materials, instead emphasizing greater use of images, videos, audio clips, interactive quizzes, and so on. Stephanie Smith Budhai and Ke'Anna Brown Skipworth, for example, argue that "typed texts and traditional lecture materials are overused in online courses, limiting the interaction learners can have with each other, the instructor, and course content" (2017: 7). Instead, such an argument runs, more dynamic and active strategies must be increasingly incorporated into online class materials. I do not challenge this positive pedagogical evolution. Rather, mine is one of those "baby/bathwater" arguments, one urging instructors not to miss every opportunity to generate positive rapport in the online classroom. Even while many online instructors rightly look for alternatives to the written word in their teaching materials, the use of written materials remains all but inevitable in most courses and we should therefore not ignore the potential of these materials to do more than communicate information.

Additionally, even amid these sensible challenges to an overdependence on written materials, it is worth noting that one emerging trend in online education may soon drive instructors to produce much *more* written material for their classrooms not less, thus making a conversation about how to best produce such materials ever more pressing. The trend in question is "open education resources" or OER, the movement to reduce or replace costly textbooks with freely available material online and additional instructor-generated materials. The logic for OER is clear and broadly irrefutable. In a changing economic and educational environment, where institutions see dwindling enrollments and students perceive dwindling financial returns on expensive educational investments, there is a moral and professional imperative on instructors to make their courses more accessible and affordable. While certainly not all of this new instructor-generated material will be in the form of written texts, much (if not most) will be. As overpriced course books begin to recede from courses, instructors will be filling the resulting gaps with their own writing and that of others shared openly online. If some of this new material is written with rapport-building in mind, it will be to the benefit of educational institutions, teachers, and students alike.

It is timely and essential, then, to talk about the possibilities of written materials in all online courses, and we will return to this broad, rapport-building focus shortly. However, any discussion of the positive potential of written materials in online classes should note that one type of online class in particular has long benefited from (and will continue to benefit from) carefully worked and calibrated written course materials: the writing class. While educators and theorists currently make a convincing case for minimizing written materials in many courses, creative writing teachers (along with all online writing teachers) have the opportunity and responsibility to craft plentiful written course materials offering unique value in active and varied ways. In addition to the specific role of rapport-building that we will discuss below, and in addition to the standard functionality of written materials to present information, such materials in writing courses offer an opportunity to *model* fundamental aspects of the discipline, from voice and audience-awareness to style and syntax.

Indeed, creative writing is a discipline in which a conscious, large-scale deemphasizing of written course materials in favor of, say, video and audio materials may deny students meaningful educational opportunities. In creative writing classes written materials can become *active demonstrations* of foundational skills and techniques within the discipline and should be prized as such. Further, writing instructors can even emphasize this aspect of the written course materials, adding commentary to their materials discussing *how* the instructor-as-writer is employing the techniques they are trying to teach. This is a significant educational opportunity bestowed upon the online creative writing instructor, one that presents her with an advantage over bricks-and-mortar colleagues. A face-to-face writing teacher, after all, communicates primarily with her students through in-class *speech*; the online writing instructor likely communicates about writing with her students primarily through the *written word*. Here, then, form and content conflate in interesting ways that are rich with pedagogical potential. While bricks-and-mortar instructors can and do supply models and demonstrations of writing, of course, online writing instructors can turn the very course itself into an extended, multifaceted *demonstration* of what writing is and how it can be utilized.

While the benefits and opportunities springing from written course materials may be greatest for the online writing instructor, then, they are plentiful for all online instructors. When creative writing instructors use course materials to model writing strategies, and particularly if they do so openly with students, commenting on the craft utilized it in the production of course materials from explanatory slides to assignment descriptions, acknowledging their own challenges and difficulties as writers, instructors reveal themselves to be ongoing learners themselves, experienced practitioners of the written word that are nonetheless prone to anxieties and struggles in their work. The creation of such an identity through course materials will certainly help foster a deeper connection between teacher and student; students enjoy seeing their faculty as experts in their discipline, but are often also thrilled by a glimpse from "behind the scenes" of the skillset they are working to develop.

This pedagogical strategy is just one way to use the written word to nurture rapport in a creative writing class, of course. There are numerous others, many of which can be utilized by instructors in various disciplines. The suggestions that follow are primarily intended for instructors who create their own learning resources and materials rather than those who use "pre-packaged" platforms from outside providers. However, even online instructors who do not create their own materials have an opportunity to utilize the written word for rapport building in email communications with students or through discussion boards included as part of pre-packaged course software.

The remainder of this short essay focuses on rapport-building pedagogical strategies that may be useful to online creative writing instructors and writing instructors more generally. Of course, the ideas here are not all presented as "best practices," but simply strategies that have proven productive in my classes over a decade of online teaching. These strategies focus specifically on how to use written materials as a way of building rapport, and I have seen many of them cited favorably by students in course evaluations. They suit my teaching style and persona, but may not feel right for every instructor, of course.

The first, most basic element of written materials in an online class is the primary course content, most likely delivered in slides prepared by the instructor for use in the class LMS. Received wisdom says that the amount of text included in such slides should be small, but I like to resist this somewhat by making at least occasional slides quite text-heavy, thereby modelling more sustained movements of writing. My self-imposed limit is two full paragraphs per slide. Key, of course, is to communicate essential information and model good writing style without overwhelming students and making progress through course units feel onerous. To help in this regard, it may be useful to subtly shift styles between slides, composing shorter chunks of text in a more formal style while making longer chunks more conversational. Rapport-building is aided by the development of a natural, "real" voice in the instructional text; such writing establishes a sense of instructor identity as the student reads through the course materials. For example, personal anecdotes, asides, and humor can all be usefully incorporated into written course materials, particularly when they tell stories of the instructor's own engagements with writing and higher education. Such moments occur naturally in face-to-face classes and do much to build connection between teacher and student, so creating space for them in content slides may improve student engagement and more vividly evokes the teacher's personality and identity as a writer. Be sure, also, to routinely review the written material in your slides, even if it has proven perfectly functional over time. It is standard practice, of course, to review course materials for broken links and outdated calendar references before each new term, but consider reviewing *all* your written content on an annual basis. Course slides can drift "out of sight, out of mind" when instructors have used them successfully for several semesters, but regular reviews are a way to make sure even small shifts in thinking make their way into the materials. Such revisions give an instructor confidence that content slides offer an accurate, current representation of where she stands within the discipline and that students are encountering and "getting to know" the instructor as a content expert, teacher, and individual.

Another kind of writing that instructors may include in learning resources, also offering both student learning opportunities and rapport-building benefits, is examples of their own writing. The addition of an instructor's published or unpublished stories, essays, or articles offer numerous advantages to students. Some instructors may balk at this move, recalling with a shudder some class they once took in which a faculty member "forced" students to read his work as part of the syllabus and sometimes even offered flattering lectures on the merits of that work. A far less questionable approach to take, however, is one that allows students to see an instructor's professional "vulnerability" as much as their talent. For example, the inclusion of a story that the instructor could never quite seem to place for publication reminds the student that all writers, even experienced and well-practiced ones, are buffeted by the same kinds of rejection, doubts, and insecurities that challenge novice writers also. Another interesting strategy might be to include an instructor-written story or essay in multiple stages of its development, thus modelling the revision process in action. Perhaps an early version of a story, one that did not connect with editors at the time, could be placed alongside a reworked version of the same piece that eventually found success or at least the author felt was much improved after alteration. The key, once again, is to use such examples as an opportunity to reveal the nuts and bolts of the writing process, the moving cogs in the works that the instructor herself assembled. With all such examples, sharing honest and earnest self-reflection on the instructor's part is essential.

In addition to examples of an instructor's own work, a small bank of sample student writings can be usefully included in the LMS, three or four examples of each assignment in the course. These are updated each semester if needed, removing old examples and adding new ones if the preceding semester has produced especially worthy pieces. I publish the examples anonymously in the LMS, student name and any other distinguishing details removed (particular care should be taken with selecting memoir-style or autobiographical pieces, and I refrain from including pieces of work that feature particularly personal themes). Importantly, I seek permission from students to include their work as a sample assignment, and students are always pleased by the thought of their work serving as an example to others in subsequent semesters. The selected pieces are always standouts, of course, but I usually preface each sample essay or story with a brief commentary outlining the pieces successes *and* one or two areas in which I feel the piece could have been even further developed. The risk of including such sample documents is that some students will use them as a crutch, modelling their work too tightly on the examples and stymying their own creativity as a result. In my experience this has not proved to be a significant problem, however, and certainly not enough of a problem to outweigh the meaningful benefits. The inclusion of student examples leads to fewer questions about an assignment from students and so is labor-saving on the instructor's part. More importantly, though, while the inclusion of student-written examples does not directly help establish rapport between instructor and student, it does potentially boost a student's sense of belonging to a community of writers past and present.

Another type of written course material worth considering in terms of rapport-building is that of written feedback on assignments. While many instructors are finding success with audio feedback on assignments, there are certainly reasons to continue offering a good amount of written feedback as well, especially when addressing the mechanics of student writing. Written feedback is labor intensive and highly time-consuming, but it offers the most precise and nuanced tool for feedback on syntax, grammar, and other writing issues. In light of the changing educational landscape referenced earlier, however, many instructors will find themselves working with more and more students each term as institutions look for ways to counter various downward economic trends. Written feedback is one place in which overstretched instructors may look to take short-cuts, and so it is important to maintain standards while maximizing efficiency and taking sensible precautions against instructor burnout as piles of written assessments mount ever higher.

In terms of rapport-building, personalized feedback, rich in commentary regarding specific and individual aspects of a student's work, is the most likely to establish connections of trust and appreciation between instructors and students. In contrast, "canned" feedback (copied and pasted from an instructor's own collection of stock comments) speaking in generalities and abstracts may be enough to communicate core concepts and ideas, but is also much more likely to produce a sense of disconnect on the student's part. While interaction between instructor and student in the face-to-face classroom is plentiful, opportunities for such in the online environment are not naturally occurring and must be deliberately generated. Assignment feedback, therefore, remains one of the most prominent points of individualized contact between teacher and student in an online course, and in addition to simply being good teaching practice, handling feedback with skill and care is a way to demonstrate compassion and commitment to student success. So how to balance the need for rapport-building, pedagogically effective commentary with the pragmatic need to work efficiently in responding to ever greater amounts of student work?

"Canned" commentary clearly has a place in the instructor's toolkit, carefully worded standard responses that address, for example, what a run-on sentence is or articulate broadly that a particular moment in the student work lacks detail. After all, there is nothing to be gained from writing anew each time some information about sentence fragments or the need to proof read work more carefully. But even canned comments such as these can be topped and/or tailed with unique comments particular to that moment in that student's essay, while a few moments of work with Microsoft Word's "Track Changes" function can add a productive and personalized element to, say, a canned comment about excessive wordiness in a paragraph. Instructors should not feel guilty about using canned commentary where there is little or nothing to be gained by writing a unique comment, then, but they should look for efficient ways to individualize feedback elsewhere in the essay or story. Sometimes this mix of unique and prepared feedback is achieved even within an individual line comment by adding a few unique sentences to a preexisting canned comment. Keeping a bank of canned common comments seems like a pragmatic necessity, but it is important to resist the slippery slope that would see the ratio of canned to original comments become increasingly unfavorable. Where students have particular problems at the sentence-level, I invest my time heavily into "track changes" markings in the first few paragraphs or more and use canned comments to give those markings context.

So if content slides, sample pieces by both instructor and past students, and instructor feedback all present formal opportunities to foster stronger connections between instructor and student, there are also countless less formal opportunities through in-course communication such as email and discussion boards. Discussion boards are another place where canned comments can be marshalled, but they are less justifiable in these forums, I think, and more easily discernable as such to students, I would say. Arguably, it is better to respond to a smaller number of posts with unique, original comments than to respond to a larger number of posts with canned comments. An instructor should look, also, to use discussion board posts as a way of "joining the dots" between student posts on a thread, identifying points of comparison and contrast between student posts in order to reinforce the dynamism of the thread's conversation. Using posts to pose new questions emerging from individual student posts, and inviting other students to answer those questions, is a way to guide the conversation in spontaneous new directions that may have begun with the discussion board prompt but have been productively extended along new avenues.

Similar care should be given to emails, both those written to individual students and to the class as a whole. I send out a weekly "Course Update" email every Monday. These are canned emails used semester after semester, but they are given the feel of unique communications by having a few sentences at the beginning of the message referring to weather, recent or upcoming holidays, new developments in the field that may be of interest to students, etc. These are not labor intensive communications, then, but hopefully still read to the students as fresh, timely, and unique moments of contact. Similarly, I send out regular "check-in" emails to the class when we are working on a particularly challenging assignment or reading, or at the beginning of the course when students are familiarizing themselves with the course structure and LMS (these emails are then republished in the LMS using its "News" feature or equivalent). While some instructors might suggest that simply posting a news item is a better approach, the email acts as an individual communication with the student in a way that posting a news item does not. Again, in online teaching it is important to embrace every opportunity to personalize interaction and to make engagements with students feel like points of communication between instructor and student. Emails also invite responses from students in a way that news postings do not. A student is more likely to ask a follow-up question in response to an email than to an update posting on the course LMS homepage.

It is important to remember that students find asking questions much easier in a face-to-face classroom, even if it is simply posing a query to the faculty member briefly as they leave the classroom. In an online class students are more likely to let important questions go unasked, leading to possible retention threats in the most vulnerable student populations; preemptive written communications inviting questions at a time when the instructor anticipates students will have them is an especially valuable way to signal an instructor's commitment to her course and her teaching. It uses targeted canned emails as a way of potentially generating meaningful individual communications soon after with students in need. Certainly any serious problems with a student should be re-directed to a phone call, Skype session, Zoom chat, etc., but many students appreciate the value of the asynchronous email communication as a way of communicating with the faculty member on their own schedule. Personally, also, remembering how the mood and tone of an email is notoriously easy to misinterpret (a reader, especially an anxious student, may see angry frustration in an instructor's reply where only professional brevity was intended), I perhaps overemphasize the friendliness of a message, being sure to begin and end with good wishes and even (eternal shame!) smiley faces every now and again to show that while the demands of the email, say, for late work to be submitted immediately were real, the message is nonetheless friendly and courteous. In other words, adding conscious, clear, and professional warmth to emails can encourage continuing student participation even when their will may be flagging. Replying to emails in a timely manner is also, of course, a good way of signaling the kind of respect that generates strong rapport in a class.

Other instructors have made great use of communication through social media platforms attached to their courses. Creative writing instructor Bronwyn Williams, for example, values Twitter for various pedagogical reasons. Not only does the limited number of characters force writers to focus on clarity and succinctness in their posts, the platform can be used to create additional pathways of discussion when workshopping a story. The asynchronous nature of the platform "can create a space for ongoing, informal responses [to a story] to take place before and after a piece is talked about" more formally in the course (2015: 252). This creates not only a forum for rapport-building casual interactions, Williams notes, but also for the kind of insights into a peer's work that only emerge sometime after an initial discussion has taken place. Here, then, is a great example of how asynchronous engagement has advantages over synchronous engagement alone, even in a discipline like creative writing that traditionally so values the synchronous, shared classroom moment.

Joseph Rein has identified another way in which asynchronous student-to-student responses to creative writing offer advantages over traditional synchronous workshopping. Imagining a creative writing course in which the workshopping of stories is done asynchronously through discussion board posts, Rein observes that such forums "democratize the workshop" (2015: 93). By this Rein means that discussion boards, unlike traditional workshop classrooms, do not create a space so easily dominated by a small number of vocal, standout participants. Because discussion boards allow participants time to reflect and measure responses, and, crucially, give all students equal "time" in the class spotlight, they "level the playing field" for students (93). "Students often feel as though they give—and receive—higher quality feedback" on discussion boards than in face-to-face seminars, Rein comments (93). Importantly, though, it should be noted that Rein achieves this outcome by breaking down large online classes into small group discussion boards of five or six students.

Whether on discussion boards or Twitter, then, asynchronous responses present rewarding opportunities. Beyond the use of social media as fora for discussing assignments, however, some creative writing teachers have even sought to place social media communication right at the heart of class projects themselves. The rationale offered for doing so is compelling, not least because many students are already highly practiced and engaged writers on these platforms. As Janelle Adsit writes, "Some of our students' Twitter feeds and Facebook accounts have a larger audience than some small-press, 'literary and little' journals will ever see" (2015: 105). Moreover, as Adsit continues, if creative writing instructors dismiss out of hand the kind of writing that many students are most engaged with, they may be fundamentally misunderstanding the motivations that prompt students to write on social media sites in the first place. Adsit herself, for example, uses social media writing in her classes as a bridge into creative nonfiction writing, particularly memoir. After all, memoir and social media posts share the same basic DNA, she argues, and by using students' familiarity with social media posts instructors can forge an exciting new route to sophisticated and self-reflexive student writing. "Putting creative non-fiction alongside online discourse is a way of refining the teaching of this genre and an opportunity to revisit the status of art—the criteria by which we separate literary personal narrative from the mundane status-update anecdote" (106).

Written texts, then, from student social media posts to instructor feedback on student work, offer opportunities not only to provide insightful creative writing instruction, but also opportunities to foster good rapport between all stakeholders in the classroom. As we have seen, across all disciplines, a worthy movement has seen written materials in online classes fall out of favor. Instead, teachers and instructional designers look for multi-modal opportunities to help them teach and build professional relationships with students. This is a generally positive trend, but the argument of this chapter has been that we should not lose sight of how written materials will continue to feature heavily in online classes for the foreseeable future. Giving thought to the creation of such materials, especially in terms of maximizing their potential as tools for community building in an online course, is something that no instructor should overlook. Creative writing instructors, along with educators across the disciplines, continue to redefine what it means to teach and learn online, building courses that match the face-to-face modality in key metrics of student success. In showing how a field bound so quintessentially to the seminar room tradition can embrace and thrive in an online setting, online creative writing instructors should feel optimistic that, with care and attention, they can continue to provide meaningful and engaging learning opportunities as the global educational landscape evolves and transforms.

Works cited

Adsit, Janelle. "Giving an Account of Oneself: Teaching Identity Construction and Authorship in Creative Nonfiction and Social Media." *Creative Writing in the Digital Age: Theory, Practice, and Pedagogy*. Michael Dean Clark, Trent Hergenrader, and Joseph Rein, eds. London: Bloomsbury Academic, 2015: 105–120.

Means, Barbara, Marianne Bakia, and Robert Murphy. *Learning Online: What Research Tells Us about Whether, When and How*. New York: Routledge, 2014.

Rein, Joseph. "Lost in Digital Translation: Navigating the Online Creative Writing Classroom." *Creative Writing in the Digital Age: Theory, Practice, and Pedagogy*. Michael Dean Clark, Trent Hergenrader, and Joseph Rein, eds. London: Bloomsbury Academic, 2015: 91–104.

Smith Budhai, Stephanie and Ke'Anna Brown Skipworth. *Best Practices in Engaging Online Learners through Active and Experiential Learning Strategies*. New York: Taylor & Francis, 2017.

Williams, Bronwyn T. "Digital Technologies and Creative Writing Pedagogy." *Creative Writing Pedagogies for the Twenty-First Century*. Alexandria Peary and Tom C. Hunley, eds. Carbondale, IL: Southern Illinois University Press, 2015: 243–268.

5 Navigating trauma in the online creative writing classroom

Laraine Herring

When I first began teaching creative writing 25 years ago, I realized that no matter the course content, many of the students were writing about their own traumas. I was also struck by how little preparation I had for teaching writing. The craft was one thing, but holding people in the journey of their own stories was something altogether different. Learning how to put a sentence together and how to pull a narrative along matters, but those things could exist without a piece of writing saying anything. For writing to have meaning, the writer had to be willing to mine their own broken places. It quickly became clear that in order to be the best writing teacher I could be, I had to learn much more about human psychology, especially the effects of trauma. I had to learn how to handle the trauma that student narratives would bring to me as an instructor, and I had to learn how to show the students how to handle the trauma that could occur as they write their stories and engage in classroom activities.

I transitioned into the online environment in the early 2000s. The software was primitive—primarily discussion boards and monochromatic pages. It was a bold, new frontier and there was little support on how to navigate this environment. In this Wild West of education, we instructors had to find ways to connect with the hearts of our students. We had to move them from zeros and ones into flesh and blood. Today, the technology is not as challenging as it was two decades ago. Most of our students now are familiar with the online environment, and in an unexpected shift, many, especially traditional-aged students, are more comfortable in the virtual world than the face-to-face one. Technological advances will continue to shape what is possible within online instruction. However, we must not lose sight of the human who might appear only as an avatar on our screens.

When I began to create courses specifically for the online environment, I drew on 25 years of teaching in a variety of modalities, my master's in psychology, and my practical experience in the field. And, I drew on the thousands of students I'd worked with over the years, who taught me more than I could ever hope to teach them. The online learning environment can provide many benefits, but in order to assure the safety and learning potential for all students, it's imperative that we apply trauma-informed practices to our creative writing classes. All members of the course are witnesses to the trauma presented in creative work and, as such, need guidelines for providing effective feedback, handling personal triggers, and managing their own mental health through the creation, revision, and workshop processes.

What is trauma and how does it impact the body?

One out of every four children attending school has been exposed to a traumatic event (National Child Traumatic Stress Network Schools Committee). Through epidemiological research, we also know that a plurality of children and youth experience one or more traumatic events in their lifetime (Fairbank, 2008). These events may include exploitation, violence, natural disasters, loss of a loved one, and military or family-related stressors. With the rise of dual-enrollment, we may find ourselves managing classrooms with an age range of 15–85. That alone exposes us to the possibility of dealing with a variety of traumas and a variety of behavioral challenges. College classes may contain people who are dealing with severe disease diagnoses, people who are in domestic violence situations, and people, such as combat veterans, who have witnessed traumatic events. To cultivate a trauma-informed classroom, we first need to understand a little bit about the trauma and stress response.

> Here are some common traumatic events, referred to as adverse childhood experiences, (ACEs):
>
> - physical abuse
> - emotional abuse
> - sexual abuse
> - an alcohol and/or drug abuser in the household
> - an incarcerated household member
> - someone who is chronically depressed, mentally ill, institutionalized, or suicidal
> - mother/father who is treated violently
> - one or no parents
> - divorced parents
> - someone with a terminal or chronic illness
> - emotional or physical neglect
> - a caregiver with a terminal illness
> - bullying

Trauma is anything which threatens one's physical or psychological integrity. It disrupts two basic human needs: safety and community. Witnessing traumatic events can also create trauma in the individual. We can develop trauma responses by watching disturbing news of global tragedies such as natural disasters, wars, and human and animal suffering.

The trauma response is a heightened and prolonged stress response. Our stress response is governed by our central nervous system, which has two primary components—the sympathetic branch and the parasympathetic branch. The sympathetic branch regulates the fight or flight response, which was intended to be used and dissipated quickly. In today's world, this stress response is often activated by events that are frustrating, but not life threatening, such as sitting in traffic or being cut off in line.

If our stress response does not dissipate as it was designed to do, physiological damage can occur. The body builds up a resistance to the stress response—meaning it re-regulates itself so that the physiological responses to the stressor, such as heightened blood pressure, shortness of breath, and constriction of the GI tract, become the new normal. Our bodies are phenomenally adaptive and able to sustain a heightened stress response for some time before physically breaking down, but eventually, things catch up.

During the physiological response to stress, the individual sees a stressor (a threat) and a message is sent to the amygdala in the limbic system of the brain. The amygdala is the part of the brain responsible for regulating and perceiving emotions. It also has a role in memory storage, which helps the individual recognize similar situations in the future. Ideally, this is a great survival strategy.

In the online classroom, however, a person might encounter another student whose word choices or even name reminds them of their abuser, or a reading assignment might be set in a location similar to the source of their trauma, such as a combat veteran reading Tim O'Brien's *The Things We Carried*. This can happen in a face-to-face classroom, of course, but the asynchronous online environment restricts us to written language and avatars that don't allow for the in-person meeting that could shift the trauma response by allowing the student to have a different, positive direct experience with someone with the same name as an abuser.

Next, the amygdala sends a message to the hypothalamus at the base of the brain to activate the appropriate response. The hypothalamus has a vital role in releasing hormones and is in constant contact with the pituitary gland. The pituitary gland is in charge of increasing or decreasing certain hormones. In a stressful situation, the pituitary gland gets a message to release stress hormones through the adrenal glands. These stress hormones are adrenaline, which increases heart rate, elevates blood pressure, and increases energy supplies, and cortisol, which helps to regulate metabolism as the body responds to stress. Wide bodies of evidence indicate that long-term trauma and stress, especially in developing brains, change the structure of the brain itself. These changes often manifest in an overdeveloped (overstimulated) amygdala, underdeveloped temporal lobes, and a shrinking hippocampus. Changes in the brain lead to changes in behaviors (Herringa, 2017).

It's important to note that the stressor need not be *real*. The individual must perceive the event or experience to be threatening, regardless of whether an outside assessment might find it to be. In other words, the threat is in the eye of the beholder.

Trauma is categorized in three primary ways. The first type of trauma is *acute* trauma, which is a single event that lasts for a short, defined time, such as a car accident. Our stress response system is designed best for acute trauma—assuming we're able to let those emotions dissipate after the threat is over. The second type of trauma is *chronic* trauma. Chronic trauma occurs when an individual experiences more than one traumatic event over a long period of time. *Complex* trauma is specific to children under the age of 5. People with complex trauma experienced multiple traumatic events at a very young age that were caused by caregivers. The final type of trauma is *historical* trauma. This is intergenerational trauma that impacts groups who have experienced long-term, systemic emotional and psychological pain. Examples of groups impacted by historical trauma are American Indians, Holocaust survivors, and African-Americans.

How stress and trauma responses translate to behaviors

Humans cope with challenging situations in the best ways they know how with the tools that they have available to them. If a person was never taught good coping skills, or if a person's trust in adults or institutions was ruptured, they are not going to behave in ways we might consider appropriate. Often a trauma response behavior becomes ingrained as part of an individual's make-up because it is familiar and effective. To the brain, a successful outcome of a trauma response is the organism's survival. It's not concerned with whether or not the pattern is healthy in the long term. People who live in chronically traumatic circumstances cultivate coping strategies that to an outsider might seem maladaptive, but are completely reasonable *within the world of the trauma*.

> Trauma impacts development, which impacts the ways students will behave and participate in class. Some common behavioral consequences of trauma are:
>
> - difficulty trusting others
> - social isolation
> - difficulty seeking help
> - hypersensitivity to physical contact
> - increase in medical, emotional, and mental problems
> - problems with coordination and balance
> - poor ability to regulate emotions
> - problems with academic achievement
> - oppositional/antisocial behaviors
> - difficulty planning for the future (Center for Substance Abuse Treatment, 2014)

Trauma isn't just something that happened in the past. For many of our students it is ongoing. For others, the experiences are repeated in their minds, creating the same physiological and psychological impact as if it were continuing to occur. Writing and reading are ways we can process trauma or relive it, and though the creative writing class is not a psychologist's office, we can provide as safe a framework as possible to best serve our students and ourselves.

Building a trauma-informed online classroom

When people write their stories, they can gain a sense of power over the narratives of their lives. This can be especially useful for trauma survivors. However, the field of creative writing, by necessity, pushes students to read texts that may recreate unsafe, unpredictable, and dramatic situations. Our job is not to be their therapists, yet we nonetheless encounter their wounds. The most effective way to manage the requirements of our discipline with the needs of our students is to build a trauma-informed online classroom.

The trauma-informed classroom, whether online or in-person, focuses on four key components: Connect, Protect, Respect, and Redirect, which I discuss in more detail later in the chapter (Hummer, 2010). We know that traumatic experiences can impact learning and behavior, and we know that a significant portion of our students will have experienced at least one ACE. Traumatic events create traumatic stress, and long-term stress impacts learning and behavior.

To understand how to work with trauma in the classroom, we must understand that it's not just about learning new tools. It's about significantly shifting the way we view the world. Most of us have been trained to look at behavior problems in isolation and to believe that correcting the behavior corrects the problem, but for the person struggling with trauma, the behavior is directly linked to that trauma and cannot be effectively resolved without understanding the reasons for its existence. That type of work involves a mental health professional, but as professors, we can help by changing our thinking. When confronted with challenging behavior, we can shift from "What is wrong with you?" to "What happened to you?" (Bloom, 1995). That switch in perspective moves from judgment to an open-ended, empathic approach.

Some common behavioral responses to being triggered are:

- Thinking one's personal space is being violated. Online, this may come across as, "You don't have any right to critique my experience."
- Overreacting when being corrected. This may present itself as extreme and volatile resistance to feedback, either from the instructor or from the class.
- Fighting when being criticized. This may manifest as aggression in discussion boards or small groups if a student disagrees with a peer's ideas or has an assumption challenged.

> - Resisting transitions or change. This may appear if the instructor needs to change assignment dates or reconfigure group assignments. The student dealing with trauma may be challenged by the "rules" or "structure" of the class changing. This interferes with their sense of safety and trust (Child Welfare Committee, 2019).

We will not be able to prevent any and all reactions from students, nor will we be able to anticipate everything that might arise in our courses. But we can structure the class from day one in a way that creates the best possible outcome for all of our students. The online environment is perfectly suited to this in one key way: you can design a course that is consistent and structured from the very first day. You can control exactly what material a student sees and when they see it, and you can control your assignments, due dates, and format requirements. This helps all students feel like they can trust their instructor and the framework of the class.

In our attempts to challenge students to dig deeper into their work, we may create more stress for that student and increase their trauma response. Be very careful trying to push through a student's walls until you know why they were built and whether or not the student is in a safe space to move deeper. We may be able to see what the student isn't yet saying on the page. We may understand what needs to deepen and what still needs to be explored in order for the story to come together. And though it is our job to help them do that, it is not our job to force them into a place that is emotionally and psychologically unsafe. We can do our best by creating an environment in which they feel safe enough to stretch.

The elements of a trauma-informed classroom: connection

Connection is about building relationships. The online environment allows us to present ourselves exactly as we'd like. We can write and rewrite our introductions and posts to the class. We can re-record our introductory videos until we have it just right. We are crafting the self that we'd like to share with all our students. Ideally, this self is warm and welcoming. Share a little bit about yourself and what you love about students, teaching, and creative writing. Mention how creative writing has helped or shaped you. Speak a bit about how you're going to structure the class. Depending on the tools available to you through your LMS, you can include screen captures of your class and show them exactly where things are to be found and why you've organized in a particular way. These actions demonstrate your competence, and they communicate to students that you are a person who is real and interested in their well-being. Your introductory video and materials should be freshly written and recorded each semester. Students can tell when something is rehashed from semester to semester.

We must also establish a safe way to connect students with one another. Depending on the type of class you're teaching (lecture, generative, workshop), there may be different levels of engagement you're expecting students to have with one another. Engaging with others may be a source of anxiety for students. You can help minimize this by having introductory discussion boards that focus not just on their names and why they're in class, but on other off-the-wall things such as favorite songs or foods or topics such as, "The silliest thing I ever did was ..." Encourage students to use video in their introductions, but understand that video may not be comfortable or possible for everyone. The introductory assignments should not induce anxiety or promote shame. Creating options for their presentation contributes to the overall sense of safety and trust. They can write their posts, or they can upload an audio or video file. These choices give the students a sense of ownership of the class, which helps them feel safe. It's important that you monitor the class activity so that you can intervene if necessary. Instructors should model a consistently respectful tone in communication, even in conflict situations.

Protection

The protection element promotes an environment of safety and trustworthiness. To best create this, use an authoritative approach to teaching and structuring your classroom. An authoritative approach is a leadership style characterized by "high acceptance" and "high control." This means that the instructor accepts the students for who they are and as they are, and they have reasonable classroom policies, rules and systems that are adhered to equitably and consistently. If the instructor does not enforce their own course rules, this diminishes their credibility in the class and impacts the sense of safety in the classroom.

Although a creative writing course thrives on the democratic approach, there still must be a leader to create and hold the space of safety. The professor is the person responsible for the educational journeys of all the students, and students, especially traumatized and marginalized students, will not feel safe to explore and own their own experiences—either on the page or in the classroom—if the space itself is not a strong, held container. If the instructor does not create these boundaries, another student with a dominant personality will fill in the vacuum, and that will vastly impact the sense of safety. Please don't confuse "authoritative" with "authoritarian" approaches. They could not be further from each other in terms of leadership styles. Within a consistent, flexible structure, there is freedom. In the section below, I discuss how instructors can include students in co-creating this structure so that all voices have input in the course design.

Respect

Respect in a trauma-informed classroom is about choice and collaboration. These tools help students feel a sense of empowerment and control over their environments. To accomplish this, have choices in your assignments and prompts. There's never only one prompt or one novel that meets the course's learning outcomes. The online environment is ideal for presenting assignment choice because you're not monitoring real time classroom management. For example, you could have two novel options to read and break the class into groups based on which text they chose. You would still have to prepare and manage the two books, but the students will have more freedom to engage in choice, which feels like collaboration and ownership in the course design. As a bonus, you're likely going to get more original engagement because the discussion boards won't be one big group where it's easy for students to get lost or repeat what was posted first.

A collaborative approach provides the student a sense of ownership and investment in the class. Some instructors use the first week of class to come up with a class-determined reading list. Consider ways of involving the students in some decision making. For example, students could vote on whether assignments were due on Fridays or Sundays.

Collaboration can also be included when designing the workshop process. The workshop can be a terrifying thing for any student, especially if it's their first time participating. No matter how much you model appropriate feedback, there's a chance someone is going to react unfavorably to it. One way to help diminish this possibility is to have the students include three craft-based questions for feedback on their submissions. This does two important things:

1 It gives the students control over *what* they want feedback on. We all know that it's not the right time for all types of feedback all the time. A first draft shouldn't be responded to in the same way as a final draft. By keeping the questions craft-based, you steer clear of the content minefields and can head off comments that could be perceived as judgmental by the writer.
2 It gives the student reviewers a solid place to start. Most beginning writers are unsure how to provide feedback. If they have three questions from the writer of the piece to work with, they have a place to start that the author has already determined was safe. The instructor can model additional feedback as warranted.

Redirection

Redirecting is an approach that encourages skill-building and competence. If we keep the focus of the assignments on craft, not content, we can help the students gain a deeper understanding of the elements of good storytelling while learning to detach from their work and not take criticism personally. We can also help build a student's writing skills through detailed, craft-based feedback. (E.g., this dialogue exchange could be more tense if the characters didn't use it to relay backstory. Consider using deflection and misdirection as we read about in chapter x of the textbook.) A feedback reply like that, as opposed to a terse comment such as *talking heads dialogue* or *info dump*, provides the recipient with the same information (the dialogue is weak), but it explains why and what to do to improve it. It doesn't address the content of the piece or the writer's choice to use dialogue. It's particularly important to be very clear in written redirections online because the student doesn't have the benefit of our body language to fill in subtext.

Assessment in our field is subjective. Clear craft-based rubrics for assessment, strong models of peer-to-peer feedback, and guidelines the workshop process help model skill-building, connection, protection, and respect. We must model that we can provide helpful feedback on pieces that are in styles or genres we don't prefer, and in doing so, we can reduce the chance a student will feel attacked.

Content warnings

The efficacy of content or trigger warnings is widely debated. Some claim these amount to coddling. Others argue that they are necessary to help people discern whether or not it is safe to access a piece of information. There have been numerous studies about the benefits of trigger warnings, but most have been using subjects who did not self-identify as trauma survivors. In 2019, Jones et al. conducted the first study using subjects who identified as having trauma histories. Their study concluded that trigger warnings don't help, and they can actually promote anxiety in folks who have experienced trauma. Though there is clinical debate about the anxiety promoted by trigger warnings, the evidence indicates that they are not helpful for most and may be significantly unhelpful for people with severe trauma.

If you choose to use content warnings, consider including a content warning conversation in your first week's collaborative activities. You can include the class in a discussion about whether or not to use these warnings, and if so, what content types should be identified. This promotes collaboration, respect, and connection.

Good, accessible, affordable mental health resources are superior to content warnings, but unfortunately, many colleges and universities do not have enough of these services. Each semester, I provide an updated resource list, and in my syllabus statement, I encourage students to take a look at the reading list and assignment list, and if they see anything that they're concerned about to reach out to me in the first few weeks of the semester so alternate assignments can be arranged. I do this for both face-to-face and online classes. This involves students in the decision-making, demonstrates respect for each student's individual process and stage, and allows me to encourage an environment of safety. Rarely do students ask for accommodations, but by inviting their participation, I've already established that I am interested in their input and willing to work with their unique needs.

Effectiveness and challenges of addressing trauma in online creative writing courses

Anonymity: benefits

People struggling with trauma may have poor social skills. They may be more withdrawn. They may not feel safe responding to people face-to-face. They may fear being touched, even by accident, and they may not be comfortable in a face-to-face classroom. Online, the student is free to create an identity that reflects their hearts. They can be seen as they wish to be seen. These benefits provide much needed control to the individual dealing with trauma. The anonymity may also help minimize implicit and explicit biases that can come into play in face-to-face classroom engagement.

Anonymity: challenges

Misunderstandings are much more likely to occur online, and the illusion of anonymity can make some people more likely to engage in conflicts they wouldn't engage in face-to-face. A person can respond to a discussion post without fear of having to deal with any replies in real time or space. This makes some people more aggressive or quicker to confront. Without the concern of real-time reprisals, certain personalities may clash more frequently online. It is also very difficult to manage subtlety online. Students who are not particularly strong writers may not know how their words are coming across. They recognize their intent, but they don't have a mature understanding of the impact of their words.

Asynchronous environment: benefits

An online classroom allows people to choose how and when they will respond—both to the material and to the other students. Controlling the time and space of engagement with a course is very beneficial for trauma survivors. An asynchronous learning environment gives them the best of all worlds—they can engage with the material when they're in the best place and frame of mind to do so.

Asynchronous environment: challenges

A key challenge to the asynchronous environment is that conflict can happen when the instructor is offline. Rarely are even a few students online at the same time. An altercation might occur in the discussion boards over the weekend, but the instructor doesn't know until they log in on Monday morning and must attempt to diffuse a conflict that might be days old, with students who are not instantly reachable. When these outbursts happen, it damages the safety of the classroom for other students.

The asynchronous environment also makes it very hard to have that all-important "first class meeting" where students get a sense of the instructor and their classmates. Because so much of our communication is non-verbal, we miss many social cues in the online world. This can make it harder for a class to bond, which can impact the sense of group safety.

Both online and face-to-face classes have the potential to trigger a trauma response in a student, no matter our best efforts. The online environment might be better for potential content challenges because the student will have control over their own environment when reading and responding to texts. They will not be put on the spot to read or respond to something, and they will be able to make choices about how and when they respond.

Communication style

An advantage unique to the online class is the method of communication. Since most class communication will be written, students have a chance to practice writing skills with each post or feedback submission. They have time to make a measured response and time to revise what they say before posting. This helps prevent potential conflicts that can occur if there is disagreement over material or feedback. We can help ensure this practice by providing a model of the writing practice—prewrite, draft, revise—that can be applied to any online communication. Also, including reminders to pause and consider the audience and impact of their posts before submitting will help take advantage of this benefit.

Tools for instructor and student success

We can give our students the tools they need for success with a comprehensive welcome letter sent out the week before class begins. When we send out a letter early, students have a chance to hear our tone, understand our class expectations, and assess how they align with their own class hopes while there's still time to change their minds about the class. The letter should present a professional, authentic, and accessible voice. The purpose of the letter is to create a connection with students, establish class policies, expectations, and an environment of mutual respect, and provide an opportunity for students to ask questions privately about the course ahead of time.

Suggestions for the letter:

- Instructor contact information, short biography, and pronouns
- Brief synopsis of the course content
- Fears students might have about a creative writing class
- Challenges and benefits of the online environment
- Diversity inclusion statement
- Workshop guidelines if applicable
- Examples of effective online communication
- Expectations for engagement
- Request for students to email you after reading the letter with an introduction and any concerns or questions they have about the class

Each of us is going to have a different level of comfort with the emotional demands of a creative writing class, and there's no one-size-fits-all approach to managing your class and your own mental health. Taking in our students' stories can build up a stress response in ourselves which we must address healthfully.

Each semester is a practice, and every combination of students is its own entity. When I was doing my internship for my graduate work in psychology, the clinical supervisor stressed the importance of each of us doing our own personal therapeutic work so that we could best serve our clients. They said, "Whatever you don't work on in yourself will walk right in your door." The warning is that we will likely project our own unresolved issues onto our clients, thereby not serving them. As instructors, we need to be aware of our own challenges so we know how to help someone or when to best refer someone to a clinician. We have to learn how to manage our own triggers so we don't unintentionally harm our students with our responses.

Trauma-informed online classroom management tools

1 Have a clear statement of inclusion on your syllabus.
2 Make sure you have a list of mental health resources and social services available at your college and in your area.
3 Be aware of your college's plan for dealing with classroom concerns. Take the time to find that resource before the first day. Recognize that your responsibility is to both student and class, and that the safety and needs of the group supersede the needs of one individual student.
4 Make sure you include your institution's student code of conduct link in your syllabus. If your institution allows variations in instructor policies, add your own that address your needs. These might include appropriate tone examples for discussion boards or critiques or a specific reference to bullying or judgment of any student's material.
5 Send out a welcome letter in the week prior to the first class that demonstrates your tone, your policies, your boundaries, and your expectations. This is the first step in establishing how you will be communicating with them and the way you expect them to communicate with you. If you're able to include a short video of you, that's also useful. This helps to create connections with the students prior to day one.
6 Establish the boundaries you are comfortable with and hold students to them. Boundaries create a sense of safety. For example, if you don't allow late work, that is not just a policy, it is a boundary. Model effective communication and boundary setting in every email, announcement, module, and video.
7 If you're feeling overwhelmed or upset, don't respond to their material until you're in a more stable space.
8 In the first week of class, be online as much as possible so that you can provide quick feedback to their introductory discussion boards and be proactive if there are any student or relational issues that you observe. If at all possible, organize a group video conference. Everyone won't be able to attend, but the ones that can will get a sense of the humanity of everyone else. You can record this and post it in the first week's module for the students who couldn't make it.

9 Stagger your assignment deadlines if you have multiple sections or multiple courses. My teaching load is 5/5 (or five sections in the fall semester and five in the spring semester), so I make sure that no week has more than one section of papers coming in. I may be grading all the time, but I'm not grading 200 papers at once. A big advantage of online teaching is that students can turn in work early and I can grade things as they come in. If this fits your style, I highly recommend it. Waiting until everything comes in can be more stressful on you than doing a few papers a day as they arrive in your grade book.

10 As professors, we are mandated reporters. Know who your campus's Title IX coordinator is. Our Title IX obligation is to report sexual misconduct, sexual harassment, and gender discrimination occurring between students, students and employees, or students and community members who are involved in the college experience. In order to comply with the law and create a sense of safety for students to write what they are compelled to write, include a clear Title IX statement in your syllabus explaining that you are a mandated reporter, as well as a statement indicating that you will make every effort to keep their work private, but that you are legally bound to report Title IX concerns. We know our students are likely to write about their traumatic experiences, and we want to create a place for them to explore their lives authentically. If you have specific questions about what must be reported, please consult with your institution's Title IX coordinator.

11 Set up as many real-time events as you can within the parameters of your institution. You could hold video office hours, for example, where students could log in and speak with you one-to-one. You could have a pop-up class through video conferencing to address an area where you found the students struggling (e.g., dialogue tags or dramatic questions). These can be recorded and uploaded to your class for viewing by students who could not attend live.

12 If your institution requires letter grades, make sure you have clear and specific rubrics for each assignment. These make sure the student knows what they will be assessed on, and it helps you in the event of a grade dispute. The rubrics should be craft-based to help minimize the subjectivity of creative writing grading. This type of grading approach will also help you avoid slipping into content-critique.

13 If you use the workshop process, make sure you have clear workshop guidelines for both writer and reviewer. Students should include three to five craft-based feedback questions on their submissions. This ensures that the writer's work is being critiqued on the basis of craft, not content. It can take some trial and error to teach students what a craft-based question means. Include question examples, such as: *I struggled once I added the third character to the bar scene on page 4. Were you able to keep track of the characters? What could I do to improve that?* Discourage questions such as: *Did you like it?* and avoid yes/no questions. This approach teaches

writers to assess their own work with a critical eye without them even realizing that's what you're teaching. Make it clear that any workshop assignment is public and, as such, don't submit anything they are not comfortable being discussed by the class.

14 Make sure you have alternate assignments and options available if a student requests them.
15 Return emails and papers within specified parameters. My college requires that we return all students' emails within 48 business hours, and that we return all graded assignments within one week of the due date unless there is a pedagogical reason for a longer time frame. If your institution doesn't have such a statement, I encourage you to create one for your own classes.
16 Remember these three elements: safety, consent, and choice. Create a sense of safety in your class through your communication, course structure, assignment structure, and topic selection. Assure student consent by having them participate in assignment construction as appropriate, and provide their own questions for feedback. You might even have them sign an agreement at the start of the semester that outlines the course and student expectations. This can lend clarity to the student and can help you in the event of a student challenge to a policy. Assure choice by providing alternate assignments when indicated and allowing them some selection in writing prompts and topics.
17 Recognize that students' problem behaviors may be trauma-related patterns. You must address the behavior and its impact on the class, but keep in mind that the behavior is likely stemming from something else. A trauma-informed approach to these behaviors might be: *I'm curious about what prompted you to reply to Dan with this intensity?* instead of: *This is an inappropriate response to Dan's post.* Reach out to "Dan" to find out how he has been impacted by the student's post and, if appropriate, assure him that you're addressing the behavior as required by your college.

Stress management tools for instructors

Instructors are human beings. Many of us are trauma survivors. Just because we have advanced degrees doesn't mean we check our humanity at the beginning of a semester. Teaching requires a great deal of energy expenditure, and it can be easy to forget to practice self-care. If you're a new teacher, you may find yourself taken aback by the amount of energy creative writing teaching takes. The depth and breadth of students' stories—their traumas—will become a part of your own narrative. I've long thought of myself as a secret keeper. I hold so many student experiences in my heart, and I've read so many encounters of trauma in their memoirs and essays, that if I didn't know how to process that energy and keep my own boundaries, I would burn out and not be able to continue teaching.

The online environment is rarely a synchronous exchange of energy. For example, for efficiency, we'll likely read all our emails at once, or grade a set of essays in a specific time block. Whereas a face-to-face student might make an appointment to visit us during office hours, online students are more likely to email us in the middle of the night with their challenges, potentially providing us with many more issues to deal with all at once when we log in.

Here are some guidelines to help you:

1 Don't assign books or create types of assignments that you know will be triggering for you. There are plenty of things to write about and plenty of things to read. If you're recently divorced or if you're dealing with a serious illness or grieving the death of a loved one, you might not want to read about those issues in a particular semester. It's OK to set your own boundaries around the content you are willing to absorb.
2 Employ good time management so that you're not always in front of the computer, always responding to student work, or always engaging in the online environment. Don't sit for more than an hour without getting up and walking around the room or the block. Take at least one day a week off from the class. Stagger deadlines.
3 Make sure that you're involved with meaningful relationships and activities that are off-screen. Stay engaged in your community. Seek support as needed.
4 Exercise and eat healthy foods.
5 Understand your own limits. You're not a machine. If you need to readjust your course calendar because of something that has come up in your own life, you can do that. New teachers often over-assign or expect that they can handle more than they actually can. Many creative writing instructors are adjuncts and feel pressure to perform over and above what full-time colleagues are doing, all while juggling multiple jobs at multiple institutions or locations. They may feel like they can't say no, but no is essential to well-being. We must learn to set and hold our own healthy boundaries if we have any hope of holding those boundaries for the students in our classes.
6 If possible, access another instructor's course shell as an observer and take note of how that instructor has set up their class, how the classroom feels, and whether or not the course promotes active engagement. This will provide insight into what you want to bring to your class and what you want to avoid.

Conclusion

Writing changes lives. Storytelling is powerful, regardless of whether or not a student finds publication. The courageous act of putting pen to paper or hands to keys transforms the writer. It can promote both inward and outward changes. I now hold in my own cells the stories I've been privileged to witness from students. I consider it a privilege to be trusted with the words of my students. We have the opportunity to bridge worlds within our students. We have the opportunity to teach healthy boundaries for them and for us. We have the opportunity to relieve and reframe some burdens, and if we really hit the jackpot, we have the opportunity to help birth an essay or a story that will fly out into the world and transform others.

We will make mistakes. We will say the wrong thing or write the wrong thing. We will put a poor match of students in a group. We will not catch a cyber-bully soon enough. When those things happen, we can model effective ways of dealing with those challenges. We can own what happened and clearly explain what is going to be different moving forward. We can show that we don't have to be ruled by what came before. We can show the students that there is another side when things go wrong. As instructors, we are also students. I believe that hiding our humanity does a disservice to the class and a disservice to our own hearts. It's possible to create and maintain healthy boundaries while still being an accessible human being. The more the students can see your authenticity, the greater their authenticity will become, and as we all know, when a writer reaches deep, their stories change the world.

Works cited

Bloom, Sandra. "Creating Sanctuary in the School." *Journal for a Just and Caring Education*, I (4): 403–433, October, 1995. http://www.sanctuaryweb.com/Publications/ListofPublications.aspx. Accessed 19 December 2019.

Center for Substance Abuse Treatment (US). "Chapter 3: Understanding the Impact of Trauma." *Trauma-Informed Care in Behavioral Health Services*. Substance Abuse and Mental Health Services Administration (US), 2014. https://www.ncbi.nlm.nih.gov/books/NBK207191/. Accessed 19 December 2019.

Child Welfare Committee, National Child Traumatic Stress Network. *Child Welfare Trauma Training Toolkit: Comprehensive Guide*, 3rd ed. Los Angeles and Durham, NC: National Center for Child Traumatic Stress, 2013. https://www.nctsn.org/resources/child-welfare-trauma-training-toolkit. Accessed 19 December 2019.

Fairbank, John. "The Epidemiology of Trauma and Trauma Related Disorders in Children and Youth." *PTSD Research Quarterly*, 19, 2008, pp. 1–7.

Herringa, Ryan J. "Trauma, PTSD, and the Developing Brain." *Current Psychiatry Reports*, U.S. National Library of Medicine, 19 August 2017, https://www.ncbi.nlm.nih.gov/pmc/articles/PMC5604756/. Accessed 19 December 2019.

Hummer, Victoria, et al. "Trauma-Informed Behavior Support: A Training and Coaching Model for Caregivers." Slide 17, 2010. http://docplayer.net/19241015-Trauma-informed-behavior-support-a-training-coaching-model-for-caregivers.html. Accessed 19 December 2019.

Jones, Payton J., et al. "Helping or Harming? The Effect of Trigger Warnings on Individuals with Trauma Histories." OSF Preprints, 10 July 2019. https://osf.io/axn6z/. Accessed 19 December 2019.

National Child Traumatic Stress Network Schools Committee. *Child Trauma Toolkit for Educators*. Los Angeles and Durham, NC: National Center for Child Traumatic Stress, 2008. https://www.nctsn.org/resources/child-trauma-toolkit-educators. Accessed 19 December 2019.

"Preventing Adverse Childhood Experiences." Centers for Disease Control and Prevention. https://www.cdc.gov/violenceprevention/childabuseandneglect/aces/fastfact.html. Accessed 19 December 2019.

6 Software and hardware tools for teaching creative writing and self-editing online

Lex Williford

Introduction: teaching self-editing in online creative writing workshops

A teaching writer and a writing teacher for almost 40 years, trying to innovate as the founding director of one of the first online MFA creative writing programs in the twenty-first century, I've experimented with many hardware and software tools to teach generative creative writing and self-editing. Since then, in all my courses, on-campus and online, graduate and undergraduate, I've taught both *macro-editing*—raising global issues of narrative process, technique and structure, characterization, theme, and generative possibilities that might further develop and deepen a narrative—and *micro-editing* at the word and sentence levels—cutting or moving text, making granular comments, and using short keystrokes to save myself time as I expand detailed boilerplate comments I've written over almost two decades of teaching. For me, it's not enough to tell students that their writing is general or vague, wordy or convoluted, but to show them, by example, how to develop their stories and how to self-edit.

Time-consuming and tedious for the teacher/editor, specific line edits throughout an entire document may also have the opposite effect one intends, overwhelming students with too many issues, perhaps even discouraging them from revising. With my students' guidance and permission, I make many detailed edits and comments for *no more than about three pages* of workshop documents in Adobe Acrobat Pro (.PDF format) to show students how to spot, locate, and correct errors, how to clarify and specify generalizations, how to move from the abstract to the concrete, from telling to showing; and how to make their own sentences as compelling and dramatic as the stories my students wish to tell. Harvard College's "A Brief Guide to Responding to Student Writing" (2009) emphasizes several important principles that I try to follow: "Make Positive Comments," "Comment on patterns … (and mark … these only once or twice)," "Ask questions," "Use a respectful tone," and "Write legibly (in any ink but red)" (Brief Guide, 3). (When I write on my iPad Pro with my Apple Pencil, I use only bright green.)

For example, using one of my most common editing techniques, I ask students to cut all the instances of "to be" and "is" verbs in their loose-boned sentences, then ask them to make their sentences more sophisticated, active and direct, transforming wordy and repetitive sentence forms into cumulative periodic sentences using appositives, participial phrases, and nominative absolutes:

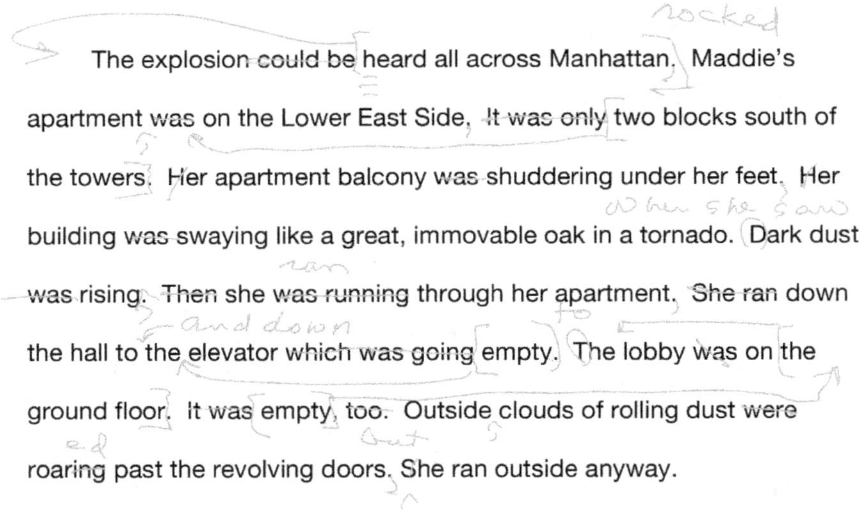

> The explosion could be heard all across Manhattan. Maddie's apartment was on the Lower East Side. It was only two blocks south of the towers. Her apartment balcony was shuddering under her feet. Her building was swaying like a great, immovable oak in a tornado. Dark dust was rising. Then she was running through her apartment. She ran down the hall to the elevator which was going empty. The lobby was on the ground floor. It was empty, too. Outside clouds of rolling dust were roaring past the revolving doors. She ran outside anyway.

Figure 6.1 Writing sample.

Despite this somewhat extreme example, working at the sentence level, my students have learned from these edits how to streamline their writing significantly:

> Heard all across Manhattan, the explosion rocked Maddie's apartment, just two blocks south of the towers on the Lower East Side, her apartment balcony shuddering under her feet, her building swaying and shaking like a great, immovable oak in a tornado. When she saw the thick dust rising, she ran through her apartment, down the empty hall and elevator to the empty lobby on the ground floor. Clouds of rolling dust roared past the revolving doors, but she ran outside anyway.

Of course, to respect a few students' preference for descriptive rather than more prescriptive critiques or line edits like these, I give my students the option to fill in a workshop cover sheet that designates the specific kinds of feedback and editing they'd prefer as demonstrated in the appendix. More often than not, when students actually see my line edits—understanding that I've streamlined their sentences without changing their sentences' meanings significantly, understanding that I'm usually showing only *one* of a countless number of ways to combine, organize, and edit sentence elements—they almost always ask for more editing, simply to see how I do it, so they can use similar techniques to edit their own work.

Why expend so much time and effort to teach students self-editing?

In one short year of graduate school, a remarkably generous professor, my MA creative thesis director, a gifted editor and writer, Fred Rodewald, taught me almost everything I know about how to edit my own work—more than all the professors I ever studied with in my BA, MA, and MFA English programs combined—and I've tried to pass along editing skills like these to my students, paying forward the time and effort my writing mentor made with the thesis drafts of my earliest stories.

In an NPR review, Stanley Fish, author of *How to Write a Sentence: And How to Read One*, recounts the story in Annie Dillard's *The Writing Life* of a fellow writer who, when asked, "Do you think I could be a writer?" said, "Do you like sentences?" For teaching writers and writing teachers wishing to learn more about editing, finding good books on sentence-level generation and self-editing can be difficult to find and even harder to teach, and as Daniel David Wallace writes, "The best books on writing good sentences [are often] quite hard to read" (2020: 3).

Wallace writes that, though he "completed an excellent MFA program in Creative Writing," after graduating, he'd realized that, like him, "those who might benefit from" sentence-writing techniques "to write with greater clarity, vividness and authority … had no idea of even those techniques' names" (3). I do not have the space here to outline other generative and self-editing techniques I teach, but for those writing teachers and teaching writers just beginning who wish to learn and teach such techniques, I recommend Wallace's free "How to Write Better Sentences" as a good starting point to learn such techniques as Christensen's cumulative sentence, parataxis, hypotaxis, etc. (3–5).

Two sources that have most influenced my sentence-building and self-editing instruction are Virginia Tufte's brilliant *Artful Sentences: Syntax as Style* and Francis Christensen's "A Generative Rhetoric of the Paragraph." Though they are difficult to find and mostly out of print, having unfairly fallen into disfavor since the sixties and seventies (and, as Ben Gunsberg (2016) writes, having "never achieved widespread application in the classroom"), Gunsberg's pedagogical essay "Schemes and Sense: Teaching Creative Writing with Design in Mind," a well-deserved corrective, discusses at length a history of the "Christensen Method" and cites several excellent examples in reference to creative writing instruction (2).

I like to joke with my students that I studied with Faulkner.

No, not *that* Faulkner, I say. (I'm not *that* old.) My late, great professor *Claude* Faulkner. He and his book *Writing Good Sentences*, still in print, taught me and other clueless MFAs at the University of Arkansas far more about how to write sentences than any of the graduate seminars we took on the novels and stories of William Faulkner.

How and why I teach self-editing in democratic workshops

As my *Poets & Writers* article "Toward a More Open, Democratic Workshop" suggests, my writing workshops, both on-campus and online, have become intensive democratic collaborations between me and my students. To teach them strong writing and self-editing skills, I ask my students to make detailed comments on each other's work in Adobe Acrobat, comments I grade as a part of their writing and editing apprenticeships.

Similar to what Rosalie Morales Kearns refers to as "non-normative" workshops, my classes give students full authority to describe how they want their creative work critiqued, eschewing "normative" workshops' tendencies to "impose gag rules" or to use "fault-finding modes" based upon "implicit aesthetic norms" or rigid rules-based instruction (2009: 796, 797, 801, 805). This approach is especially important in online classes—where some students may easily misread or take offense at any editing of their work at all, unless they've specifically requested such editing.

My workshops give student-writers the opportunity to discuss the problems they've encountered writing their stories as a part of positive brainstorming sessions in discussion boards which focus on process, development, structure, and revision along with specific discussions of technique and craft, referring to the work of professional writers who've experimented with narrative techniques and whose names my students may not know of yet.

Intensely aware of how my own authority as a so-called "expert" writer and workshop director can undermine my desire to give students the freedom to risk voicing those issues in which they've inadvertently been silenced or even bullied about in other workshops—Kearns cites my comparison of "the workshop dynamic to that found in authoritarian families" (806). Some students prefer a prescriptive approach, a preference I respect, but, when necessary, I channel the discussions away from students' unsupported subjective judgments and focus instead mostly on writing and editing technique. If students want a strictly descriptive critique with no editing, I respect their preferences as well.

Teaching writing and self-editing in on-campus workshops can be time-consuming and challenging enough, I think, at either the graduate or undergraduate levels, but teaching those same skills to online MFA students since 2006 has presented significant technological challenges to the kinds of detailed line-by-line commenting and editing I use to help students learn how to edit their own work. Even so, through a lot of trial and error, expensive hardware and software, and countless hours of technical support, I've adapted many of the time-saving methods and technologies, and my students consistently respond positively to the technologies I've chosen and the techniques I teach.

Preferred hardware and software for teaching creative writing workshops

Directing the online creative writing MFA at the University of Texas at El Paso and designing its first online MFA creative writing course, I faced many of the same daunting questions online creative writing teachers face for the first time:

- What software applications and other technologies could best help my students and me make line edits and detailed comments which automatically sync in a single shared weekly electronic document?

- Which of these applications were compatible with most Internet browsers, computers, and operating systems, including tablets and smartphones?
- Which of these would be the most widely used and the easiest to find, download, and install?
- Which of these could my students use for free with little technological expertise or technical support?

Despite some of Adobe Acrobat's disadvantages over the years—many of them now eliminated—I'm glad that I made Adobe Acrobat Pro my first and final choice. Admittedly, some online writing instructors may balk at using Acrobat Pro because of its expense—a subscription-based price of about $15 a month—but because it's evolved as the default electronic document exchange and commenting software over the last few decades—still retaining the exact formatting of documents as written—I've also found using Acrobat Pro just as useful for creating professional-looking documents for poetry, fiction, and creative nonfiction as it is for the correctly formatted screenplays film producers, directors, and agents require. More importantly, since many universities have recently contracted with Adobe to make its Creative Cloud and/or Adobe Acrobat free to faculty, it's become perhaps the most effective and least expensive option now available.

Hardware and software I've used to design online creative writing workshops

I wanted to create high-quality images and presentations for my courses myself, and I decided to expend more of my own funding and time buying, experimenting with, and teaching myself about software and hardware to develop and teach the additional courses I've designed, to create rich online MFA courses and hybrid on-campus courses in UTEP's first-of-its-kind bilingual MFA program, the bilingual option now also online, as well as the hybrid graduate and undergraduate classes I now also teach on UTEP's Blackboard platform.

After considerable trial, error, and expense—and a considerable number of bad choices about hardware and software too glitchy, expensive, or complicated to use—the preferred software and hardware I currently use include:

- Blackboard Ultra's Web Instruction Platform:
  - Which I use mostly for asynchronous instruction, except for Collaborate, which I use for synchronous online office hours and conferences.
- Software applications:
  - Which I use for professional online presentations and lectures on my ad-free YouTube channel:
    - Apple's Keynote:

- More sophisticated and beautiful than Microsoft's presentation software but also exportable to PowerPoint (free, Mac only).
- TechSmith's Camtasia:
  - Expensive but well worth the Education price ($169 for two computers, Windows, or Mac).
- The Adobe Creative Suite:
  - Free at some universities or, for instructors where it's not free, reduced Student & Teacher monthly ($19) and annual ($240) subscriptions, including the much-improved Document Cloud for syncing shared Acrobat comments.
  - Photoshop (pixel-based artwork) and Illustrator (vector-based artwork):
    - For course logos, banners and presentations.
  - Acrobat Pro:
    - For electronic document handling, distribution, and shared commenting.
  - InDesign:
    - For sophisticated professional pamphlets, books, booklets, and numerous other course documents—all exportable to .PDF.
- Affinity Photo (pixel-based), Design (vector-based), and Publisher (each $50 for Mac or Windows/$20 for iPad and other iOS devices).
  - For images, logos, banners and pamphlets, books, booklets, etc.
- Art Text 3:
  - For beautiful 3D text banners and logos (Mac only, $30).
- TextExpander ($3.33 monthly) or other text-expansion programs available at various prices:
  - For snippets of three- or four-letter keyboard shortcuts to save time with repetitive tasks, long class e-mail lists, detailed boilerplate comments and mini-lessons I've written over a dozen years on writing technique, grammar, sentence-editing, etc.
- Computer hardware:
  - A 12.9" iPad Pro (starting around $1,000) and an Apple Pencil ($99).
    - My primary tablet for commenting and illustrating.
  - A Wacom tablet, available starting with the Wacom One ($399.95) and the pricier Cintiq or Intuos tablets (prices varying based upon on size and quality).

- I still occasionally use the first commenting and illustrating hardware I used, a Wacom Cintiq Hybrid Companion (an independent Android operating system with options to connection to Windows and Mac computers).
- Two Mac Pros (2008 and 2013) and a 2014 Mac Mini (with a Thunderbolt monitor), all installed with fast solid-state drives.

Since teachers of online writing and editing may find hardware and software costs of these applications prohibitive, I recommend that faculty contact their institution's academic technologies and/or college grants departments. I also recommend adapting the equipment teachers already have to the task of commenting and editing; fortunately, Adobe now works with almost any hardware or operating system, but for those who can afford it, the best investments I've made over the last ten years—Adobe Acrobat Pro, the iPad Pro, and the Apple pencil—have been well worth the cost and have made teaching self-editing in writing workshops much less difficult, ideal for teaching courses online.

A comparison of software for shared commenting in online classes and creative writing workshops

I've tried a number of different kinds of software enabled for shared commenting but have settled on only one, first out of necessity, then by preference: Adobe Acrobat Pro.

My online MFA colleagues who don't make line-by-line comments and edits rely mostly on Blackboard Discussion Boards for global comments on workshop documents, especially when courses are asynchronous. Because these discussion boards can't make the kind of line-by-line editing and comments I prefer, I rely on them mostly for general discussions of readings and heuristic writing exercises, particularly useful in brainstorming sessions that focus on possible ways of developing creative writing projects further. Blackboard's interface has become more sophisticated when grading essays and the like, but Blackboard's commenting and editing functions for graded assignments remain quite basic, with only a few markup tools, not intended for commenting from anyone other than the instructor.

Google Docs and Microsoft Word commenting features

Perhaps the most widely used applications for making detailed, line-by-line shared comments on students' writing in the online creative writing workshop have been the free Google Docs (including Google Drive) and Microsoft Word (including Office 365), a free platform at many universities like my own using Word, SharePoint, Teams, and OneDrive. Each has its own distinctive advantages and disadvantages, but except for collaborations outside the classroom, I rarely use these.

Google Docs is perhaps the simplest, most accessible shared commenting interface to teachers and students with little expertise or those who prefer not to work with technologies that have anything but the most basic learning curves, but this web-based application doesn't include the kinds of sophisticated line-by-line edits and comments I prefer to make available to all my students.

Microsoft Word is perhaps the best among these for making granular comments in both its software and web-based services (and, yes, one may write comments in Word directly with an Apple Pencil or stylus on iPad Pros, Wacom and Microsoft Surface devices), but Word's comments-in-the-margins interface seems cluttered, making comments within wide margins difficult to read, especially when the professors and classes are making shared comments together on small devices. While I find Word's ability to compare different drafts of documents useful for my own personal use as a writer, and recommend it to students struggling with many drafts, I find Word less suitable for teaching online because its interface can become cluttered and because it forces writers to accept, reject, or delete others' comments just to strip them out of their documents, a tedious, time-consuming process.

Preferred document-sharing applications

Unlike having to print, copy, collate, staple, distribute, and shuffle paper documents in an on-campus workshop—something I stopped doing altogether almost two decades ago—I've found exchanging electronic documents for workshops, both on- and off-campus, far easier, more convenient, and, when the software works, much more efficient, mostly because students can share all their comments in one unified, uncluttered electronic document.

Preferred methods for students to submit documents for weekly workshops: Blackboard or Dropbox

Trying to avoid the complexity of receiving many e-mails with attachments from many different workshop students scheduled each week, I've relied on both Dropbox shared folders (or at times Microsoft's OneDrive, supported by my university) and Blackboard links to Dropbox as places for students to upload their workshop documents by a specific weekly deadline (usually midnight Sunday the weekend before we workshop their documents). At the beginning of each semester, I share distinctive links to weekly workshop Dropbox folders in my syllabi and occasionally with links to Dropbox folders from Blackboard itself.

Using Dropbox, a fast, remarkably reliable way of syncing and sharing documents outside the Blackboard interface, students may download the Dropbox app to use shared folders directly on their computers, where they may copy their workshop documents directly, or they may use web-based Dropbox shared folders where they may upload their documents to the appropriate weekly shared folder with almost any Internet browser or device.

It can be problematic to ask students, especially "those ... not as digitally literate as others," to adjust to too many different technologies outside the online classroom, overwhelming them with new interfaces and software apps to learn (McMurtrie, 2020). Fortunately, my students may call the UTEP Help Desk with technical problems for either Blackboard or other university-supported applications. When possible, giving students access to university tech support makes risking these technological solutions a bit more productive and worthwhile, but for unsupported university applications, I recommend creating simple presentations that help students learn unfamiliar interfaces. For example, I create YouTube videos to show students how to use the free Adobe Acrobat commenting tools with workshop documents. For these applications, I also ask students to contact me directly with any technical support questions the Help Desk can't answer. If I can't troubleshoot these issues, I call the application's tech support myself to find solutions which an entire class may find confusing.

Problems I've encountered with Adobe Acrobat Pro's previous methods of sharing document comments

In 2018, Adobe came out with a completely revamped version of Acrobat Pro, a newly simplified interface using Adobe's Document Cloud service—included as a secure stand-alone comments server as part of Creative Cloud subscriptions—which syncs comments, a significant improvement over the previous versions I've used, when it works, and it usually does, quite well, if teachers and students have relatively fast Internet connections. For those students who can't afford Internet services, I suggest that they make their comments using the university's relatively fast Wi-Fi network.

At the beginning, the most significant problems I've encountered with Adobe Acrobat Pro, despite its sophisticated shared commenting functions, have arisen from the difficulty of creating a secure university WebDAV comments server and my university's increasingly restrictive security demands, but with the newest updates I can recommend this application with far fewer reservations:

1   With Adobe's own secure dedicated server, it's now far simpler and a great deal faster to send shared documents for comments in just a few steps. Better yet, though students may have to create a free Adobe ID, this process has eliminated the complexity of and the need for the complex security settings I've confronted in the past.
2   Because the new version of Adobe Acrobat Pro allows my students and I to access the Document Cloud in a greater variety of ways—via any web browser or device including Mac or Windows, iPhones or iPads, and other tablets or smart phones, with the additional advantage of the ability to make comments—the program is accessible to all my students in a way it never has been before. And students can choose the most convenient and comfortable method for their distinctive technology needs. The ability to draft on a smartphone is beneficial to students without consistent access to a computer.
3   Because Adobe doesn't always sync well with my handwritten edits and comments and because those edits can clutter documents shared with

students' comments, I now create a duplicate, unshared weekly workshop document which I use exclusively for my handwritten iPad Pro and Apple Pencil comments. I e-mail those comments to all my students directly so everyone can see how I've edited and read my suggested boilerplate comments about numerous grammatical, editing, and other issues they may share.

Setting up a shared review with Acrobat Pro directly from a Mac or PC

After each week's workshop deadline, usually at the beginning of each week, I combine that week's scheduled workshop documents into a single shared document, converting different document types directly into .PDF, then e-mailing a Document Cloud download link and setting a deadline to students at least a week to make comments.

The principal disadvantages of using Adobe Acrobat Pro for shared commenting

Like many who use Acrobat Pro, I've had to become accustomed to the yearly expense of paying for the software subscription as a part of the Adobe Creative Cloud, which I use for many other tasks, including teaching, writing, and illustrating, but for online instructors interested in using an Acrobat Pro subscription to give their students and themselves the ability to make detailed comments on workshop documents, the subscription might be worth a try, even if the price of just an Acrobat Pro subscription itself may seem prohibitive. For me, it's a price worth paying, though my focus on editing at the sentence level—and the additional work of sending out documents for class comments—may be far more work than many instructors have the time or patience to do. This is time I'm willing to spend because teaching writing and editing at the sentence level has helped many of my students surprise themselves as their writing has become more specific, concise, dramatic, and readable than before. And countless former students have published or produced many articles, stories, novels, memoirs, and film scripts.

Setting up a clear collaborative student-commenting protocol

Acrobat Pro's shared reviews automatically sync all student comments in a single document, giving students the opportunity to mention each other or to reply directly to others' comments—an especially useful feature to help students see that their own comments may be subjective or that they may disagree not only about suggestions for revision but also with each other's basic cultural, racial, religious, and gender assumptions.

All students have to do to make comments is to download the latest free version of Adobe Acrobat Reader on their computers, tablets, or phones to gain access to the same commenting tools as everyone else in the class, including me—a convenient process that democratizes learning in fascinating ways and offers opportunities to create a dialogue rather than unnecessary conflict, even as students write about deep conflicts within their own lives. These freedoms carry with them important responsibilities.

For this reason, it's important to give students a clear protocol for how to collaborate with each other, making comments that focus primarily on writing technique rather than individuals' subjective judgments, not simply to avoid offending students (political correctness!), but to share culture difference, empathy, and mutual respect by being open to highly divergent issues that may be important to their peers but may consciously or unconsciously conflict with others' cultural backgrounds and upbringings.

A white professor who teaches in a bilingual program at a famously diverse university and city with an 80 percent Hispanic student population as well as many students online writing in English, Spanish, or bilingually, many from different parts of the Americas, I've spent years trying to teach students to give themselves permission to risk writing about their own distinctive traumas and truths—students who've seen the worst of the drug wars in Mexico and horrific prejudice against immigrants for centuries—and effective collaborative pedagogy must above all be open-minded and respectful, the teacher emulating dignity, empathy, and complex critical thinking:

> Learning occurs most effectively when experts and novices work together for a common product or goal, and are therefore motivated to assist one another …. Working together allows conversation, which teaches language, meaning, and values …. This is especially important when the teacher and the students are not of the same background.
> ("Five Standards of Effective Pedagogy")

I've been incredibly fortunate to teach such a diverse group of students for the last 20 years, students who must cross the border to take my classes, students who've traveled from Peru or Colombia, Uruguay, or Nicaragua, from Central to South America, many of them students who meet in an online environment I've tried to create suited to teaching writing collaboratively. In many respects, despite whatever work I may have done to discover technological solutions to teach online with such a remarkably diverse group of students, my students have taught me far more than I could ever teach them.

Appendix

Workshop Cover Sheet

Prof. Lex Williford

Your Name:
The Title of Your Work:
Workshop Week:
Number of Words/Pages:

Please use this handout as a cover sheet for manuscripts you submit for workshop discussion, *especially if you want to give the class specific instructions about how you want your writing critiqued.* This sheet is optional but highly recommended: it gives you a chance to say something about how you want us to critique your specific workshop pieces. If you don't use this cover sheet, you may assume that we'll discuss your work both descriptively *and* prescriptively, focusing primarily on narrative writing techniques and specific issues of craft and credibility.

For the two weekly scheduled workshop slots you signed up for at the beginning of the semester (one before and one after midsemester), click on the designated link to Dropbox for the appropriate week listed under Ungraded Weekly Workshops Assignments in Blackboard or in the syllabus; then upload your original workshop documents *to Dropbox only* no later than *midnight Sunday* before the week it's due for workshop discussion. Please don't upload your workshops to Blackboard, *only to the weekly Blackboard weblink to Dropbox*; please don't e-mail me your workshop documents or upload them to Graded Assignments (Final Drafts Only). I assemble all weekly workshop documents *only* from the weekly Dropbox folders synced to my computer. *If you don't meet your scheduled weekly deadline, the class won't discuss your workshop piece.*

If you have a legitimate reason for turning in your work any later than this deadline, please text or call me and let me know with sufficient lead-time *so that I can arrange another student's submission for workshop that week.*

The easiest way to use this cover sheet is to open it in Word, type *Control A/ Command A* to mark all the text, then to copy and paste it into the beginning of your workshop document. I'll download and combine all the weekly workshop documents and convert them to Adobe Acrobat (.PDF) format, then enable them for students' shared comments in the free Adobe Acrobat Reader (https://get.adobe.com/reader).

When you submit this cover sheet, please mark the kinds of critique you'd prefer (double-click on the underline and type *x*):

__ *Descriptive*

> Using *critical analysis*, readers describe the piece as they read it, identifying what they think the piece is about, describing the piece's narrative elements

and techniques, then discussing the piece's themes, images, etc., *as if they were reading critically any piece of literature we read in class, using textual examples from the piece as evidence of their assertions.*

__ **Prescriptive**

Using *critical evaluation*, readers critique a workshop document, discussing *what they believe the author's intended effects are in crafting the piece and how well the author has succeeded in achieving those effects.* Depending on the author's questions at the end of this cover sheet, readers may then *discuss two or three specific issues they found with the text* (typos, grammatical or spelling errors, lack of clarity, credibility, two-dimensional characterization, imprecision of detail and the like), then *supply textual evidence and concrete suggestions for change.* It's not enough simply to say that a manuscript "works"; please qualify every subjective judgment with the phrase "does or doesn't work for *me*," and then discuss why. *Not everyone will read or interpret every piece in the same way, and that's* why writing workshops can be so effective—because there's room for respectful disagreement. *Those receiving critiques may take whatever suggestions they can use and set aside the rest.* Try to imagine the story the author's trying to tell, not necessarily the story as you would tell it. Feel free to brainstorm ideas for editing, developing and deepening the stories you read. In your comments, consider writers' right to write their own truths as they wish and respect their dignity and beliefs, even if you don't share the same worldview. This class includes everyone.

__ **Both**
__ **Other** (describe below)

Also check off all that apply:

__ **Please don't edit.** Write marginal and end commentary focusing on content only.
__ **Please edit for wordiness and imprecision** ("is" verbs, prepositional phrases, abstract nouns, etc.)
__ **Please mark typos and grammatical errors.**
__ **Extensively comment on the manuscript paragraph by paragraph.**
__ **Other** (describe below)

As your instructor, I usually don't mark or edit every page, simply because I don't want to overwhelm writers or take away anyone's incentives to write.

Please list several specific questions you have about your piece to help the workshop focus our discussion.

This course will not have a "gag rule" or silence the writer of workshop documents, which means the author may ask questions for suggestions about process, clarification, development, and editing as long as they focus on craft and technical issues and resist the temptation to defend their work. There's no need to feel defensive in this class because we'll respect all writers at whatever stage their writing is the moment they first enter class

Works cited

Christensen, Francis. "A Generative Rhetoric of the Sentence." *College Composition and Communication* 14. 3, 1963, pp. 155–161.

Christensen, Francis. "A Generative Rhetoric of the Paragraph." *College Composition and Communication* 16. 3, 1965, pp. 144–156.

Christensen, Francis. *Notes toward a New Rhetoric: Six Essays for Teachers*. New York: Harper & Row, 1967.

Christensen, Francis and Christensen, Bonniejean. *A New Rhetoric*. New York: Harper & Row, 1976.

Dillard, Annie. *The Writing Life*. New York: HarperPerennial, 2013.

Faulkner, Claude. *Writing Good Sentences*. New York: Pearson, 1981.

Fish, Stanley. *How to Write a Sentence: And How to Read One*. New York: HarperCollins, 2011.

"Five Standards of Effective Pedagogy." Teach Tolerance. Reprinted with permission from the Center for Research on Education, Diversity and Excellence, University of California. https://www.tolerance.org/professional-development/five-standards-of-effective-pedagogy.

Gunsberg, Ben. "Schemes and Sense: Teaching Creative Writing with Design in Mind." *Journal of Creative Writing Studies*. RIT Scholar Works, 2016. https://scholarworks.rit.edu/cgi/viewcontent.cgi?article=1039&context=jcws.

Harvard College Writing Program. "*A Brief Guide to Responding to Student Writing*." 2009. https://writingproject.fas.harvard.edu/files/hwp/files/bg_responding_to_student_writing.pdf.

Kearns, Rosalie Morales. "Voice of Authority: Theorizing Creative Writing Pedagogy," *College Composition and Communication*, National Council of Teachers of English, 6. 4, June 2009, pp. 790–806.

McMurtrie, Beth. "How to Help Struggling Students Succeed Online." *The Chronicle of Higher Education*, March 20, 2020. https://www.chronicle.com/article/How-to-Help-Struggling/248325.

Wallace, David Daniel. *How to Write Better Sentences: A Simple Ten-Part Guide to Writing Really, Really Well*. 2020. http://jtancredi.weebly.com/uploads/1/0/4/5/104511429/howtowritebettersentences_danieldavidwallace.pdf.

Williford, Lex. "Toward a More Open, Democratic Workshop," *Poets & Writers*, 26. 2 (March/April, 1998): 52–54, 56, 60, 62, 67, 69, 73, 75, 77.

7 Zoom in and Zoom out

Virtual creative writing classroom pedagogy using Zoom

Nicole Anae

The growing international reach of creative writing as an academic discipline is becoming more and more apparent (Harper, 2015). While the presence of creative writing in an "increasingly internationalised academy" (Mort, 2013: 220) had led to greater "inflections of cultural identity [which] colour the creative and critical work of staff and students" (Kroll and Harper, 2013: 10), the advent of the "virtualization"—the process referring to the change or creation of a real-form object or thing into a version discernible using computer technologies—of creative writing, has precipitated a veritable explosion in the compositional tools available to would-be and operative writers. As various models in online creative writing pedagogy continue to evolve, understandings of what creative writing is and does, as much as the modes and forms of creative writing techniques, styles, and genres, ever-expand well beyond conventional understandings of time and space; into synchronous and asynchronous synaptic realms and virtual platforms. This chapter focuses specifically on the unique and ideal aspects of the online environment for exploring potential avenues for developing an online creative writing pedagogy, including practical approaches to incorporating collaborative online writing workshops utilizing video communications technologies.

By adopting a practice-led case study approach, this chapter maps the ways in which creative writing pedagogy incorporating online video communications technologies not only builds rapport between teacher and student-writers, but how these synchronous online experiences encourage peer networks within the synaptic-technologic creative writing environment, including developing trust relationships in the self-assessment of creative work. The discussion focuses specifically on how online video communications technologies have been embedded within a fully online offering of a second-year undergraduate course in Creative Writing at an Australian university. That this course is offered fully online is an important point of difference compared to other courses, while also signaling an increased pedagogical reliance on synaptic technologies, such as Zoom, a real-time video conferencing platform. This course regularly embeds 90-minute video conferencing sessions between the lecturer and students over the 12-week duration of the semester, typically one session every two to three weeks, in the form of ZoomLive creative writing workshops in which students participate in regular supportive and collaborative review of draft work-in-progress. During these sessions, students are invited to experiment with their own digital applications, and often do, resulting in practical experiences (largely without extensive technical expertise or knowledge) combining more conventional literary applications with forms of digital writing.

Feedback data, in the form of Course Evaluation Instrument (CEI) and Student Evaluation of Teaching (SET) responses, as well as personal emails and e-unit forum posts, evidence the high popularity of these ZoomLive creative writing workshop sessions as much as their effectiveness; not only as regards creative writing skills development, but engaging students in a community of writers. What characterizes the Zoom video-conferencing application is not only its literal focus on sharing, but its agency as a way of students speaking to the world through and about *their* writing—an impulse of creative production centering on personal experience, self-reflection, and collaborative reading.

Literature

Before commencing the discussion, it is helpful to briefly overview general trends in the scholarship regarding developments in online creative writing pedagogy within undergraduate tertiary education, including the approaches to teaching the various forms and genres of creative writing, before going on to explain the synaptic technology called Zoom. While there exists emergent scholarship examining the utility of writing in various genres among undergraduate students to include alternative creative writing styles—such as fictocriticism (Hancox and Muller, 2011), auto-ethnography (Mawhinney and Petchauer, 2013), studies in self-narration, using autobiographies, and self-reflexive examinations of the postmodern self (Ostman, 2013)—a critical gap in the scholarship concerning completely online creative writing pedagogies in undergraduate tertiary degrees is apparent. The body of contemporary literature about online writing pedagogy in the main includes research specific to writing (rather than "creative writing") pedagogies for masters and doctoral students (Badenhorst and Guerin, 2016); developing online pedagogies sensitive to culturally diverse contexts (Chambers, 2016); together with considering the question of "creativity" in the online learning environment (Baxter et al., 2018); as well as approaches adopting a "non-linear," or non-final-outcomes-based methods focusing on the intrinsic goals of creative writing (Clark et al., 2015). Some consider utilizing the online platform to offer "individualized feedback and mentoring" to practicing and aspiring writers (Venis, 2010: 98), while others expound gathering together student contributions to publish "a virtual class anthology" of creative writing (Moneyhun, 2015: 234). That said, although not specific to online creative writing pedagogies in undergraduate tertiary degrees, texts such as Graeme Harper's *The Future for Creative Writing* (2014), *Creative Writing in the Digital Age: Theory, Practice, and Pedagogy*, edited by Michael Dean Clark, Trent Hergenrader, and Joseph Rein (2015), and *Creative Writing Pedagogies for the Twenty-First Century*, edited by Alexandria Peary and Tom C. Hunley (2015), among others, represent very important contributions to the critical scholarship around the opportunities for emergent creative writing pedagogies within and beyond the twenty-first century. The concerns of this current chapter therefore offer an original contribution to a critical gap in the scholarship specific to online creative writing pedagogies in undergraduate tertiary degrees.

Zoom

Zoom is a user-friendly "cloud platform for video and audio conferencing, collaboration, chat, and webinars across mobile devices, desktops, telephones, and room systems" (Zoom 2020). The course under discussion here, the undergraduate elective in creative writing called "Creative Writing II: Writing Beyond the Page," integrated regular online Writing Workshops (via Zoom) incorporating a part-Amherst and part-Iowa approach as a form of "self-assessment" as much as a mode of formative feedback.

Writers interested in participating in a supportive critique of their work by the group were invited to send an anonymized version of either a section of their work, or a full draft, to the course coordinator. The work might consist of a chapter of a story, a series of creative writing exercises the student aims to incorporate into a major creative piece, a series of poems, a dramatic script, a short story, etc. The course coordinator then distributed all anonymized work to the group electronically one week before the workshop and led the discussions. Each session was around 90 minutes in duration, allowing sufficient time for around nine supportive critiques of around 10 minutes in duration. During the course of the session, each workshop participant shared impressions, advice, and analysis for each piece in a balanced way; there was as much a stress on affirmation as on suggestions for change.

It is important to note at this point that, while students enroll in online classes due to their flexibility and their asynchronous nature, it was also possible to receive feedback on draft work in the event that a student could not physically attend the Zoom session/s. In that case, students submitted their section to the course coordinator via email as per the description for the Zoom session one week before the next scheduled session. Students then received a single file containing all submitted (anonymized) sections for discussion at the next workshop and were expected to provide comments on each piece (using "track changes" function in Word). Students submitted their file containing all feedback to other students' work to the course coordinator via email by 9:00am on the morning of the Zoom session, and the coordinator then shared this feedback to peers on the students' behalf during the session itself. Sessions were recorded and links to the film clips made available to students for download and later viewing. This presented another issue in consideration: recording students without permission, which could present a potential barrier. In this case, students were notified both via Moodle notifications and prior to sessions via email that online Zoom sessions are recorded for educational purposes. Notifications stipulated that: 1) recordings of Zoom sessions conducted over the course of the unit may be uploaded and appear on YouTube, Moodle, and Microsoft Teams; 2) that if students had any concerns about being recorded could they please turn off their webcam or audio, or both, during the session; and 3) that their participation in any Zoom sessions will signify the student's consent to the recording and publication for educational purposes.

> WRIT12010_2192 -> Week 8 Discussion -> Feedback from my Zoom Critique
> by - Sxxxx Wxxx - Wednesday, 11 February 2020, 1:49PM
>
> Thank you for recording the zoom session, it was so informative and fun. I wish I could have joined you, but I must say it was fun to see you guessing about all my confusing experimental techniques and me not being there to put you out of your confusion.
>
> Thank you for your awesome feedback. It was very insightful and helpful.
>
> When I started this story I had a vague idea of researching into the history of food and the bohemian lifestyle of the 1920's and travel. All things I love.
>
> This is why it has difficulties with transitions and is what I was particularly concerned with.
>
> I thought where do I start? Paris has such a colourful history of food and the arts. So many artistic movements were created at this time. So it was fun researching this.
>
> Now where do I go? I need to get on a ship, so I research and write about Marseilles.
>
> Now I have to describe the boat as it is going to be the scene of the murders.
>
> So I research boats at that time and came up with this historical yacht that came to its fate on rocks at a lighthouse.
>
> I better get on with the characters and the cooking challenges. I need to throw in a few clues and get on with the murders so I can get back to my mystery.
>
> Janet you were so right about, whoops I only have a few more words left to fit into the word count. Let's get the murders over with quickly. You were so funny with your comments re the Game of Thrones
>
> But I still have about 200 words left and the story is not finished.
>
> I plan to do as Nicole suggested and use the economy of language to try and free up more words to end the story with.
>
> Experimental writing does not always work and my transitions between scenes and multiple viewpoints are not working. So I have to try and get these to flow better. I tried to give hints as to who was speaking but these are not strong enough for the reader to grasp.
>
> Because the story was supposed to be humorous I thought realist and antirealist types of exaggerated behaviour may help. The Unsinkable Barley Soup
>
> Capitalisations are my mistakes not experimental. I am not sure how that is experimental Absinth instead of absinth, except I suppose I wanted to accentuate it was a drink of the 1920's and the art movement.
>
> So my friends you will have to see who DUNN it? I am not 100% sure yet either.
>
> Thank you again for your feedback. It is a relief to know you enjoyed it.
>
> I hope I have answered some of your questions I would have supplied in the zoom meeting. Cheers Sally
>
> Permalink Edit Delete
> See this post in context

Figure 7.1 Screen-snip of commentary posted on a weekly forum via the course Moodle site—an open-source Learning Platform (LP) or course management system (CMS)—by a student (Student A) who could not attend a ZoomLive session in real-time (synchronously). Note, in this case, in responding to the feedback of peers, Student A herself alludes to the polyphonic dimensions underlying the online creative writing pedagogy utilized in this course; one having "many voices," and indeed, inspiring various "texts which are not dominated by a single narrative or authorial authority" (Hunt, 2006: 179).

In reflecting on the feedback of peers, via a "Critical Reflection Journal" (an assessable item of the course) students regularly meditated on the aural and oral scope of the online creative writing pedagogy utilized in this course; one having multidimensional perspectives of and about a particular text, rather than the piece having a uniform meaning, dominant reading, or complexity.

Similarly, again in reflecting on the peer feedback process (via a "Critical Reflection Journal"), students also regularly meditated on their own processes of responding to, and providing peer feedback; "I see the issues being raised but I also see what I am trying to do very clearly ... thank you. I will have to work hard to make what I see into something that everyone sees" (Student A).

Rather than "digital," the term "synaptic" best describes the pedagogic implications of the Zoom technology in the virtual creative writing classroom:

> In essence, contemporary technologies are synaptic; meaning they are technologies of flow, of bringing together, of transmission, exchange, networking, of social, financial, political, cultural and personal activity. The experience-focus of these technologies has long superseded any logical reason for a continued reference to the digital.
>
> (Harper, 2012: 13)

Together with its synaptic qualities and purposes, Zoom promotes this application as "frictionless" (Zoom 2020). "Friction is usually considered to be the tendency shown by bodies in contact, whether moving or at rest, to adhere or stick to each other" (Bureau of Naval Personnel, 1964: 246). Because "friction" is by definition integral to elements of creative writing, particularly regards creating conflict and tension in characterization, pace, scene, and plot (Ackerman, 2014), the nature of Zoom as somehow "frictionless" presents very interesting possibilities in the development of creative writing approaches and online pedagogies. Terms such as "non-friction" writing define a mode of writing free of pressure, interruption, distraction, and inhibition (Brown, 2020), while its opposite, "friction writing," has become a powerful form of creative enterprise focusing on free-thinking, imagination, and developing a "self empowered state of mind" (Chambers, 2019). Online literary journals such as *F(r)iction* also appeal to this trend in applying concepts of friction for creative purposes to push genre boundaries and challenge literary conventions "to create just that—*friction* in the mind of the reader, *friction* in the industry, *friction* in our own hearts" (Hedlund, 2019). Even monographs such as Michael Shermer's *Science Friction: Where the Known Meets the Unknown* (2005) investigate belief systems, perceptions about news and history, and how one, or both, can create empirical discord. Of course, while Zoom promoters utilize the term "frictionless" to underscore the user-end friendliness of its cloud platform, the concept of what "friction" *is* and *does* in the context of the online creative writing classroom utilizing Zoom bears more than a coincidental relationship between user access to a virtual application and the creative enterprise of writing creatively. In this sense, not only can formulating, incorporating and adopting an approach to Zoom as pedagogy prove effective in capitalizing on the unique and

Zoom Tip Sheet for Collaborative Feedback –
"A Children's Fairytale" (Student C)

The following points have been adapted from John Hodgins *A Passion for Narrative: A Guide to Writing Fiction* **(2001) as a checklist in responding to draft work (via Zoom or some other platform):**

1. Has the writer chosen specific and concrete words throughout, aware of their sounds and rhythms and connotations as well as all their dictionary meanings? There are relevant terms. Some words may be complex depending on the reader. I would also include more sensory words – use alliteration and onomatopoeic words
2. Has the writer chosen words that are honest — that is, specific, direct, unadorned, and tangible? Yes
3. Has the writer used words necessary for the effect desired? If so, consider an example. If not, consider an example and suggest a possible alternative/s.
4. Has the writer chosen language that appeals to more than just one or two of the five senses? Include more sensory words e.g.: what did certain perceptions feel, taste, smell, or look like?
5. Has the writer chosen 'energy' words, in particular verbs that move the prose/poetry? Yes … maybe more action verbs to give the piece a sense of rhythm and action. Words to excite the senses. Have fun with the words. This will inspire younger readers and ignite their imaginations.
6. Where applicable, has the writer conveyed their (or the character's) feelings directly and indirectly? Yes … again … a little more emotion …this will help build the characters more. Though your use of idiosyncratic speech patterns and colloquial terms did give your characters a strong and individualised sense of voice.
7. Has the writer established a clear narrative voice? Yes … enhance on this a little more to create rich unique characters between the protagonist and antagonist.
8. Is the point of view of the piece easily identifiable? Yes
9. Is the narrator 'believable'; that is, authentic, realistic, a figure you can relate to/with? Yes
10. Does the writer's sentences/lines of poetry, etc., imply some depth of meaning for the reader who is sensitive to subtext and implication? I do wonder about some of the complexity of the concepts for the younger reader. Will there be a glossary at the end of the book?
11. Has the writer varied the lengths and patterns of word/sentences/phrases, lines of poetry, etc.? I would like to see more variety in sentences to help with tempo changes and shifts in mood and emotions. A lot of block of words … add more white space … will the illustrations be on their own page?
12. Has the writer experimented with the effects of following long sentences/word sequences with short sentence/word sequence, or following short sentences/word sequences with a long sentence/word sequence? More experimenting with this? The use of the clip art is good … maybe separate this with a good amount of white space.
13. Has the writer considered arranging events/plot sequences/progressions in ascending order of importance, of saving the best for last? Yes … there is a good sense of tension when the protagonist has an opportunity to escape because of a weather event (a storm).
14. Are the writer's transitions between ideas smooth, flowing, fluid, coherent, etc.? Yes … I gather some exciting moments will follow on the next page to increase the tension for the reader (?)
15. Has the writer used techniques such as comparison, contrast, metaphor, figurative language, symbolism, or analogy, etc., to sharpen meaning? I would like to see more of this to really colour the piece and enhance all the senses in the reading experience
16. Do you, as the reader, get a clear sense of the genre of the work (e.g., poetry, 1st chapter of an intended novel, a short story, creative non-fiction, personal essay, a novella, etc.) and the mode (ode, pastoral, flash fiction, horror, pastoral, magic realism, speculative, etc.,) in which it is told? Yes, it's a chapter book in the genre of a fairytale for children. I would say for 9 to 12 years olds if you take into consideration the concepts and the language.

Figure 7.2 Students could use the "Zoom Tip-Sheet for Collaborative Feedback" to assist them in organizing their peer feedback along conceptual, literary lines. This example is one student's response to a children's fairytale using elements of postmodernism as literary experimentation.

ideal aspects of the online environment for creative writing. Instructional methods utilizing Zoom can also successfully produce a student-centered environment encouraging strong peer networks amongst a community of writers while encouraging "friction" in the mind of both the reader and the writer for creative purposes.

Figure 7.3 shows a screen-snip of a ZoomLive session with students. The course coordinator has shared her desktop to display the collaborative feedback document with all participants, including commentary. Note, in this case, the student's use of intertextual elements created with synaptic technologies (online Newspaper generator, together with a Letter Generator tool [Vintage Mail Maker]) and "virtualized" as/into another textual form. These tools are themselves synaptic technologies specifically because they are "technologies that are producing new human experiences, ideas and ideals ... technologies involving multi-directional exchange (what has often been called 'networking'), a grid of activities that might include the social, financial, political, cultural and personal, all in the same flow of exchanges" (Harper, 2013: 217, 218).

Case study: discussion

The description for the undergraduate course in creative writing, "Creative Writing II: Writing Beyond the Page," stipulated that students would undertake a writing project, building on the skills acquired in its prerequisite course ("Creative Writing I: Fundamentals of Writing") which may take the form of a short story, play, suite of poems, or any approved mixture of these, using experimental writing techniques (e.g., stream of consciousness, multiple viewpoint, anti-realism, impressionism, cut-ups, metafiction, microfictions). Over the previous offerings of the course, students conceived "experimentation" as a

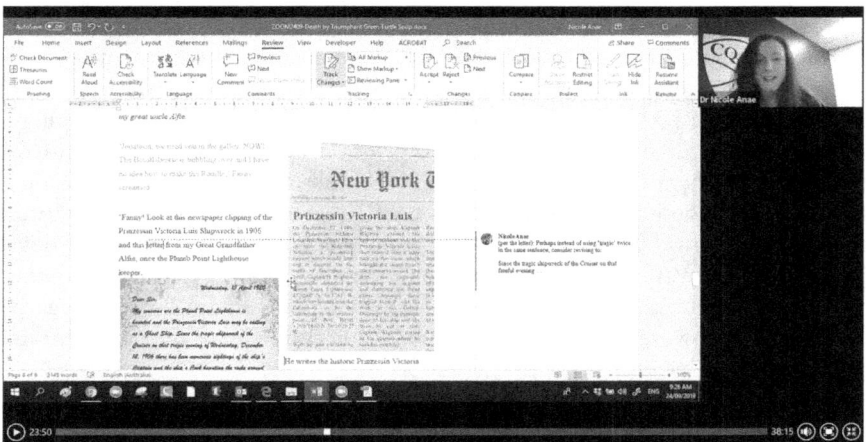

Figure 7.3 Screen-snip of a ZoomLive session with students.

quite alarming concept and therefore approached conceptualizing their potential project with some caution. As one student put it: "Meandering frantically is that me trying to write experimentally?" (Student B). Another student (Student C) described her approach to conceptualizing the project through the "A peculiarity of mess" analogy:

> All mess is not created equal. My mess is tiered into the acceptable and the gross. Paint mess, the stain of Lamp Black oil, is a treasured mess; a symbol of creativity. Fingers celebrate the birth of an artefact and wear this mess with pride. It is strange how an identical mess, the smear of motor oil, creates only repulsion. Fingers scrape against clothes, dispelling this mess, like a dog decanting fleas.
>
> (Student C)

That student, (Student C), sought to embrace experimental writing as a way of satisfying her interest in writing stories for children. Given that her concept involved utilizing an online platform for creating interactive digital fiction, my advice to Student A in the first instance focused specifically on storytelling; considering how the plot might include a "story within a story" motif to provide a bigger message in simplified terms (the student's ideological message was the impact of urbanization on wildlife); how this inner story might be written in terms of genre (the student's genre of choice was the fairy tale); the possibilities for creating and incorporating simple illustrations to provide visual clues that support the writing (the student opted to create monochromatic, stylized images in black and red); and the form the writing itself might take (the student integrated first-person limited point of view with stream-of-consciousness passages, and sections of dialogue).

To that end, the student initially opted to build a hype-text interactive fiction using "Twine"—"an open-source tool for telling interactive, nonlinear stories" (Twine)—incorporating an illustrated frame tale (e.g., story within a story). She sourced online resources to help realize her conception, such as Melissa Ford's *Writing Interactive Fiction with Twine* (2016), to ensure interactive and visually interesting elements. In formulating her story, the student drew on her experiences travelling to Alaska the previous year, creating a "mood board" of photos she had taken on the trip: a large black bear brazenly crossing the road in front of her; an ebony raven holding a bright red lollipop; children playing on a skidoo. The mood board included post-it notes on which she had written snippets of a conversation she had had with a Ketchikan local. She undertook a Google search on Alaskan Black bears, pinning to the board article printouts of the food they ate, their hibernation cycles; references alluding to the negative effects of global warming and how seasonal changes can leave the bears starving and force them into town to scavenge food.

In researching her experimental writing ideas, the student entertained the idea of including a virtual "cut-up" to represent seasonal change. She read some disturbing newspaper headlines about global warming. She discovered a "Newspaper Headline generator" and noted its URL, eventually using the generator to display the headlines within the creative projects she planned to write. She settled on including metafiction to draw the reader's attention to the story's qualities and characteristics as an "artefact" (Harreveld et al., 2016: 8). She started writing fragments for the opening; jotting down everything and trying not to be too judgmental as suggested by Singleton (2014) in his description of the necessity of mess to the process of creativity. She devised to explore the wayward, fragmentary nature of thoughts displayed in a stream-of-consciousness monologue as a device to introduce her characters, their setting, an incident happening within the context of the story, and foreshadowing the twist concluding the story.

What the account of Student A's creative enterprise shows is the extent to which the online environment presents for instructors unique instances for exploring potential avenues for developing an online creative writing pedagogy, while simultaneously highlighting how the environment itself offers students ideal methods for creating, and realizing, rich and innovative "artefacts" of creative endeavor via synaptic applications and technologies.

Attending ZoomLive sessions

In catering to the need for in-progress draft critiques, semi-structured 90-minute video-conferencing sessions (via Zoom) between the lecturer and students presented students with opportunities to participate in regular supportive and collaborative peer review of draft work-in-progress. These (voluntary) sessions—given the lack of structure in the critical literature about online creative writing pedagogy—incorporated a part-Amherst and part-Iowa approach (Elbow, 1973; Schneider, 2003):

1 A nonhierarchical spirit (how we treat writing) in the workshop is maintained while at the same time an appropriate discipline (how we interact as a group) keeps writers safe (Amherst philosophy).
2 At all times writers are free to refrain from reading their work aloud (Amherst philosophy)
3 Collaborative group feedback is offered only when the writer asks for it (Amherst philosophy).
4 Feedback is balanced; there is as much affirmation as suggestion for change (Amherst philosophy).
5 The unit coordinator/lecturer leads a discussion about a work written by a member of the class; workshop students share impressions, advice, and analysis (Iowa philosophy).
6 Within these workshops, writing students receive candid and instant feedback about their writing and in so doing, reportedly become better critics of their own work (Iowa philosophy)
7 Many writers also established long-lasting relationships with other group members whom acted as 'critical readers' (Iowa philosophy).

This philosophical underpinning of the "workshop" context represented a form of "self-assessment" as much as a mode of formative feedback. Here, students were invited to reflect on their own and others processes of creative practice therefore offering students individualized feedback as much as mentoring experiences as aspiring writers.

> After attending a very constructive and encouraging drafting zoom session, I have decided on a change of direction for my writing piece. The story will no longer be published as a Twine hypertext ... The Zoom session has given me the confidence that my writing explores the experimental requirements of the course without resorting to hypertext.
>
> (Student C)

The student's reflection illustrates how, in using the Zoom video-conferencing within the pedagogy of teaching an online creative writing course, the unique and ideal aspects of the online environment for creative writing are emphasized. For instance, as it is within the Zoom context that a unique form of "joining," to coin Ulmer, occurs; that is, where student writers not only establish an immediate connection between literacy and orality through their involvement with electronic media (Madden, 2018: 53), but where electronic media itself, as a form of writing, "concerns all disciplines to the extent that it is the interface of all pedagogy" (Ulmer, quoted in Figueiredo, 2020: 64). Further, with respect to how this interface might shape and develop students' writing, Student B's commentary also presents a vivid example of how "synaptic technologies are those contemporary technologies that support reciprocal human experiences, not material manifestations, of our human presence in the world" (Harper, 2015: 8). While synaptic technologies *can* be utilized productively for material, creative writing, ends (textual products such as books, short stories, novellas, novels, poetry and dramatic scripts, among other artefacts), students can, in the context of a wholly online creative writing course using Zoom, consider and reconsider their programming choices utilizing synaptic technologies as aspiring creative writers. In the case of Student B, her decision to reconsider the use of Twine to create a hypertext—"a term that refers to the systems and contents that operate on a computer to organise information in a non-linear manner" (Comte)—precipitated a ground-shift in apprehending the possibilities for author programming as an experimental frame for open-ended story-making: "I think that this is the value of experimental writing. It invites the reader to contribute their own experiences to construct meaning that wasn't necessarily planned by the author" (Student C).

Gregory Ulmer's concept of "electracy" (2008) is a useful term in theorizing how the Zoom video-conferencing system can be applied pedagogically to cut across the interface between information and communications technology (ICT) and creative expression. For Ulmer, "electracy" is to digital media what literacy is to print:

> In the digital age, there is potential for more than the progression of "writing" from a text-driven literacy to multimedia electracy—what

Zoom in and Zoom out 81

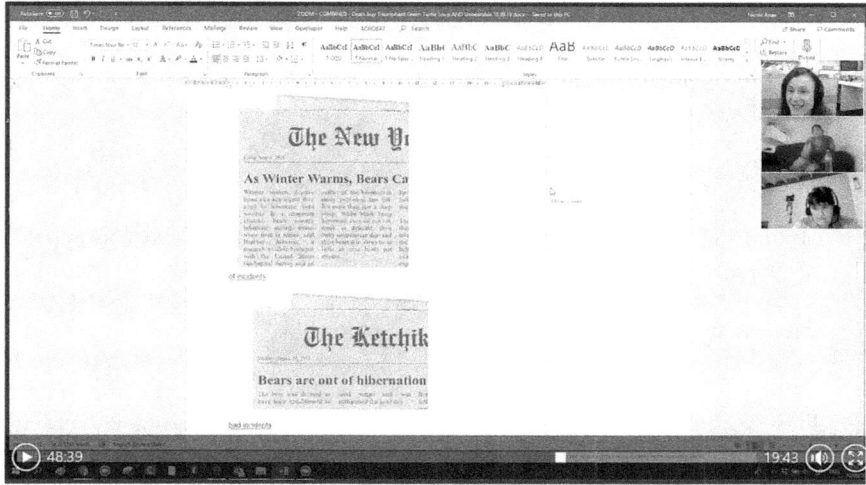

Figure 7.4 In this screen-snip of a ZoomLive session with students, the course coordinator has shared her desktop to display the collaborative feedback document with all participants, including commentary. Note, in this case, the student's (Student C) use of a Newspaper headline generator to add intertextual elements within the piece.

electracy signifies is a potential seismic shift between the structures of writing (object) and the individual who writes (subject). This means more than new tools in the toolbox—there is a new "organism" in place. As Ulmer notes, the "group subject" and a new public sphere become "writable."

(Kuhn and Callahan, 2012: 293)

Because creative writing typically encompasses a solo enterprise on the part of the creative writer, Student B's commentary also shows the "creative writer's personal desire to discover and develop knowledge that can assist their creative practice" (Harper. 2015: 118). As another student later commented;

> I am so appreciative we have been able to do these [Zoom sessions]. Feedback and interaction is so important for me to learn and grow. Otherwise, I would be stuck with my own interpretation of things which is very one sided and insular.
>
> (Student B)

The level of peer support and trust relationship driven by Zoom participation is also clearly evident in the commentary of other students:

> I have learned a valuable lesson through the process of writing and receiving feedback ... I originally asked a friend, who also had this knowledge of my characters, to read my work. She saw no problem. Participants in the

[Zoom] Creative Writing workshops do not have this context and could pick up gaps in my writing instantly. I see now why Leach (2014) recommends avoiding having close friends and family in writing groups and workshops.

(Student D)

I found the 2nd Zoom Workshop session extremely beneficial and appreciate the advice of the lecturer and other participants. Thank you for taking precious time to read and give constructive feedback. I would be struggling if it was not for the Zoom Workshop Sessions.

(Student E)

This week's zoom session was definitely worth participating in, and the feedback I received from my lecturer and class mates was fantastic. During the session, I took notes of what the group had said so I have a hard copy to refer to as I make changes to my artefact. Some of what the group said I had already taken into consideration, and I began researching some finer details to make sure I had my facts right.

(Student F)

Incorporating the Zoom platform as a complement to other online platforms (e.g., e-unit Moodle forums and blogs) capitalizes on the unique and ideal aspects of the online environment for creative writing given it emphasizes the broad dimensions of "transmedia" as both tool and application. While the term

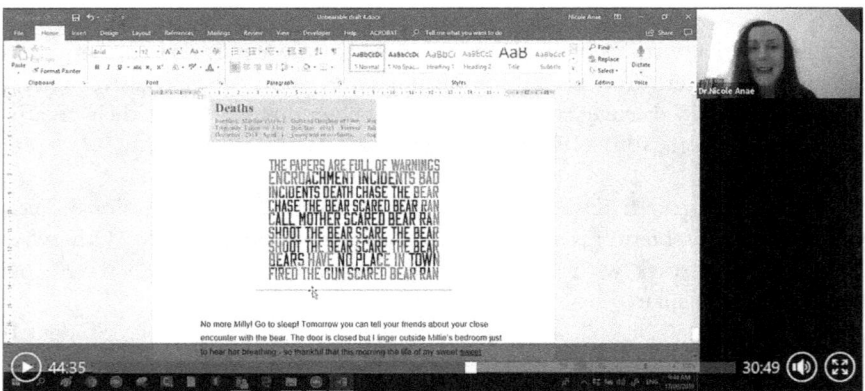

Figure 7.5 In this screen-snip of a ZoomLive session with students, the course coordinator has once again shared her desktop to display the collaborative feedback document with all participants, including commentary. Note, in this case, the student's (C) combined use of a Newspaper headline generator, as well as her use of Word.Art—an online word cloud creator—to add two separate, but interrelated, intertextual elements within the piece: graphic and concrete.

"transmedia" (from the Latin) denotes "works about the same content that are produced in different media and modes" (Williams, 2015: 255), "transmedia," unlike the other terms, "is meant to denote not only a collection or a relationship between various media, but a new 'whole' that is greater than its parts" (Falzon, 2012: 926). Thus, in relation to student's draft work, even though it is of the same content, it is disseminated across various platforms (Zoom, Moodle, forums and blogs, etc.), in various modes (as e-document, as a living document [via Google Docs], as attachment via email, as storyboard, etc., and/or as image or clip in recordings of a Zoom session). These processes of the dissemination create another kind of "text," one greater than the sum of these various material and virtual iterations.

While a storyboard is characteristically used as a pre-production tool giving "a frame-by-frame, shot-by-shot series of sequential drawings" (Hart 1), typically mapping the story arc of a feature film or similar product, for this student, her storyboard illustrations proved an integral element of her creative writing piece as they not only provided visual clues for the reader to use to construct meaning, but also, in submitting the draft to a Zoom session, brought to the (writer's) fore "how many interpretations could and were made about the story" (Student C).

Conclusion

The breadth of functionality offered by the Zoom cloud platform makes this application particularly ideal in the context of an online environment for creative writing instruction. Virtual live classrooms enable content sharing, whiteboard,

Figure 7.6 Example of the storyboard Student C created to accompany her story.

and chat functionality, and opportunities for webinars using software Zoom applications (or App); either running on a desktop or laptop computer (via Windows, Mac, or Linux), or the introduction to the Zoom application (or App) running on a mobile tablet or phone (via Apple [iOS] or Google [Android]). That the host of a meeting or webinar can make a recording, or allow participants to record, means that the possible pedagogic applications of this synaptic technology are limited only by the imagination.

Josie Barnard has suggested that in the "postdigital age," "the remediation of a writer's own practice is key" (2017: 275). By this, Barnard argues that the new challenges to creative writing borne by advancing digital technologies present new opportunities for pedagogical approaches in which the writer both draws on, and challenges, elements of creative writing praxis within a process of self-collaboration. While the word "remediation" implies some sense of correction, rectification, or improvement, the term also suggests a return, or revisitation, to current abilities and past practice as a locus for the adaptation and (re)application of competencies within contemporary frameworks and interactive writing environments.

Zoom, as an essentially synaptic, interactive cloud platform, offers students a sense of structure to the sessions that can help them guide and organize peer feedback, while allowing them to exercise creativity within this structure. Here, students can utilize elements of the platform structure to set their presentations of feedback apart from others by devising different approach styles: while some students might prefer an informal, conversational style, others might employ whiteboard functionality or desktop sharing to present a more formal approach to providing peer feedback (using PowerPoint presentations or word.doc expositions, etc.). The peer feedback students provide within the context of a ZoomLive collaborative workshop session is formative, and typically ongoing, as students focus on the continuing development of a single creative artefact over time. By extension, formative feedback builds students' self-confidence in moving toward the final submission of the creative artefact for summative assessment, assuring them that they have done all they could to improve the piece. That lecturers/instructors can connect with students synchronously directly opens up possibilities to identify those needing more intensive support, as well as encouraging a sense of self-direction. Self-recording becomes a key process within, and beyond, the online collaborative writing sessions as students problem-solve how they will respond to the draft work of peers *as a writer*. These are the self-evaluative responses, that is, the "personal judgements" (Kaplan, 1986: 82) students make about a creative piece, including how they decide on an approach that best communicates their responses effectively *as a reader*. A student's self-evaluative responses conveying the effect of the transaction between precision of language and narrative meaning.

In the final analysis, conceiving and implementing an approach to Zoom within a structured creative writing pedagogy effectively capitalizes on the unique and ideal aspects of the online environment for creative writing precisely because it provides a synchronous space facilitating the creation of an "interpretive community." This mobilization of a community of writers/readers who share the same strategies for "writing texts, for constituting their properties and assigning their intentions," means that "[while] these strategies exist prior to the act of reading and therefore determine the shape of what is read" (Fish , 1980: 71), what is being written is ultimately left to the writer's own imaginative practice.

> I finally managed to emotionally separate myself from my work and welcome others' perspectives! I keenly seek their feedback because they were the only people who could read this work objectively, without prior knowledge of my characters. There was group consensus that the source of my characters' conflict was a sibling rivalry between my protagonist and her sister. This was not the message I was trying to send. This occurrence is summed up well by Don Murray (2004, quoted in Williams, "Writing Creative Nonfiction" 32) who says "the writer sits down intending to say one thing and hears the writing saying something more, or less, or completely different." I will rewrite this section.
>
> (Student G)

Here, the student touches on an analogy resonating with Michel de Certeau's concept of the "writing-reading" context: "A different world (the reader's) slips into the author's place. This mutation makes the text habitable, like a rented apartment. It transforms another person's property into a space borrowed for the moment by a transient" (1984: xxi). The writer's text is occupied but the reader, and in the duration of the lease, the reader furnishes the text with their own "acts and memories." Within this online community, structured as it is within a synaptic cloud platform, creative writing pedagogy both embraces and emphasizes the various human experiences student writers themselves encounter, as much as the experiences these technologies simultaneously form and facilitate.

Works cited

"About Zoom." *Zoom Video Communications*, 2019. zoom.us/about. Accessed 11 June 2020.

Ackerman, Angela. "Writing Fiction: Creating Friction with Clashing Personalities." *The Creative Penn*, 4 January 2014. www.thecreativepenn.com/2014/01/04/clashing-personalities/#comments. Accessed 11 June 2020.

Badenhorst, Cecile, and Cally Guerin. *Research Literacies and Writing Pedagogies for Masters and Doctoral Writers*. Koninklijke Brill, 2016.

Barnard, Josie. "Testing Possibilities: On Negotiating Writing Practices in a 'Postdigital' Age (Tools and Methods)." *New Writing: The International Journal for the Practice and Theory of Creative Writing*, vol. 14, no. 2, 2017, pp. 275–289.

Baxter, Jacqueline, et al. *Creativity and Critique in Online Learning: Exploring and Examining Innovations in Online Pedagogy*. Bloomsbury, 2018.

Brown, Mike. "Creative Thinking: Friction or Non-Friction Writing?" *The Brainzooming Group*, brainzooming.com/creative-thinking-friction-or-non-friction-writing/21401/. Accessed 10 June 2020.

Bureau of Naval Personnel. *Computer Basics: Analog Computer Fundamentals*. Bureau of Naval Personnel, 1964.

Chambers, Mary-Lynn. "A Rhetorical Mandate: A Look at Multi-Ethic/Multimodal Online Pedagogy." *Applied Pedagogies: Strategies for Online Writing Instruction*, edited by Daniel Ruefman and Abigail G. Scheg. Utah State University Press, 2016, pp. 75–89.

Clark, Michael Dean, et al. *Creative Writing in the Digital Age: Theory, Practice, and Pedagogy*. Bloomsbury, 2015.

Comte, Annette. "Hyperfiction: A New Literary Poetics?" *TEXT: Journal of Writing and Writing Courses*, vol. 5, no. 2, 2001. www.textjournal.com.au/oct01/comte.htm. Accessed 10 June 2020.

de Certeau, Michel. *The Practice of Everyday Life*. Translated by Steven Rendall. Berkeley University Press, 1984.

Elbow, Peter. *Writing Without Teachers*. Oxford Univeristy Press, 1973.

Falzon, Charles. "Brand Development and Transmedia Production." *Journalism and Mass Communication*, vol. 2, no. 9, 2012, pp. 925–938.

Figueiredo, Sergio C. "Theopraxesis and the Future of H'MMM in the University: An Interview with Gregory L. Ulmer." *Journal for Cultural and Religious Theory*, vol. 16, no. 1, 2016, pp. 58–73. jcrt.org/archives/16.1/InterviewUlmer.pdf. Accessed 11 June 2020.

Fish, Stanley Eugene. *Is There a Text in This Class? The Authority of Interpretive Communities*. Harvard University Press, 1980.

Ford, Melissa. *Writing Interactive Fiction with Twine*. E-book, Que, 2016, www.oreilly.com/library/view/writing-interactive-fiction/9780134303116/.

Graham, Robert et al. *The Road to Somewhere: A Creative Writing Companion*, 2nd ed. Palgrave Macmillan, 2014.

Hancox, Donna Marie, and Vivenne Muller. "Excursions into New Territory: Fictocriticism and Undergraduate Writing." *New Writing: International Journal for the Practice and Theory of Creative Writing*, vol. 8, no. 2, 2011, pp. 147–158.

Harper, Graeme. "Creative Writing: Words as Practice-led Research." *Journal of Visual Art Practice*, vol. 7, no. 2, 2008, pp. 161–171. www.tandfonline.com/doi/abs/10.1386/jvap.7.2.161_1?journalCode=rjvp20. Accessed 11 June 2020.

Harper, Graeme. "Digital Is Dead: Synaptic Technologies Rule." *Campus Review*, 22 June, vol. 20, no. 12, 2010, p. 13.

Harper, Graeme. "Synaptic Landscapes: Exploring the 21st Century Moving Image." *Film Landscapes: Cinema, Environment and Visual Culture*, edited by Graeme Harper and Jonathan Rayner. Cambridge Scholars Publishing, 2013, pp. 216–220.

Harper, Graeme. *The Future for Creative Writing*. Wiley Blackwell, 2014.

Harper, Graeme. Ed. *Creative Writing and Education*, New Writing Viewpoints 11. Multilingual Matters, 2015.

Harper, Graeme. "Creative Writing in the Age of Synapses." *Creative Writing in the Digital Age: Theory, Practice, and Technology*, edited by Michael Dean Clark, et al. Bloomsbury, 2015, pp. 7–16.

Harreveld, Bobby, et al. Introduction. *Constructing Methodology for Qualitative Research: Researching Education and Social Practices*, edited by Bobby Harreveld, et al. Palgrave Macmillan, 2016, pp. 1–14.

Hart, John. *The Art of the Storyboard: A Filmmaker's Introduction*. Elsevier, 2008.

Hedlund, Dani. "Editor's Note." *F(r)iction*, 28 February 2019. frictionlit.org/friction-12-editors-note/. Accessed 11 Jun. 2020.

Hunt, Peter, ed. *Understanding Children's Literature*. Routledge, 2006.

Kaplan, Howard B. *Social Psychology of Self-Reliant Behavior*. Springer Science+Business Media, 1986.

Kroll, Jeri, and Graeme Harper. Introduction. *Research Methods in Creative Writing*, edited by Jeri Kroll and Graeme Harper. Globe Press, 2013, pp. 1–13.

Kuhn, Virginia, and Vicki Callahan. "Nomadic Archives: Remix and the Drift to Praxis." *Digital Humanities Pedagogy: Practices, Principles and Politics*, edited by Brett D. Hirson. Open Book, 2012, pp. 291–308.

Library London. "Friction Conviction. Creative Writing with Geoffrey Chambers." Eventbrite, January 16, 2019, St Martin's Lane. https://www.eventbrite.com/e/friction-conviction-creative-writing-with-geoffrey-chambers-tickets-53813338143#.

McCallum, Robyn. "Very Advanced Texts: Metafictions and Experimental Work." *Understanding Children's Literature*, edited by Peter Hunt. Routledge, 2002, pp. 138–150.

Madden, Mary C. "Class Matters: Examining Class, Gender, Race, and Social Justice in Modernist Literature." *Teaching Modernist Anglophone Literature*, edited by Mary C. Madden and Precious McKenzie. Brill, 2018, pp. 51–98.

Mawhinney, Lynnette, and Emery Marc Petchauer. "Coping with the Crickets: A Fusion Autoethnography of Silence, Schooling, and the Continuum of Biracial Identity Formation." *International Journal of Qualitative Studies in Education*, vol. 26, no. 10, 2013, pp. 1309–1329. www.tandfonline.com/doi/abs/10.1080/09518398.2012.731537. Accessed 11 June 2020.

Moneyhun, Clyde. "A Basic Writing Teacher Teaches Creative Writing." *Creative Writing Pedagogies for the Twenty-First Century*, edited by Alexandria Peary and Tom C. Hunley. Southern Illinois University Press, 2015, pp. 221–242.

Mort, Graham. "Transcultural Writing and Research." *Research Methods in Creative Writing*, edited by Jeri Kroll and Graeme Harper. Globe Press, 2013, pp. 201–222.

Ostman, Heather Elaine. "Self-narrative as Performative Act: Student Autobiographies and the Postmodern Self." *New Writing: International Journal for the Practice and Theory of Creative Writing*, vol. 10, no. 3, 2013, pp. 336–344.

Peary, Alexandria. "The Pedagogy of Creative Writing across the Curriculum." *Creative Writing Pedagogies for the Twenty-First Century*, edited by Alexandria Peary and Tom C. Hunley. Southern Illinois University Press, 2015, pp. 194–220.

Schneider, Pat. *Writing Alone and With Others*. Oxford University Press, 2003.

Shermer, Michael. *Science Friction: Where the Known Meets the Unknown*. Holt Paperbacks, 2005.

Singleton, John. "The Necessity of Mess." *The Road to Somewhere: A Creative Writing Companion*, edited by Robert Graham et al. Palgrave Macmillan, 2014, pp. 35–36.

Twine, Interactive Fiction Technology Foundation, 2020, https://twinery.org/. Accessed 11 June 2020.

Ulmer, Gregory. *Electronic Monuments*. University of Minnesota Press, 2005.

Ulmer, Gregory. *Internet Intervention: From Literacy to Electracy*. Pearson, 2008.

Venis, Linda. "E-Mentoring the Individual Writer within a Global Creative Community." *Cases on Online Tutoring, Mentoring, and Educational Services: Practices and Applications*, edited by Gary A. Berg, Information Science Reference, 2010, pp. 98–116.

Williams, Bronwyn T. "Writing Creative Nonfiction." *A Companion to Creative Writing*, edited by Graeme Harper. John Wiley & Sons, 2013, pp. 24–39.

Williams, Bronwyn T. "Digital Technologies and Creative Writing Pedagogy." *Creative Writing Pedagogies for the Twenty-First Century*, edited by Alexandria Peary and Tom C. Hunley. Southern Illinois University Press, 2015, pp. 243–268.

Weldon, Fay. "On Assessing Creative Writing." *New Writing*, vol. 6, no. 3, 2009, pp. 168–174 (doi:10.1080/14790720903556734) Accessed 11 June 2020.

8 Digital pedagogy in the online creative writing classroom
An integrative, interdisciplinary approach

Cynthia Pengilly

As a scholar and practitioner of professional and technical writing, I am likely the most puzzling participant in an essay collection about online creative writing pedagogy. A brief introduction should suffice to explain my pedagogical and disciplinary underpinnings as well as my interest and background in teaching creative writing students. Online pedagogy and, more specifically, online writing instruction (OWI) are indeed my comfort zones when it comes to teaching (Hewett and DePew and Warnock). This unique pedagogical uptake is because, unlike many of my colleagues, I began my academic career teaching online and shifted to the classroom several years later having already honed my pedagogical focus in OWI and digital pedagogy. My background in industry is also important to note, having worked as a technical writer with specialized training in coding, web design, audio/sound writing, and video editing/production, and this background definitely undergirds my *approach to, comfort with*, and *interest in* digital pedagogy courses.

One of my greatest academic and pedagogical challenges, however, occurs only after accepting a tenure-track position in professional and technical writing with Central Washington University's English Department. In this position, I am responsible for designing, revising, and teaching professional writing courses in the B.A. in Professional and Creative Writing (PCW), of which there is a face-to-face and fully online option for students. The uniqueness of this program lies in the fact that students do not select tracks or areas of emphasis and are required to take a large number of core classes from both disciplinary areas, and this combination makes the program truly integrative and interdisciplinary in structure. Even though the PCW program is offered in both modalities, the online modality has more declared majors (150 vs. 30), resulting in more online course offerings and increased opportunity for infusing digital pedagogy and creative composing projects. If we accept Harper's account in "Creative Writing in the Age of Synapses," that creative writing is meant to challenge convention at its core, then it only makes sense for creative writing studies to embrace digital pedagogy and online learning—thus challenging the idea of the craft, the workshop, and the broadening definitions of the creative industry for students. In these innovative courses, I found commonalities between myself and my creative writing students, thus why I like to frame the process taking place in the online classroom as one of critical creative composing—inclusive of the many genres, forms, and modalities of writing expected of everyone in the new creative industry.

In this chapter, I discuss my experience guiding creative writing students through the creative composing process, thus enabling them to imagine a creative life worth pursuing, to borrow from Carol Lloyd. Similarly, Clark, Hergenrader, and Rein assert that creative writing is about exploration and play, concepts that extend to the digital realm as well. It is of my opinion that the courses mentioned in this chapter fuse "creative play" with the parameters of the course itself, thereby creating an atmosphere in which creative writers thrive. And, the longer I teach in the Online PCW program, the more I recognize the beneficial and integrative aspects of *professional* and *creative* writing, as well as the unique affordances of the online classroom for both disciplines. As such, I will explore the following questions in this chapter: What role does interdisciplinary collaboration play in pedagogical invention? How might online spaces contribute to the study of creative writing pedagogy and/or creative composing?

This chapter will explore these questions by highlighting the significance of interdisciplinary approaches to teaching two different online creative writing courses by one technical and professional writing professor: ENG 454 Studies in Nonfiction (Graphic Novels) and ENG 474/574 Professional Writing with New Media (Writing with Sound). With regard to B.T. Williams' critique of the lack of creative writing scholarship involving digital pedagogy, this chapter describes the interdisciplinary aspects of two new courses in a program that is both fully online and intentional in its use of digital pedagogy, courses that resulted in a range of final creative projects such as graphic narratives, autographies, audio essays, and digital oral histories. For the readers of this collection, I hope to provide useful strategies for incorporating critical creative digital projects such as these in the online creative writing classroom.

PCW program context: an interdisciplinary approach

As previously stated, the PCW program is completed in either a face-to-face or online modality, but an overwhelming majority of our student population exists online and thus many of the courses are only offered in the online modality, such as ENG 474/574: Professional Writing with New Media. The online and onsite programs are identical in structure and make use of the same faculty (mostly tenured and tenure-line), which is a practice particularly noteworthy for online programs. The growth of the online PCW program is likely due to a combination of factors, including the high ranking of the program compared to other online programs (with almost all faculty being tenured or TT), geographic location of the institution (on the other side of the Cascade mountains, approximately 1.5 hours from Seattle), faculty credentials with academic publications in both professional and creative writing, faculty training and expertise in online pedagogy (through previous online teaching experience as well as institutional and department training), and innovative and practical elements of the program that blend creative and professional writing disciplines.

In terms of program content, students take courses in both areas or disciplines of study as well as literature and/or film. There are 32 credits of core courses—a mixture of creative writing, professional writing, and general writing studies courses—as shown in Table 8.1. The program is rounded out by 27 credits of additional creative and professional writing courses; 15 credits of literature, linguistics, or film courses; and one practicum course (2+ credits).

The elective courses in creative writing, professional writing, and literature combine for a total of 42 credits and are designed to build upon one another, infusing critical-creative composing projects that ask students to retain knowledge from previous courses and apply them to new disciplinary contexts. For example, students openly share their reflections with program faculty about the seemingly coherent integration of visual concepts learned in ENG 315: Visual Rhetoric and Document Design, ENG 465: Advanced Poetry Writing (visual poetry), and ENG 454: Studies in Nonfiction (graphic novels)—interdisciplinary courses in professional writing, creative writing, and literary studies respectively. Such feedback has led to increased efforts to integrate course concepts across courses, to share or duplicate textbooks when possible, and to increase co-teaching opportunities such as the design of a new graphic memoirs course that draws on expertise from creative writing, professional writing, and art and design faculty. I would argue that the interdisciplinary nature of the program, coupled with its mostly online modality, has contributed to the innovative pedagogy in the PCW program such as my use of critical-creative digital projects.

A primer on teaching critical creative digital projects

During my years of teaching both online and face-to-face courses, I have come to recognize a pattern for teaching critical-creative-digital projects. The first hurdle, so to speak, is getting students to recognize the new genre as something worthy of *academic* study. I place the emphasis on *academic* because for the topic to be "cool" or "hip," especially for serious students, such as adult learners and creative writers, is often not enough. This problem is not unlike Koehler's recognition of

Table 8.1 Listing of required core classes in the PCW program, catalog year 2020–2021

Core Classes	Credits
ENG 263/264/265: Intro to Creative Writing	5
ENG 301: Rhetoric for Professional Writers	5
ENG 302: Poetry and Poetics	5
ENG 303: Principles of English Studies	5
ENG 320: English Grammar	5
ENG 323: Writing and Editing for Publication	5
ENG 489: Senior Colloquium	2

student's categorization of high-brow (print) and low-brow (digital) culture in their discussion and privileging of certain texts. In short, the topic must either have some greater status or merit, or provide unique insights into an underserved or under-represented community in ways that other creative genres do not. This recognition gives the course value to creative writing students and later aids them in their critical analysis of the genre and practice with the genre (i.e., their craft).

I would also mention the importance of a textbook of some kind, whether the text exists physically or digitally. In my experience, I have found that students need and often prefer reference material, especially when tasked with new forms of composing; and because the online environment already comes with enough uncertainty for students, I find it is best to avoid contributing to those feelings. To clarify, I am not advocating for locating texts that teach a specific technology, as doing so would be a fruitless endeavor. In today's digital age, any technology is likely obsolete before the text is even published; instead, I tend to focus on finding texts that explore the genre and craft itself, from a critical perspective. This focus often requires that I cobble together readings, and scanned PDFs from several different sources, but anthologies are also a great starting place too and are surprisingly available for even newer creative genres such as *The Sound Studies Reader* or *Reality Radio*, for use in a podcasting or soundwriting class.

The final aspect of establishing academic merit or credibility for a new creative genre is the selection and timely release of critical readings. I often set aside the first few weeks of course instruction for engaged critical scholarship of the new creative genre be it video games, graphic novels, documentary filmmaking, or podcasts. For example, in ENG 454 Studies in Nonfiction (Graphic Novels), we read McCloud's *Understanding Comics* alongside critical pieces about the value (or not) of graphic novels to the literary tradition such as Chute's "Comic as Literature." I use a similar approach in ENG 474 Writing with Sound, a class in which I front-load many of the critical readings to help students better visualize themselves, and their work in the class, as part of a larger creative community. We begin our academic vetting of the genre by using required audio readings from *Soundwriting Pedagogies,* written by Courtney Danforth and Kyle Stedman, alongside other seminal pieces such as Rodrigue's "Navigating the Soundscape" to give students a sense of the depth and breadth of this burgeoning field. Students are appreciative of the fact that we read and discuss these seminal texts as a class because the discussion allows them to easily follow, in the later weeks of the course, the scholarly conversations in literary journals.

After students gain a solid foundation of the genre and open their minds to the beauty of the genre—as something that can be practiced, learned, and honed as a craft—guiding students through the study of the genre, of its many forms and functions, is much easier. This process is not unlike teaching other genres, such as literature, but the difference lies in the critical-creative-production process that takes place in a digital publishing space often located outside of the online classroom, to which I will turn my attention next.

ENG 454: Studies in NonFiction (Graphic Novels)

To provide a bit of context, the ENG 454 Studies in NonFiction class has a unique function within our English Department because it serves majors from several different programs: Professional and Creative Writing (face-to-face and online), English Language Arts/Teaching, and English Language and Literature. Professional and Creative Writing students take 15 credits of literature, language, or film courses at the 300-level or above, so ENG 454 is not necessarily required, but is often used to fulfill this program area. I taught the course online in Spring 2018, and 23 students completed the course. The breakdown of majors is as follows: 15 online PCW majors, 3 face-to-face PCW majors, 1 English Language & Literature major, and 5 English Language Arts Teaching majors.

The interdisciplinary aspects of the course stems from the fact that it serves multiple majors and is intentionally designed with interdisciplinary concepts in mind, drawing from literature, creative writing, and professional writing (specifically visual rhetoric and design aspects when I teach the course). In the course, students write two critical essays (first analyzing comic/design concepts and then a literary criticism paper) and compose a short graphic narrative as the culminating, critical-creative project in the course. The graphic novels selected include Spiegelman's *Maus: A Complete Story*, Marchetto's *Cancer Vixen*, Bechdel's *Fun Home*, Ledesma's *Diary of a Reluctant Dreamer*, and Guibert's *The Photographer*. The graphic novels include several forms of creative nonfiction: memoir, autobiography, experimental personal essay, travel narrative, and literary journalism as well as some forms unique to graphic novels, such as graphic medicine (*Cancer Vixen*) and graphic reportage (*The Photographer*). The variety in selection is meant to engage all program majors and to provide a solid foundation for the critical essays and critical-creative project where students are expected to approach their craft using interdisciplinary concepts from all three fields.

Since the course is geared toward studying literary forms, and not necessarily producing them, I had anticipated the creative project receiving push back from my new colleagues and/or being met with some apprehension and resistance from students (neither of which occurred). Yet while some students struggled with the literary criticism papers, mostly due to their lack of practice caused by the shortage of online literary courses offered in the department, the majority of students thrived and flourished while completing the creative project. Since we only had time for one creative project, I opted to scaffold the creative composing process itself: students submitted a proposal including a storyboard or plot sequence, worked on drafts in small groups to receive additional feedback on their content and graphical design considerations (in addition to weekly class-wide discussions), published their graphic narratives to the online Wix website (by group deadlines instead of class-wide deadlines), and submitted written reflections at the end of the project. There are five different deadlines for the graphic narrative creative project (by group), and students sign up in advance

Digital pedagogy 93

for whichever group due date is most flexible with their personal schedules. This flexibility means that four to five completed graphic narratives are published each week, over the final five weeks of the course, allowing for extended opportunity for feedback, revision, and admiration of/from fellow classmates.

Specifically, I employed a process and invention focused pedagogy, not unlike Mayers' work with multi-genre creative writing courses, that shifts the class-wide foci "on how and where works of creative writing *start* (invention) and how they *develop in their earliest phases* in ways both guided by and sometimes outside of or contrary to the writers' intentions (process)" (Mayers, 2017: 11). This pedagogical strategy is especially noteworthy in this course in which students worked in small groups workshopping their critical-creative projects with varied final due dates throughout the quarter that allow each group to "peer inside" another group's invention and writing process. The unexpected benefits of the staggered workshop strategy speaks to the uniqueness of online pedagogy in a creative writing classroom, as the online modality has certain affordances that lend itself well to group work, community-building, and a focus on the writing process over a longer period of time and in earlier stages of the writing process, as advocated by Mayers.

An important note is that I do not explicitly teach students to use a specific technology or platform for the graphic narrative creative project. Instead, I provide them with the tools they need to understand visual rhetoric, generally speaking, basic design principles, and introductory comic design concepts. As Smith states in *Creative Writing Innovations*, the "emphasis is on conceptual understanding rather than technical prowess" (67). In terms of visual and comic concepts, we rely on McCloud's *Understanding Comics* as a primary text, which is supplemented with other key readings both on the form and craft of graphic novels. For the technology itself, I guide students toward *Pixton*, *ToonDoo*, and *StoryBoardThat* as possible platforms for their critical-creative projects, but I do not require a specific platform nor provide training beyond offering a list of links to online tutorials. Many students use one of the three platforms, while more artistically inclined or digitally talented students opt to free-hand draw and color their narratives either on paper or using Adobe's In-Design platform. Daniel Craig's "Desaparecido" is one such narrative, for example, as it is drawn and colored by hand then uploaded to Pixton for frames and captions (see Figure 8.1). By the end of the course, the critical-creative project fuses several disciplines of study as students apply genre studies, creative nonfiction writing, and visual design/professional writing concepts to their own and their classmates' work via drafting, peer review, and critical reflection at the end of the project.

The course is interdisciplinary in nature and particularly well-suited for the online classroom due to the community-building aspects of Canvas combined with the seamless incorporation of online graphic/comic building platforms— spaces that do not require repeated shifts between modalities. As Borgman and McArdle advocate in their model for online writing instruction, online learning should be personal, accessible, responsive, and strategic (PARS model), and I believe the design of this course achieves PARS by demanding active student participation in the creative spirit of the classroom. For example, as students

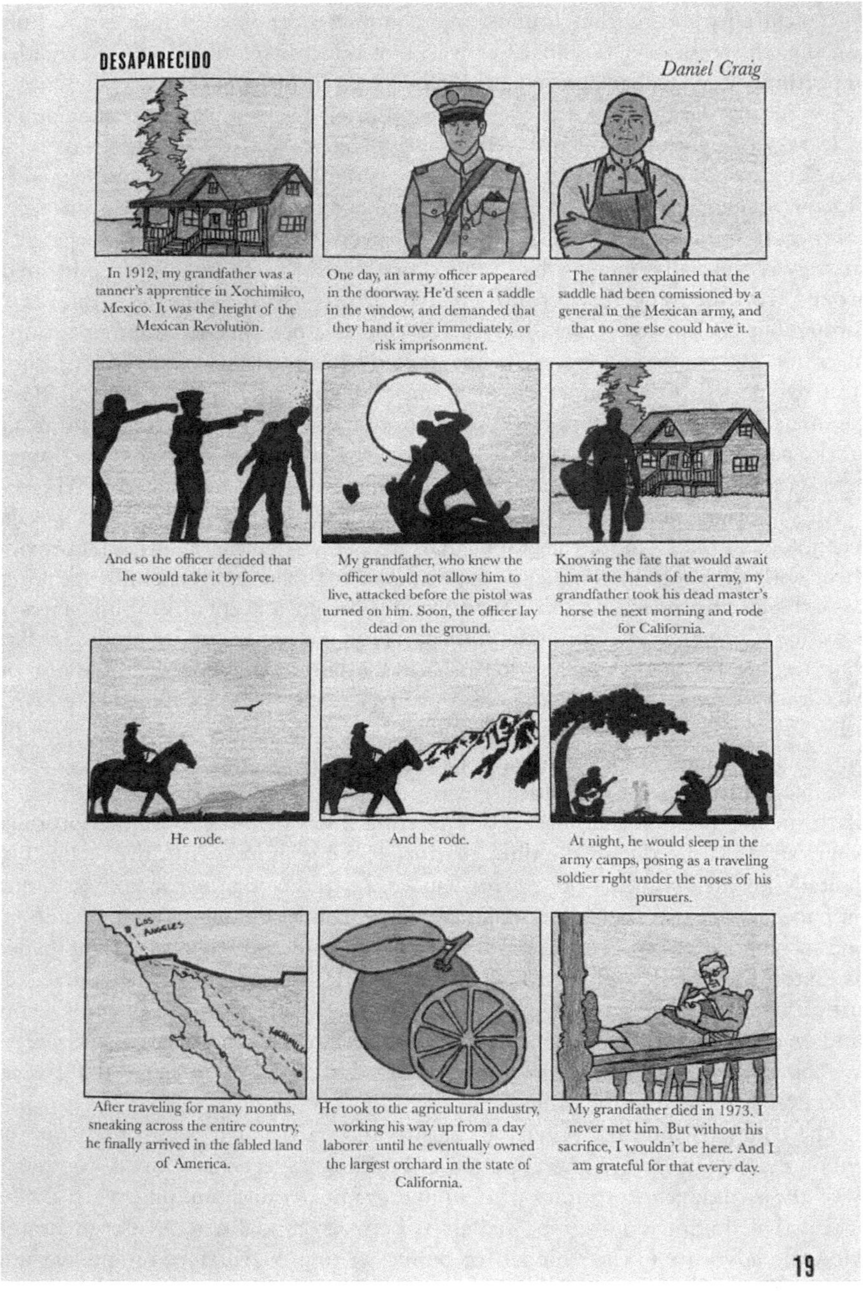

94 Cynthia Pengilly

Figure 8.1 "Desaparecido" written and illustrated by Daniel Craig in ENG 454, Group 1, Spring 2018. Later published in *Manastash: A Journal of Writing and Art*, Volume 29, Spring 2019, page 19.

work in small creative groups via Canvas group discussion boards (and share the same deadline for their graphic narrative with their group members), they share tips and strategies amongst themselves about how to use the platform(s) along with other visual, cultural, and design considerations ("This reminds me of Ledesma's experiential memoir both in spirit and unique style ... Does your platform have something called weighted lines? Look for a feature with a similar name"). Indeed, I find that creative writing students are particularly well-versed and well-poised for such active learning spaces because they are familiar with pedagogical models, such as the workshop, that require such personal and interactive responses between fellow classmates, a collaboration that is only further enhanced by the online modality.

In short, I am simply building upon the foundation of the workshop model that is already familiar to creative writing students while expanding their abilities to craft critical-creative composing.

ENG 474/574: Professional Writing with New Media (Writing with Sound)

The ENG 474/574 course is a product of a need to align the professional writing course offerings with the professional writing discipline; in other words, as a member of the professional writing faculty, we believe the lack of courses dealing specifically with new media would place students graduating from our program at a disadvantage. So, the course, and its outcomes, are focused on students learning a professional writing *genre* through a series of rotating topics. I planned to run topics through the course such as Writing with Sound, Writing with Video, and Digital Writing, and though I did not anticipate the course appealing to creative writers, even in an interdisciplinary program such as ours, I was gladly mistaken. The course was offered in Winter 2020 under the topic of "Writing with Sound," and it enrolled 17 students (13 undergrads and 4 graduate students), nearly all of whom had a strong interest in creative writing.

Because this course is designed with equal parts genre study/criticism and equal parts practice, I strategically use class discussion for smaller, sound-writing practice exercises as opposed to having students submit such activities privately to the instructor (see Table 8.2).

This strategy helps students to see themselves as a community of learners, practicing and learning a new genre together. (In fact, the initial practice exercise in my version of the course is borrowed and adapted from the DS106 Assignment Bank, "A Life in Two Minutes.") This intentional pedagogical strategy has also made troubleshooting a bit easier, as needed, but the explicit "teaching of the technology" is not a required element of digital pedagogy, in my opinion, and is therefore not built into the course design. Finally, a simple shifting of these assignments to the class discussion turns them into low-stakes creative composing activities because students receive a single grade as they would for any other class discussion; students either practice the craft and respond to fellow classmates, or they do not. I found this strategy particularly useful because it affords more

Table 8.2 Listing of soundwriting practice exercises and major assignments in ENG 474/574 Writing with Sound, Winter 2020

Assignment or activity	Length	Submission location(s)
1. Voice-only Introduction: share a personal story or life-defining moment with the class, adapted from the *My Life is True* series	2 minutes	• Week 1 Discussion
2. Soundscape or Sound Effects Story: capture an on-site location recording, no voice allowed	1–2 minutes	• Week 2 Discussion
3. Revised Audio Intro: take the audio from Week 1 Discussion and revise it by layering voice with music	2 minutes	• Week 3 Discussion
4. Sonic Remediation: take a printed text such as a poem, short story, or news article, and remediate it using voice, music, and sound effects	3–5 minutes	• Canvas Assignment to the instructor (Week 4), and • Optional Discussion Board, requested by students to facilitate sharing with classmates
5. Podcast Analysis: analyze the theme, genre, and technical dimensions of a podcast series (student selections cannot overlap)	4–5 minutes	• Discussion-based peer review of partial draft (Week 5), and • Canvas Assignment to the instructor (Week 6)
6. Digital Oral History Podcast Series: create a two-episode podcast series on a digital oral history topic of the student's choosing	5–10 minutes per episode	• Discussion-based peer review of first episode (Week 9), and • Canvas Assignment to the instructor (Week 10)

soundwriting practice opportunities before the larger assignments are due (i.e., sonic remediation, podcast analysis, and digital oral history podcast series), thereby allowing students to gain valuable practice with increasingly advanced soundwriting strategies, such as layering, ducking, and sound interaction, in a safe, low-stakes environment with minimal impact to their overall course grade. I believe the online aspect of the class aided students during these practice opportunities because they could listen to their own submission as well as their classmates' contributions as often as needed, thus facilitating peer learning, peer review, and integration of interdisciplinary concepts.

The more advanced assignments, items 4–6 above, have weighted percentages associated with them, but students work on them over time with drafts, feedback, and the opportunity for revision, if desired. The first of these assignments, the Sonic Remediation, was initially scheduled to be submitted only to the instructor for grading, but the students wanted the ability to share it with classmates too, so I created an optional discussion for this assignment. Out of the 17 students in the course, ten participated in this optional discussion board, which I found fascinating on many levels. First, students are choosing to participate and engage with their community of learners beyond what is being graded or assessed, and secondly, students are choosing how that interaction takes place. Some students asked for guidance and feedback on a particular element ("Does the audio level sound okay to you?") and other students just wanted to share their growth in soundwriting ("I'm so proud of how far I've come in this class"). I truly believe the online nature of this class contributes to such an overwhelmingly positive experience for students, and the creative writing background of many students further aided them in forging their own creative community at moments when I lacked the forethought to do so.

As another added layer of interaction and community-building, I integrate graduate students through weekly discussion board moderation activities in a way that allows me to take advantage of the layered aspects of the course between undergraduate and graduate students. The practice of allowing graduate students to moderate online discussions is considered to be quite successful in terms of the research that exists on the subject; it could be argued, in fact, that the online environment is likely the best modality for such leadership opportunities because it provides graduate students with the opportunity to engage with their peers over a prolonged duration of time, creating more meaningful for long-term academic growth (Thormann and Fidalgo, 2014). In other words, face-to-face classes rarely have enough time for graduate students to take the lead on a topic for more than a small portion of a class period, but such a strategy is easily achieved in the online classroom. In this course, for example, the discussion board moderation assignment includes three parts: 1) providing a preliminary analysis of that week's topic one week in advance (4–5 minute audio analysis); 2) developing discussion questions for the class to engage with; and 3) moderating that week's class discussion by asking and/or answering questions and encouraging deeper thinking (minimum of six posts spread throughout the week). The audio analysis element affords graduate students even more practice in soundwriting. As such, graduate students work on their discussion board moderation activity across a span of 7–10 days, if not longer, leading to a stronger foundational understanding of course content and improved peer interaction.

To my surprise, the graduate student audio analyses range from 7 to 10 minutes, due to the contextualizing made by the graduate students to better connect with peers and identify their positionality to the weekly topic. Pedagogically speaking, if I modify the assignment parameters in the future, then it would be to extend the time limit since the longer critical analyses have been beneficial, strategic, and necessary in every case. One student, for example, discusses his background as a privileged, white male raised in a politically conservative environment (but who has since moved left politically and socially) as a way to contextualize his introduction of that week's topic about racial sound resistance and its potential to disrupt, dismantle, and decenter the mainstream or status quo; this introductory framing is well received by classmates and opens up the conversation in unique, interesting, and thoughtful ways—ways that I, alone, may not have been able to garner. The introductory framing is repeated in future weekly discussion board moderations, such as the topic on disability and accessibility matters, which is particularly refreshing, as someone who identifies as a minoritized faculty of color living with a chronic illness. So, this assignment allows the class, by way of graduate student leadership, to explore how "word–sound relationships can facilitate ideas about disability, gender, and ethnicity" (Smith, 2017: 57) and touch on Rein's point about the shift in authority, and increased contributions, that takes place when students moderate discussion ("Lost in Digital Translation"). In light of this finding, it appears that the introductory framing techniques initiated by graduate students serve as both a practical and critically reflexive approach, thus demonstrating the unique pedagogical potential of student-led discussions, particularly those that take place in the online classroom.

This course demonstrates another interdisciplinary course design for the online creative writing classroom in that it fuses principles of professional writing, via that of aural or sound rhetoric, with that of creative writing. From the perspective of professional writing faculty, specifically, the goal is that students leave the program with some familiarity with activities expected of them in the new creative economy, namely audio editing, video editing, and digital writing to name just a few. It is my belief that the achievements and areas of student growth shared here are not only aided by the online classroom but also enhanced by it.

Final thoughts

I am not a creative writer, nor do I pretend to be. I do, however, see myself as a creative composer—an identity I now share with my creative writing students to their surprise ("How could this be? The technical writing professor is a creative digital composer?!"). Admittedly, when I first accepted my position at CWU, I was not prepared for the pedagogical undertaking it would entail—blending digital pedagogy, creative writing pedagogy, professional writing pedagogy, and the pedagogy of online writing instruction. I likely would not have believed such an endeavor possible and definitely not with the level of success we have achieved in the program, considering our ranking as one of the nation's top 15 online English programs (according to Best Schools, an independent organization).

As someone with many years of experience teaching creative composing projects online, the most notable changes in the aforementioned courses at

CWU is the overall quality and polished nature of the creative projects, which I believe speaks to students' foundational background and training in the creative writing craft. I draw upon that foundation, as well as print culture, offering a pedagogical framework for incorporating digital creative projects into the online classroom alongside traditional, print-based exercises, thus offering students "a multi-genre, process-based approach to workshop" (Mayers, 2017).

The variety of critical creative digital projects incorporated into my classes—from graphic narratives and autographies to audio essays and digital oral histories—speaks to the intricacies of creative writing craft as well as the increasing expectations for students in the creative industry. In light of my experiences in the online PCW program, I would argue that the management of the breadth and depth of such projects are possible due, in large part, to the online modality of the class. As several authors in *Creative Writing Innovations* contend, creative writing is no longer limited to words on a printed page—if it ever has been—and my hope is that this chapter contributes to the growing body of scholarship on creative composing in the online creative writing classroom.

Works cited

Best Online Bachelor's in English Degree Programs. Best Schools, January 2020, https://thebestschools.org/rankings/best-online-bachelors-english/.

Borgman, Jessie, and Casey McArdle. *Personal, Accessible, Responsive, Strategic: Resources and Strategies for Online Writing Instructors*. Practices & Possibilities Series. University Press of Colorado, 2019.

Chute, Hillary. "Comics as Literature? Reading Graphic Narrative." *PMLA*, vol. 123, no. 2, 2008, pp. 452–465. *JSTOR*, www.jstor.org/stable/25501865. Accessed 28 February 2020.

Clark, Hergenrader, and Joseph Rein. "Introduction." *Creative Writing in the Digital Age*, edited by Michael Dean Clark, Trent Hergenrader, and Joseph Rein, Bloomsbury, 2015, pp. 1–4.

Danforth, Courtney S., Kyle D. Stedman, and Michael J. Faris (Eds.). *Soundwriting Pedagogies*. Computers and Composition Digital Press/Utah State University Press, 2018, http://ccdigitalpress.org/soundwriting.

DS106 Digital Storytelling Assignment Bank. Audio Assignments, Open Resource, http://assignments.ds106.us/types/AudioAssignments/.

Harper, Graeme. "Creative Writing in the Age of Synapses." *Creative Writing in the Digital Age*, edited by Michael Dean Clark, Trent Hergenrader, and Joseph Rein, Bloomsbury, 2015, pp. 7–16.

Hewett, Beth L., and DePew, Kevin Eric (Eds.). *Foundational Practices of Online Writing Instruction*. Perspectives on Writing Series. Parlor Press, 2015.

Koehler, Adam. "Screening Subjects: Workshop pedagogy, media ecologies, and (new) student subjectivities." *Creative Writing in the Digital Age*, edited by Michael Dean Clark, Trent Hergenrader, and Joseph Rein, Bloomsbury, 2015, pp. 17–28.

Mayers, Tim. "Notes toward an Inventive, Process-Oriented Pedagogy for Introductory Multigenre Creative Writing Courses." *Creative Writing Innovations*, edited by Michael Dean Clark, Trent Hergenrader, and Joseph Rein, Bloomsbury, 2017, pp. 7–20.

McCloud, Scott. *Understanding Comics: The Invisible Art.* William Morrow, 1993.
Rein, Joseph. "Lost in Digital Translation: Navigating the Online Creative Writing Classroom." *Creative Writing in the Digital Age*, edited by Michael Dean Clark, Trent Hergenrader, and Joseph Rein, Bloomsbury, 2015, pp. 91–104.
Rodrigue, Tanya. "Teaching Writing and Rhetoric with Sound." Macmillan Community, 2017, https://community.macmillan.com/community/the-english-community/bedford-bits/blog/2017/11/29/teaching-writing-and-rhetoric-with-sound.
Rodrigue, Tanya, et al. "Navigating the Soundscape, Composing with Audio." *Kairos: A Journal of Rhetoric, Technology, and Pedagogy*, vol. 21, no. 1, Fall 2016.
Smith, Hazel. "Musico-Litrary Miscegenations: Word and Sound Relationships in Creative Writing Pedagogy." *Creative Writing Innovations*, edited by Michael Dean Clark, Trent Hergenrader, and Joseph Rein, Bloomsbury, 2017, pp. 57–72.
Thormann, Joan and Patricia Fidalgo. "Guidelines for Online Course Moderation and Community Building from a Student's Perspective." *MERLOT Journal of Online Learning and Teaching*, vol. 10, no. 3, Sept. 2014.
Warnock, Scott. *Teaching Writing Online: How and Why.* National Council for Teachers of English, 2009.
Williams, B.T. "Digital Technologies and Creative Writing Pedagogies." *Creative Writing Pedagogies for the Twenty-First Century*, edited by Alexandria Peary and Tom Hunley, Southern Illinois University Press, 2015, pp. 243–268.

9 Designing peer review

Research and intentional practices for effective online creative writing workshops

Lori Ostergaard and Marshall Kitchens

> I really appreciate that everyone seemed to take an interest in one another's writing, and that the peer reviews and other replies were written well and taken seriously. I realize that posting your writing for your classmates to see can be intimidating and lead you to want to open up less, because I experience that myself, but I loved that everyone seemed comfortable enough to be open in telling their stories, as well as respectful in replying to stories that clearly came from a hard or emotional place. I think that everyone's ability to open up in their writing this semester and be serious about responding to each other's writing is what made the semester a great one. Good job everyone!
>
> (Becky, online student, fall 2019)[1]

It is commonplace to speak of the workshop as the "signature pedagogy in creative writing" (Stukenberg, 2017: 277), to laud the workshop's role in helping students to shape texts and introducing them to the craft of creative writing. As Jill Stukenberg observes, through the workshop, creative writing students "develop many key habits of mind, including awareness of how readers interpret, and even co-create, texts ... and the intimate understanding that drafts are drafts, [and] that manuscripts ... are created through play, revision, choice, and even accident" (278). Workshopping is a common practice for writing faculty across many specializations, but faculty in diverse fields outside of writing have also begun to recognize its effectiveness. For example, in a 2014 study, Raoul A. Mulder, Jon M. Pearce, and Chi Baik examined student perceptions prior to and following the use of peer review in four disciplines: zoology, information systems, engineering, and environmental science. Chief among their findings was a significant increase in their students' recognition that in reviewing their classmates' papers, they had also learned how to revise their own texts (163). Mulder, Pearce, and Baik's conclusions will not surprise the readers of this collection who understand that, in offering observations and recommendations to their classmates, our students "return to their own work with those fresh eyes and sharpened perspectives" necessary for improvement (Stukenberg, 2017: 283). Indeed, most of the students in this study reported that their papers had improved as a result of both their peers' feedback and their own "self-reflection after reviewing their peers' work" (166). Mulder, Pearce, and Baik make a number of recommendations for improving face-to-face peer reviews that echo our own approach to designing online workshops, including providing training prior to the first workshop, offering models for effective review, outlining "clear and detailed criteria and guidelines" for student reviewers, and assessing students' reviews of their classmates' work (2014: 167–168).

Most of the students in a creative nonfiction course we teach at Oakland University (an R2 university in southeast Michigan) have already encountered some kind of writing workshop model in their high school English classes or in their first-year writing classes, and many, like our student quoted in the epigraph above, are apprehensive about participating in their first creative writing workshop. Indeed, students' concerns about workshopping may be compounded when their creative writing class is offered online, in a space where they are required to offer substantive feedback in written form to classmates who they may never meet in person.

Current research into peer response practices demonstrates what many of us have long understood: when they conduct their first workshop, many creative writing students "lack the confidence and commitment to engage in peer review" (Dixon and Hawe, 2017: 8). These insecurities may be multiplied in online classes where they may not have an opportunity to participate in both formal writing workshops and more informal conversations before, during, and after class that can help to establish trust and build rapport. As Stukenberg notes, workshopping is a social process: "workshop for some necessarily encompasses not just the in-class sessions of critique but the conversations between students and faculty that spill over afterward, at the bar or guest writer's reading" (2017: 280). But as Joseph Rein observes, in the online classroom, "creative writing instructors face a multitude of issues when attempting to recreate the human elements, the personal connections so prevalent, so necessary to the traditional creative writing classroom" (2015: 93). Rein highlights the essential, human aspects of the face-to-face workshop by suggesting that

> the online classroom often cannot deliver, among other things, the immediacy of face-to-face peer interaction; the joy and discomfort of each individual student when [their] work becomes the center of a pointed, live discussion; the vocal tones and facial expressions so often necessary in deciphering said discussion; the improvised but necessary tangents; and for instructors, those teachable moments where an issue in one student's work highlights a larger course concept.
>
> (92–93)

In the online class, absent too are the shared bonding experiences that many of us take for granted in our face-to-face classes—a student cracking a joke that makes everyone laugh together or students complaining together about campus parking or the lines in the campus food court.

These casual and communal bonding experiences are often initially absent from online classes. However, as Marcelle Freiman suggests, although the creative writing workshop "is an extremely exposed situation for students to learn in" (para. 12), the absence of face-to-face contact in an online class may actually facilitate more meaningful workshop engagement. She argues that "behind the 'screen' of the internet, a comfortable interactive and collaborative space is created where personal differences and issues of confidence are less likely to interfere with learning" (para. 14). Heather Beck further argues that online classes may be "more democratic and less intimidating" for students because the online medium gives students time to think about how they want to respond and craft their responses to peers (35). Rein's observations echo Beck's as he posits that online creative writing classes may be more democratic than face-to-face classes. He praises the "asynchronous nature of online feedback [that] … levels the playing field" and where "everyone in class has a voice" (93). He further suggests that "the immediacy of the face-to-face workshop, and its inclination toward the extroverted, can challenge even the most democratic of instructors" (93).

While some aspects of the online class medium may facilitate more meaningful and democratic interactions between our writers, in our experience as teachers of online creative writing, we have found that intentional online workshop design may also aid in (1) building student engagement, (2) increasing student–student and professor–student trust and rapport in the online classroom, and (3) supporting students' growth from novice to more experienced writers. To be successful, such course design must take into account the fact that "developing an online community is paramount to student engagement" and that "additional efforts at engaging students are necessary in the online environment" compared to the traditional brick and mortar classroom (Girardi, 2016: 60). In the following sections, we overview some of our strategies for the intentional design of online workshops, including information about how to prepare students for active and collaborative engagement in the workshop, develop clear guidelines for student responses, provide effective feedback on workshop responses, and assess those responses. Because we believe reflection is a required component of the learning students do in the online workshop, throughout this chapter, we also include some excerpts from our students' process reflections and from the acknowledgments they write to their peers at the end of the semester.

Course design

Before we introduce how we approach online workshops, it is necessary to briefly describe our course and online course management system. While ours is a third-year creative nonfiction course, because of the student population—a combination of majors from creative writing, professional and digital writing, journalism, communication, and education—the class serves both as an introduction to creative nonfiction and as a prerequisite for our online advanced creative nonfiction class. Our online classes are delivered asynchronously through Moodle, an open source course management system that includes discussion forums, chat rooms, announcements, assignment uploads, and other digital affordances, including the ability for students and instructors to easily record audio or video feedback.

In the creative nonfiction classes we teach online, students compose works in new discussion forums every week and then they provide one another with feedback on those creative works in threaded discussions. Some weeks we assign students to workshop in groups of three or four or we require them to respond to a certain number of works across the entire class. Both of us have extensive reading lists that include a variety of "craft" readings providing students with introductions to creative techniques as well as a collection of sample creative nonfiction readings that demonstrate those techniques, and we frequently ask students to reference concepts from those works in their workshop reviews. Students also revise two of their weekly works into longer stories that undergo multiple workshops before they are finally submitted to us, and they write reflections about both the process they used to write those longer works and the revision suggestions they received from their peers.

The majority of the class grade is related to the work students produce in the discussion forums, including their weekly original works, their workshop responses, their reading responses, and their reflections on the writing and revision process. The remaining percentage of the course grade is divided evenly among the two larger, more polished, works students revise: a memoir and either a family story or a travel piece.

Preparing the online workshop

In designing our asynchronous workshops, we have found that rather than stultifying the creative writing workshop, the online medium increases student interaction, engagement, and critique compared to face-to-face workshops. As with face-to-face workshops, though, a considerable amount of front-loading of expectations and modeling of effective response is required to encourage meaningful engagement from students. In addition, as we discuss in the next section, some unique affordances are available to us in the online medium to prepare our students for workshopping, including informal spaces for students to share information and ideas that are not directly connected to the course and mechanisms for providing ground rules for respectful response.

Our course design deliberately builds toward risk tolerance, beginning with low-risk assignments that ensure success and escalating risk with structured rewards for student engagement throughout the semester. We supply students with direct instruction in the goals and structure of the review process in the early weeks of the course, we offer clear instructions for each workshop, and we provide the rubrics we use to evaluate students' responses to one another. In our own responses to our students' story drafts, we model good feedback practices, responding to students as we hope they will respond to one another. For example, if we provide students with specific questions to answer about their peers' drafts, we will also answer those questions when we provide feedback on their drafts. At the beginning of the semester, we allow students to decide for themselves which pieces they will peer review. This gives our students some flexibility to respond to pieces that particularly move them or that they find compelling, but we ask that they also respond as "good online citizens" and find works that have not yet received a response.

To facilitate more casual connections among students, we provide a question and answer forum where students can post general questions about the course and receive answers from either us or their classmates. We also set aside a single forum, a "writers' lounge," where students can post questions or information relevant to the course, announcements about campus activities, and even links to their blogs or social media sites. While we see some interaction in both of these forums, the majority of the connections our students form develop organically within the weekly workshops. In these spaces, we find our students forming microcommunities that emerge from their familiarity with one another's creative work. As they revise individual pieces into longer works, some of our students will seek out peers whose work they appreciated or reviewed in draft form. For example, in Lori's winter 2019 class, Angus[2] re-reviewed a story Tammy had chosen to revise, praising her for the refinements she made to the story and offering new suggestions. Angus opened by acknowledging his familiarity with Tammy's work, before offering some additional revision advice, telling Tammy, "You always write so passionately about your family and it really came through in this piece. I remember reading this when you first wrote it and you were somehow able to make it even more compelling this time around and it's incredible, seriously." In her response to Angus—which was not required for this workshop—Tammy thanked him for the feedback, noting that he was her "biggest fan" in the class.

Before participating in their first workshop, we provide students with directions to maintain a tone of civility, compassion, and encouragement. They're advised to acknowledge when someone is being brave by sharing deeply personal stories and to avoid moral judgments. While they're advised against being negative or hyper-critical, we also explicitly caution them to avoid evasive responses such as "It looks perfect as it is" or "I wouldn't change a thing." We also prepare our students to encounter stories that push them out of their comfort zone or challenge their beliefs with the following advice:

- If you read something that offends you, take a constructive approach in your response. Talk about the positives of the piece first, and then gently point out passages where the tone or content may have made you feel puzzled or uncomfortable as a reader or that you think others might find offensive. Suggest ways in which someone else might have seen things differently. Avoid accusations against the writer and instead favor explanations that describe your response as a reader.
- Don't take feedback personally. If a classmate was a little snarky in their response to your work, try to give them the benefit of the doubt. Consider first how technology might be leading you to misconstrue their tone and intent. If something your reviewer said offended you, consider that they may have misunderstood you or you may have misunderstood their response. Take what is helpful from their feedback and leave the rest.

Designing the workshop

We both have come to recognize that our students' microcommunities enable them to make positive personal connections in a seemingly impersonal space, which in turn creates the conditions for success in our online workshops. In this section, we discuss some of the elements of an effective online writing workshop, including how to set up formal response guidelines and word counts, set expectations for these exchanges, and provide clear evaluation standards.

Before we compose the instructions for an online workshop, we begin by asking ourselves the following questions:

- What creative skills did we intend for students to develop with this writing assignment?
- What types of feedback might benefit students at this stage of their writing process, and how can we facilitate that kind of feedback?
- Given the questions above, what characterizes an effective peer response for this particular workshop?

Because we cannot be in the room with our students when they read and respond to their peers' work and because we cannot remedy asynchronous workshops that have gone astray until after the reviews are completed, the answers to the questions above guide the directions we provide our students and determine both the roles or stances we ask our students to assume in the workshop and the kinds of questions we ask them to answer for their peers. Our directions for the workshops include all of the following elements:

1. An explanation for the creative writing assignment that students will post for review.
2. A list of the multiple deadlines for this work—typically one deadline for stories to be posted to the discussion forum and another deadline for the reviews of those stories.
3. Instructions for how to respond to their peers' work and a required word count for each of their responses.
4. The number of peers whose work they will need to respond to.
5. The rubric that we will use to evaluate their responses.

Four stances: compliment, connect, contribute, question

Prior to the first workshop, Lori introduces students to four stances to take in their reviews—compliment, connect, contribute, and question—and she defines them as follows:

> To compliment, identify the strengths in the work, address only the positive aspects of the writer's storytelling style, and praise their use of specific stylistic elements that were introduced in course materials.

To connect with a classmate's story, write about how the story's characters, situations, plot, resolutions, etc. affected you: sparked memories, thoughts, or emotions.

To contribute to your classmate's story, offer specific suggestions for ways they can improve their storytelling and the story itself.

To question, provide five to six good, open-ended questions about the story that will help the writer fill in some of the blanks for their readers, explain more, or improve their characters, settings, etc.

In her feedback to her students' stories, Lori models each stance, and in her feedback on their responses to their classmates, she offers suggestions for how they might improve their feedback while assuming each stance. We both emphasize the importance of the workshop by not responding to every story our students write so that they will recognize the value of their peers' feedback. We also base the majority of our workshop grades on how well students responded to their peers' work. Notably, the majority of the grade students receive on each workshop is shaped by the quality of their feedback rather than on the quality of their own creative works.

Lori asks students to assume certain stances in their reviews, and Marshall likewise provides a structure for workshopping drafts by asking his students to provide a combination of positive affirmations, questions and suggestions, and encouragement. He first asks students to provide positive affirmations, prompting students to:

- Address the author directly and sign your name at the end.
- Acknowledge what you think the story is about, whether or not it's fully articulated. Point out some of the parts of the work that you thought especially vivid or effectively detailed or that resonated with you in some way.
- Point out ways that what they've written reflects advice given in any of the craft readings or reminds you of some of the model readings.
- Let the writer know that you appreciated the work and know that you got what they were trying to say.

Marshall then prompts students to ask questions and make suggestions:

- Give the writer something to work with when they go back to revise — particularly ideas about how to expand and reorganize. The goal isn't to be critical, but to offer constructive feedback from a reader's point of view about how they might revise and polish their piece.
- Avoid any variation of the line "I don't really have any suggestions," or "it looks great as it is." That's not helpful and will cost you points for the workshop. You might start out passages with "If you were to revise this ..."

- Point out anything that might be missing by asking clarifying questions. What factual questions do you have? What details should be added? What confused you? What more might they tell you about the setting, the people, the event?
- Point out any stylistic challenges. Is the beginning effective at creating a visual scene or jump starting the narrative? Is there another paragraph that might better serve as the beginning? Does the conclusion resonate? Or is it more summary and "moral of the story"?
- Look for other stylistic or content issues. Try to balance out the positive comments from the first section with constructive suggestions in this section.
- Is there any particular advice from the craft readings that you think might be helpful for them, or examples from the model readings? Be specific.

Finally, Marshall prompts students to provide a strong ending for their review:

- End on a positive note—your goal is to allow the writer to be excited about the possibilities of the piece rather than to shut them down.
- Push past clarifying questions to ask probing questions. What deeper questions does this piece raise for you about interpersonal relationships, about culture, about human nature? You might speculate on what the story is really about rather than just what it appears to be about on the surface. Try to push a little on what their theme might be.
- Give the writer encouragement to revise by pointing out what's valuable about the piece or what potential it has to offer.

By the end of the semester, we find that our online students require less of this overt guidance in providing feedback, and they uniformly have a better feel for what is or is not working in their own stories. But we both require a set number of peer responses each week (each with a high required word count) and we incorporate those requirements into our evaluation criteria so that students continue to improve their responses in the online workshop. Of course, requiring students to respond at length is no guarantee of a quality response, but over the years we have found that pushing students to write more, particularly early in the semester, yields better, more thorough and engaged, responses throughout the term. Along with the guidelines and word counts, our workshop directions also include our full evaluation rubric. In the next section, we discuss providing feedback on workshops and present more detail on how we evaluate our students' responses.

Workshop feedback

One benefit of teaching creative writing in a fully online format is that the learning students do is arguably more visible than in traditional face-to-face environments. This makes the instructor's dual tasks of providing constructive formative feedback and of assessing students' work a little easier. As Freiman notes, online creative writing workshops create "an environment for active learning in which it is possible to see what students actually do in their learning," something that can be challenging to observe in face-to-face classes "given the diversity of students and the way they convey their understanding and engagement" (para. 8). In fact, Freiman notes that the "active and student-centered processes in creative writing" may actually "make it especially suited to online teaching and learning" (para. 9).

Our students begin workshops in the second week of the semester and these continue weekly throughout the term. Each week students produce one or two new stories (or revise earlier stories into their longer projects) and then workshop those stories with a small number of classmates. Early in the semester, we both spend as much time responding to the workshop responses as we do to the stories our students have written. And in our own responses to students, we strive both to provide our writers with feedback on their work and to model best practices for peer responses. For example, with some reviews Lori will assume the stance of a connector and questioner, answer the questions the writer asked of their workshop partners, or connect her suggestions to the craft and style readings the students have completed. Marshall uses a similar model of affirmations and suggestions for development, making connections to craft readings and pointing out similarities with model readings. One of his responses to a fall 2019 student unpacks many of these elements:

> Good work getting this posted. What I'm looking for in particular with this forum is the degree to which you are building on storytelling and sensory details by incorporating some of those craft skills from the readings on settings and characterization: developing the sense of people and places as fully fleshed out, three-dimensional characters and locations, as well as the storytelling structure. I'm looking to see who the characters are in this piece and how well you've described them and captured their sense of personality, and for your story's settings, I'm looking for descriptive details about your environment as well as the ways that you establish a sense of place in the sense that Dorothy Allison was describing: the larger cultural and social sense of the neighborhood or city or region and what it reflects in the cultural imagination.
>
> If you were to revise, you might develop other characters more fully within the narrative structure. Provide some more nuanced physical descriptions, maybe some bits of dialogue, background details, or mannerisms.

In terms of setting, think about both sensory details about the setting where this takes place, as well as the geographical setting. You might develop the cultural context. Look back at Dorothy Allison and David Hood for tips about setting. Think about the way that Lance Arthur creates a psychological profile of suburban Bakersfield, CA in the 1970s.

Finally, pay careful attention to the feedback you get from your classmates (not that you should necessarily follow all the advice you get), and review the craft articles on characterization and setting, beginnings and endings, and dialogue to get some ideas about revision possibilities if you decide to revise this story into a longer work.

One additional way we demonstrate our respect for the feedback our students provide is by pointing out when a classmate has made an especially astute observation about a work or echoing, in our own reviews, the recommendations our students provided to the writer.

Online workshop assessment

Given the amount of writing students do in their online workshops (an average of 2,500 words per student, per week), we have had to develop strategies for dealing with a staggering amount of text to read, respond to, and assess. One simple strategy is to avoid false precision in our evaluations. Rather than parse whether a response is, for example, a B or a B–, we provide more holistic grades for the workshops. This gives us time to focus more on providing feedback to our students' stories and workshop responses. For example, Lori uses the following three-point scale:

- Exceeds Expectations: All replies are robustly developed and meet (or exceed) the word (or question) count; address the author/work directly; push the author to think more deeply about their writing by responding as a complimenter, connector, contributor, or questioner to develop an engaged, thorough, and constructive response.
- Meets Expectations: All required replies are adequately developed and meet (or exceed) the word (or question) count; address the author/work directly; push the author to think more intentionally about their writing by responding as a complimenter, connector, contributor, or questioner to develop an engaged and constructive response.
- Does Not Meet Expectations: An underdeveloped (under the required word or question limit) response; may be missing one of the required responses; may duplicate elements of a response another classmate has already posted; or does not push the author to think deeply about their writing.

In our comments to students, we use language from the rubric to identify where they produced a successful or unsuccessful response. Marshall will praise students for writing effective responses at the beginning of the semester, for example, by pointing out when their responses to this workshop maintain a positive tone, have compassionate affirmations and personal connections, and ask some good questions. Keep that up. Work on asking probing and clarifying questions and providing suggestions for further development. You might look back at the guidelines and rubric for ideas on developing those suggestions more fully. One tip I have for everyone as we move forward is to make more connections to the craft readings and the model essays in your feedback when you're giving suggestions for specific improvements. Good start here—I'm sure you'll see your feedback getting stronger as we progress.

In the face-to-face classroom, students receive more immediate feedback on their responses to other writers. In addition to hearing the writers respond with thanks and an echo back of the helpful critiques they received, in the physical spaces we occupy with students, students can read their classmates' facial expressions and body language. Because this kind of positive affirmation of their critique is absent in the online space, our feedback and assessment of their workshop responses must provide students with both specific praise for their responses and detailed suggestions for improvement.

Conclusion

While it is challenging to build community and generate trust between students in the online classroom, after years of trial and error we have both come to prefer teaching our creative nonfiction classes online. When given the time to develop their responses to their classmates' texts, and when provided with clear directions for and individualized feedback on their responses, we find that our online students engage more—and more deliberately, thoughtfully, and thoroughly—with both their classmates' work and with one another.

We opened this chapter with Becky's reflection on her initial trepidation sharing her personal creative work with her classmates, so it seems fitting to close with another of our student's reflections on the role her online classmates played in her development as a writer. In her final class acknowledgments, "Ellen" recognized both her classmates and the online classroom conditions that contributed to her experience with the class and her growth as a writer:

> This was one of my craziest semesters here at Oakland. However, this class was a safe place for me to temporarily forget everything else that was going on around me and really reflect and get creative with the life events that I've experienced. The advice I received from both my classmates and the professor were more than helpful, they were motivational. In the sense that they pushed me to think more outside of what I was comfortable writing and really master the skill of writing in a way that would inspire or change the mindset of my readers. I wouldn't say just one or two people were

especially encouraging, but there were some strategies that really helped me to take advice more gratefully. When my peers explained what they liked most about my story first, it really made me feel that they had actually read my work. Then following with some constructive criticism, in a respectful way, made me feel that they weren't just pointing out what was wrong with it, but what I could improve on as a writer .... . I have had such a fun time learning more about writing in regards to creative non-fiction and also getting the experience of reading others' works. I'm proud of, not only myself, but everyone else in this online class for pushing themselves and always improving.

(Ellen, online student, winter 2019)

Notes

1 This study has been approved by the Oakland University IRB (#1540187) and uses an archive of existing student work from the authors' online creative nonfiction classes.
2 All student names used in this chapter are pseudonyms.

Works cited

Allison, Dorothy. "Place." *The Writer's Notebook: Craft Essays from Tin House*. Tin House Books, 2013, pp. 5–16.
Arthur, Lance. "My Stupid Childhood." *The Fray*, 2000. fray.com/hope/childhood/. Accessed 15 June 2020.
Beck, Heather. "Teaching Creative Writing Online." *New Writing: The International Journal for the Practice and Theory of Creative Writing*, vol. 1, 2004, pp. 23–36.
Dixon, Helen, and Eleanor Hawe. "Creating the Climate and Space for Peer Review within the Writing Classroom." *Journal of Response to Writing*, vol. 3, no. 1, 2017, pp. 6–30.
Freiman, Marcelle. "Learning through Dialogue: Teaching and Assessing Creative Writing Online." *Text*, vol. 6, no. 2, 2002. textjournal.com.au/oct02/freiman.htm. Accessed 15 June 2020.
Girardi, Tamara. "Lost in Cyberspace: Addressing Issues of Student Engagement in the Online Classroom Community," *Applied Pedagogies: Strategies for Online Writing Instruction*, edited by Daniel Ruefman and Abigail G.Scheg. UtahState University Press, 2016, pp. 59–74.
Hood, Dave. "Creative Nonfiction: Writing About Place." *Find Your Creative Muse: Learn to Write Poetry, Fiction, Personal Essays and More*, 2012. davehood59.wordpress.com/2012/04/23/creative-nonfiction-writing-about-place/. Accessed 15 June 2020.
Mulder, Raoul A., Jon M. Pearce, and Chi Baik. "Peer Review in Higher Education: Student Perceptions Before and After Participation." *Active Learning in Higher Education*, vol. 15, no. 2, 2014, pp. 157–171.
Rein, Joseph. "Lost in Digital Translation: Navigating the Online Creative Writing Workshop." *Creative Writing in the Digital Age: Theory, Practice, and Pedagogy*, edited by Michael Dean Clark, Trent Hergenrader, and Joseph Rein. Bloomsbury, 2015, pp. 91–104.
Stukenberg, Jill. "Deep Habits: Workshop as Critique in Creative Writing." *Arts and Humanities in Higher Education*, vol. 16, no. 3, 2017, pp. 277–292.

Appendix A: Course bibliography

What is creative nonfiction?

Craft readings

Gutkind, Lee. "What Is Creative Nonfiction?" *Creative Nonfiction*, www.creativenonfiction.org/ online-reading/what-creative-nonfiction. Accessed 15 June 2020.

Moore, Dinty. "A Genre by Any Other Name? The Story Behind 'Creative Nonfiction.'" *Creative Nonfiction*, Summer 2015. www.creativenonfiction.org/online-reading/ genre-any-other-name. Accessed 15 June 2020.

Snow, Shane. "Why Storytelling Will be the Biggest Business Skill of the Next Five Years." *Contently*, 3 February 2014. contently.com/2014/02/03/ this-will-be-the-top-business-skill-of-the-next-5-years/. Accessed 15 June 2020.

UVM Writing Center. "Creative Nonfiction." www.uvm.edu/wid/writingcenter/tutortips/ nonfiction.html. Accessed 15 June 2020.

Wallace, David Foster. "English 183D Syllabus." *Salon*, 11 November 2014. www.salon.com/test2/2014/11/10/david_foster_wallaces_mind_blowing_creative_nonfiction_syllabus_this_does_not_mean_an_essayist%25E2%2580%2599s_goal_is_to_share_or_express_herself_or_whatever_feel_good_term_you_got_taught_in_h/. Accessed 15 June 2020.

Model readings

Arthur, Lance. "My Stupid Childhood." *The Fray*, May 2000. fray.com/hope/childhood/. Accessed 15 June 2020.

Daily, Ryan C. "Candy Thief." *River Teeth: A Journal of Nonfiction Narrative*, 25 July 2016. www.riverteethjournal.com/blog/2016/07/25/candy-thief. Accessed15 June 2020.

Horyn, Cathy. "Snooki's Time." *The New York Times*, 23 June 2010. www.nytimes.com/2010/07/25/fashion/25Snooki.html. Accessed15 June 2020.

Norquist, Richard. "100 Major Works of Modern Creative Nonfiction." *Thoughtco*, 19 November 2018. www.thoughtco.com/major-works-of-modern-creative-nonfiction-1688768. Accessed 15 June 2020.

Porterfield, Kay Marie. "Second Breakfast." *Hippocampus Magazine*, 1 January 2016. www.hippocampusmagazine.com/2016/01/second-breakfast-by-kay-marie-porterfield/. Accessed 15 June 2020.

Rice, Jeff. "A Table Essay." *Medium*, 5 May 2019. medium.com/@drfabulous/a-table-essay- a7093b0bfd3d. Accessed 15 June 2020.

Twombly, Sarah. "The Strongest Cookie." *Hippocampus Magazine*, 1 December 2016. www.hippocampusmagazine.com/2016/12/the-strongest-cookie-by-sarah-twombly/. Accessed 15 June 2020.

Washington, Glynn. "The Tribe." *Snap Judgment*, 21 February 2014. www.npr.org/2014/02/21/ 280696431/the-tribe. Accessed 15 June 2020.

Writing processes

Craft readings

Biederman, Roseann. "The Writing Process: Step One." *Writer's Digest*, 29 February 2012. www.writersdigest.com/there-are-no-rules/the-writing-process-step-one. Accessed 15 June 2020.

Lamott, Anne. "Shitty First Drafts." *Bird by Bird: Some Instructions on Writing and Life*. Anchor, 1994, pp. 21–27.

Miller, Brenda and Suzanne Paola. "The Body of Memory." *Tell It Slant: Creating, Refining, and Publishing Creative Nonfiction*. 3rd ed., McGraw Hill, 2019, pp. 3–22.

Moore, Dinty. "The Personal (Not Private) Essay." *Crafting the Personal Essay: A Guide for Writing and Publishing Creative Non-Fiction* (Kindle Locations 187–193). F+W Media. Kindle Edition.

National Council of Teachers of English. *NCTE Beliefs about the Teaching of Writing*. February 2016. ncte.org/statement/teaching-writing/. Accessed 15 June 2020.

Raisin, Ross. "7 Methods for Writing Your First Draft." *Literary Hub*, 1 May 2018. lithub.com/7-methods-for-writing-your-first-draft. Accessed 15 June 2020.

Sitko, Barbara. "Knowing How to Write: Metacognition and Writing Instruction." *Metacognition in Educational Theory and Practice*, edited by D. J. Hacker, J. Dunlosky, & A. C. Graesser, Lawrence Erlbaum, 1998, pp. 93–115.

Wright, Zach. "A Handy Strategy for Teaching Theme." *Edutopia*, 25 February 2020. www.edutopia.org/article/handy-strategy-teaching-theme. Accessed 15 June 2020.

Beginnings and endings

Craft readings

Bloch, Hanna. "A Good Lead Is Everything." *NPR*, 12 October 2016. training.npr.org/2016/10/12/leads-are-hard-heres-how-to-write-a-good-one/. Accessed 15 June 2020.

Hood, Dave. "Writing Creative Nonfiction: Beginning and Ending." *Find Your Creative Muse*, 16 August 2012. davehood59.wordpress.com/2012/08/16/writing-creative-nonfiction-beginning-and-ending/. Accessed 15 June 2020.

Rogers, Tony. "How to Write Great Ledes for Feature Stories." *Thoughtco.*, 22 February 2019. www.thoughtco.com/how-to-write-ledes-for-feature-stories-2074318. Accessed 15 June 2020.

Rogers, Tony. "How Feature Writers Use Delayed Leads." *Thoughtco.*, 22 February 2019, www.thoughtco.com/the-definition-of-a-delayed-lede-2073761. Accessed 15 June 2020.

Model readings

Chambers, Jennifer. "Refuges Find Detroit a 'Paradise,' Hope More Syrians Come." *The Detroit News*, 21 September 2015. www.detroitnews.com/story/news/local/detroit-city/2015/09/21/refugees-find-detroit-paradise-hope-syrians/72602340/. Accessed 15 June 2020.

McCrummen, Stephanie. "An American Void." *The Washington Post*, 12 September 2015. www.washingtonpost.com/sf/national/2015/09/12/an-american-void/. Accessed 15 June 2020.

Setting and characterization

Craft readings

Allison, Dorothy. "Place." *The Writer's Notebook: Craft Essays from Tin House*. Tin House Books, 2009, pp. 5–16.

Corriveau, Erin. "Separating the Person from the Persona: Details and Distance in Creative Nonfiction – An Interview with Kim Dana Kupperman." *Causeway Lit/ Mason's Road*, Issue 5. causewaylit.com/masons-road-2/issue-5-characterization/. Accessed 15 June 2020.

Hood, Dave. "Creative Nonfiction: Writing about Place." *Find Your Creative Muse*, 17 March 2010. davehood59.wordpress.com/2010/03/17/how-to-write-creative-nonfiction-writing-about-place/.Accessed 15 June 2020.

Hood, Dave. "Creative Nonfiction: Writing about Place, Part 2." *Find Your Creative Muse*, 23 April 2012. davehood59.wordpress.com/2012/04/23/creative-nonfiction-writing-about-place/. Accessed 15 June 2020.

Roorbach, Bill and Kristen Keckler. "Crafting True to Life Nonfiction Characters." *Writer's Digest*, May/June 2009. www.writersdigest.com/improve-my-writing/craft-true-to-life- nonfiction-characters. Accessed 15 June 2020.

Model readings

Bellanti, Courtney. "Meeting the Folks." *Moth Radio Hour*, 23 September 2010, themoth.org/ stories/meeting-the-folks. Accessed 15 June 2020.

Buntin, Julie. "She's Still Dying on Facebook." *The Atlantic*, 6 July 2014, www.theatlantic.com/ technology/archive/2014/07/shes-still-dying-on-facebook/373904/. Accessed 15 June 2020.

Montano, Armando. "The Unexpected Lessons of Mexican Food." *Salon*, 18 March 2012, www.salon.com/test2/2012/03/17/the_unexpected_lessons_of_mexican_food/. Accessed 15 June 2020.

Preston, Douglas. "My Search for a Boyhood Friend Led to a Dark Discovery." *Wired*, 22 April 2019, www.wired.com/story/my-search-for-boyhood-friend-led-to-dark-discovery/ . Accessed 15 June 2020.

Romig, Rollo. "When You've Had Detroit." *The New Yorker*, 17 June 2014, www.newyorker.com/culture/culture-desk/when-youve-had-detroit. Accessed 15 June 2020.

Dialogue

Craft readings

Hood, Dave. "Dialogue and Action." *Find Your Creative Muse*, 18 March 2010, davehood59.wordpress.com/2010/03/18/how-to-write-creative-nonfiction-dialogue-and-action/. Accessed 15 June 2020.

Luke, Pearl. "Space and Punctuate Dialogue Correctly: Creative Writing Success Tips." *Be a Better Writer*, www.be-a-better-writer.com/punctuate-dialogue.html. Accessed 15 June 2020.

Weihardt, Ginny. "How to Punctuate Dialogue in Fiction Writing." *The Balance Careers*, 28 May 2019, www.thebalancecareers.com/punctuating-dialogue-properly-in-fiction-writing-1277721. Accessed 15 June 2020.

Model readings

Cronkite, Sue Riddle. "Blood Kin." *The Bitter Southerner*, n.d., bittersoutherner.com/ folklore-project/blood-kin-apalachicola-florida. Accessed 15 June 2020.

Dietrich, Sean. "A FEMA Trailer for Mother." *The Bitter Southerner*, n.d., bittersoutherner.com/ folklore-project/a-fema-trailer-for-mother/. Accessed 15 June 2020.

Gil, Sean. "A Temporary Shelf Life." *Hippocampus Magazine*, 1 September 2015, www.hippocampusmagazine.com/2015/09/a-temporary-shelf-life-by-sean-gill/. Accessed 15 June 2020.

Travel writing

Craft readings

Bowes, Gemma. "Tips for Travel Writing." *The Guardian*, 23 September 2011, hwww.theguardian.com/travel/2011/sep/23/travel-writing-tips-expert-advice. Accessed 15 June 2020.

Fox, Dave. "Travel Writing Tips for Beginners: Get Specific." *Globe Jotting*, 29 July 2012, www.globejotting.com/travel-writing-tips-for-beginners-get-specific/. Accessed 15 June 2020.

Fox, Dave. "Travel Writing Tips for Beginners: How to Structure Your Travel Tales." *Globe Jotting*, 31 July 2012, www.globejotting.com/travel-writing-tips-for-beginners-beginnings-middles-and-endings/. Accessed 15 June 2020.

Fox, Dave. "Travel Writing Tips for Beginners: Putting the Final Sparkle in Your Story." *Globe Jotting*, 2 August 2012, www.globejotting.com/travel-writing-tips-for-beginners-putting-the-final-sparkle-in-your-stories/. Accessed 15 June 2020.

Model readings

Carlisle, John. "At U.P.'s. Only Strip Club, Hunters are Big Business." *Detroit Free Press*, 25 November 2015. www.freep.com/story/news/columnists/john-carlisle/2015/ 11/25/hunting-season-at-upper-peninsula-strip-club/76114570/. Accessed 15 June 2020.

Randall, Laura. "In Los Angeles, Sriracha Fans Line Up for the Hottest Tour in Town." *The Washington Post*, 7 June 2018. www.washingtonpost.com/lifestyle/travel/ in-los-angeles-sriracha-fans-line-up-for-the-hottest-tour-in-town/2018/06/06/c4e18dd2–64ff-11e8–99d2–0d678ec08c2f_story.html. Accessed 15 June 2020.

Sedaris, David. "Santa Barbara." *Conde Nast Traveller*, September 2014. www.cntraveller.com/ gallery/david-sedaris-guide-santa-barbara. Accessed 15 June 2020.

Smith, Brian. "Tucson Salvage: A Wandering Escape." *Tucson Weekly*, 19 May 2016. www.tucsonweekly.com/tucson/tucson-salvage/Content?oid=6225127. Accessed 15 June 2020.

Sullivan, John Jeremiah. "Upon this Rock." *Gentlemen's Quarterly*, 25 January 2004. www.gq.com/story/rock-music-jesus. Accessed 15 June 2020.

Sullivan, John Jeremiah. "You Blow My Mind. Hey, Mickey! A Rough Guide to Disney World." *The New York Times Magazine*, 12 June 2011. www.nytimes.com/2011/06/ 12/magazine/ a-rough-guide-to-disney-world.html. Accessed 15 June 2020.

Tower, Wells. "The Old Man at Burning Man." *Gentleman's Quarterly*, February 2013, www.gq.com/story/burning-man-experiences-wells-tower-gq-february-2013. Accessed 15 June 2020.

Wallace, David Foster. "Stepping Out: On the (Nearly Lethal) Comforts of a Luxury Cruise." *Harper's Magazine*, September 2008. harpers.org/wp-content/uploads/ 2008/ 09/HarpersMagazine-1996–1901-0007859.pdf. Accessed 15 June 2020.

Wallace, David Foster. "Ticket to the Fair: Getting Away from Already Being Pretty Much Away from It All." *Harper's Magazine*, July 1994. harpers.org/wp-content/ uploads/ HarpersMagazine-1994–1907-0001729.pdf. Accessed 15 June 2020.

Profiles

Craft readings

Hong, Binh and Susan Ager. "Hearts and Guts: Writing the Personal Profile." *The Poynter Institute*, 22 August 2002. www.poynter.org/archive/2002/ hearts-and-guts-writing-the-personal-profile/. Accessed 15 June 2020.

"How to Write a Profile Feature Article." *The New York Times Learning Network*, 2 July 2019. web.archive.org/web/20190717103021/https://archive.nytimes.com/www. nytimes.com/learning/students/writing/voices.html. Accessed 15 June 2020.

Model readings

Orlean, Susan. "The American Man at Age 10." *Esquire*, December 1992. classic.esquire. com/ article/19921201100/print. Accessed 15 June 2020.

Ross, Lillian. "How Do You Like It Now, Gentlemen: The Moods of Ernest Hemingway." *The New Yorker*, 6 May 1950. www.newyorker.com/magazine/1950/05/13/ how-do-you-like-it-now-gentlemen. Accessed 15 June 2020.

Saslow, Eli. "'How's Amanda?' A Story of Truth, Lies and an American Addiction." *The Washington Post*, 23 July 2016. www.washingtonpost.com/classic-apps/ hows-amanda-a-story-of-truth-lies-and-an-american-addiction/2016/07/23/7be9ee40–43fa8–11e6-a66f-aa6c1883b6b1_story.html. Accessed 15 June 2020.

Singh, Perpreet. "Choking Out the Natives." *The Bitter Southerner*, n.d., bittersoutherner.com/ folklore-project/choking-out-the-natives/. Accessed 15 June 2020.

Telese, Gay. "Frank Sinatra Has a Cold." *Esquire*, April 1966, classic.esquire.com/ article/ 1966/4/1/frank-sinatra-has-a-cold. Accessed 15 June 2020.

Wang, Frances Kai-Hwa. "Carrying our Courage, From Immigrant Stories to Refugee Stories." *NBC News*, 24 November 2015. www.nbcnews.com/news/asian-america/ essay-carrying-our-courage-immigrant-stories-refugee-stories-n467611.

Life during the pandemic

Craft readings

Proulx, Natalie. "12 Ideas for Writing through the Pandemic with *The New York Times*." *The New York Times*, 15 April 2020. www.nytimes.com/2020/04/15/learning/ 12-ideas-for-writing-through-the-pandemic-with-the-new-york-times.html. Accessed 15 June 2020.

Model readings

Collins, Laura. "Missed Calls: Reinventing Grief in an Era of Enforced Isolation." *New Yorker*, 11 May 2020. www.newyorker.com/magazine/2020/05/11/ reinventing-grief-in-an-era-of-enforced-isolation. Accessed 15 June 2020.

Coppins, McKay. "I Just Flew. It was Worse than I Thought It Would Be." *The Atlantic*, May 2020. www.theatlantic.com/politics/archive/2020/05/is-flying-safe-coronavirus/611335/. Accessed 15 June 2020.

Kurlyandchik, Mark. "I Got an Early Glimpse of the Future of Dining." *Detroit Free Press*, 26 May 2020. www.freep.com/story/entertainment/dining/mark-kurlyandchik/2020/05/26/ got-early-glimpse-future-dining-heres-what-looks-like/5250024002/. Accessed 15 June 2020.

Martins, Kristin F. "Running Out of Outlets." *Wordpress*, 21 April 2020. kristenfmartins.wordpress.com/2020/04/21/running-out-of-outlets/. Accessed 15 June 2020.

Purdum, Todd. "Stuck at Home with my 20-Year-Old Daughter." *The Atlantic*, May 2020. www.theatlantic.com/politics/archive/2020/05/college-students-home-coronavirus/611665/. Accessed 15 June 2020.

Sizemore, Tony (as told to Eli Saslow). "Anything Good I Could Say about This Would Be a Lie." *The Washington Post*, 28 March 2020. www.washingtonpost.com/nation/2020/03/28/voices-from-the-pandemic-indiana-man-recounts-partners-death-from-coronavirus/. Accessed 15 June 2020.

10 Taking the poetry exercise online

Carrie Etter

On March 17, 2020, I received an email from my university's vice chancellor informing me that the institution would be moving online in *days* in response to the spread of Covid-19. While I had anticipated the move, I was surprised it was happening so quickly and without a break from teaching, and I had yet to consider fully how to render my weekly freshman and senior poetry seminars as online courses.[1]

Students had also received word of the shift and begun sending panicked emails akin to: *I'm returning to my family out in the country, and we have a poor internet connection—I don't know if I'll be able to participate in video chats.* Another: *I'm on my way back to Seattle, and our 10 a.m. seminar time in the UK is 2 a.m. back there.* After reading a number of such messages, I decided to begin with asynchronous seminars, using online workshops to replace the ones we had in class and discussion boards to engage students in thinking about the assigned reading.

Alongside these elements, I wanted to include something that would give students a sense of my presence and availability, something that would help to continue the relationship begun in the classroom and that would make the online seminars less impersonal. The slender handbook of advice we received about moving to online teaching suggested that recorded videos be no longer than six to eight minutes, on account of the resulting file size. Anticipating that the use of videos would allow me to be present "in person" to my students in asynchronous teaching, I began thinking about what I could offer within the parameters of a 6–8-minute video and considered what would best complement the online workshops and discussion boards. As I thought about the other activities we regularly took part in in our seminars, I remembered how much my students appreciated my providing poetry exercises to help them with inspiration to write and engagement with different poetic techniques, and I decided I'd try creating short videos of individual poetry exercises.

My plan was to base each exercise on a poem or poems, in part to continue implicitly both classes' emphasis on reading. As Mary Oliver writes in *A Poetry Handbook*, "to write well it is entirely necessary to read widely and deeply. Good poems are the best teachers" (1994: 10). More specifically, addressing the problem of new poets' overreliance on first-person, personal narrative, Claire Hero observes, "Reading widely is one way to counteract the excessive focus on the personal 'I', for through reading students gain an appreciation of what a poem can do, what it can incorporate of the world, what it can create" (2005: 4). I planned to use poems both from the students' assigned reading and from other works, to help them more fully appreciate the craft in some of the poems they were studying as well as to encourage exploration beyond the set texts.

Employing poetry exercises based on specific poems would, I thought, also help students understand elements of craft "from the inside out," so to speak. Exercises based on specific pieces of writing might help students, as Jason Wirtz found, "see writing as examples of craft at work, examples that could be reverse engineered in a move that lent insight into how they were made" (2010: 72). By working through multiple poetry exercises based on individual poems, students might not only generate new work, but also begin to see all poems they read as "examples of craft at work" that they could analyze to appreciate both "how they were made" as well as how they might use elements in their future writing.

Yet for all this consideration about the poetry exercises' design, I wanted the videos themselves to be amateur. I knew my video-making skills were limited and figured that with some research as well as help from my university's IT department, I could make something more professional, but I decided against it. I supposed that if the videos' production quality was relatively amateur and if I spoke in the video as I would to the students in a class discussion, those qualities would enhance the senses of immediacy and social presence that would in turn foster a stronger sense of community in an asynchronous, online environment. This is to say that while professionalism matters, I think instructor-made videos can convey a stronger sense of social presence if they aren't perfect, if the instructor sometimes says, "Um," loses their place in the book they were reading from, and so on—just as they might in a face-to-face class.

The exercises

Since the university chose to continue teaching remotely until the end of the semester, I ultimately had to create eight poetry videos for my students. I have focused on the first six here, since at the time of drafting this essay, those are the videos my students had the opportunity to view and respond to. Through creating these exercises for my students and sometime later sharing them online with other instructors, I hoped to show how writing exercises can do much more than simply generate new writing. They can, as I mentioned earlier, illustrate the benefits of wide reading; they can improve understanding of specific techniques, different approaches to a poem's structure, etc.; and they can help students explore subjects they might not otherwise have considered. Or indeed, as with the first, such an exercise might take material students often use—their own personal experience—and demonstrate a new way to articulate it.

Exercise 1: Poem as self-portrait

The first video exercise takes a poem from one of the seniors' set texts, *Kismet* by Jennifer Lee Tsai. The prose poem "Self-Portrait at Four Years Old" begins the chapbook and introduces a number of the themes emerging from its speaker's struggle for identity as a Chinese girl and later woman living in largely white areas of Britain. In the poem, as the speaker recounts reading fairy tales, she notes, "Only Snow White has black hair / Her eyes are brown, like mine / but her skin is white" (2019: 1). The conversational register helps make engaging a form that might at first seem strange to new poets, a prose poem with slashes, and the focus on childhood memories presents territory any student can mine. In the video, I read the poem and note its form, clarifying that I understand the slashes to operate like juddering pauses in the text, signaling shifts among thoughts. Of course, this is akin to how line breaks themselves operate, "record[ing]," as Denise Levertov writes, "the slight (but meaningful) hesitations between word and word that are characteristic of the mind's dance among perceptions but which are not noted by grammatical punctuation" (1979: 266). In a prose poem, I suggest, the slashes indicate those hesitations with a more jarring effect amid the fluency of prose.

I follow with a very different poem as self-portrait, Claire Crowther's "Self Portrait as Windscreen." In this poem of consistently shaped tercets, the poet whimsically plays on the meaning of her first name as clarity. The poem opens:

> Do you think I'm clear on every issue
> just because I'm glass?
> Have you heard yourself calling 'Claire,
> Claire, Claire, Claire' when you're confused?
> A name is lulling
> when you aren't clear on every issue.
> (2015: 42)

After reading Crowther's poem and pointing up the two poems' different approaches to the poem as self-portrait, I urge the students to take either as a model: to try a poem as a self-portrait at a particular age or to try a self-portrait in the form of something that represents some aspect of their personality, say, self-portrait as dandelion or self-portrait as tiger. Students' poems in response to this exercise included "The Year You Learned to Hate Your Voice," "Self-Portrait with an Apple at Fifteen Years Old," and "Self-Portrait as Daisy." As one student commented:

> I viewed this exercise when I was having trouble creating a new poem. This exercise gave me some guidance by providing a title and I was able to unlock my creativity from there. What resulted was a strong first draft of a poem [...]. I will also explore the other poetry video exercises because I find having prompts so helpful.

After a few weeks, the university surveyed our students about their experiences moving from face-to-face to online teaching, and in my classes the most common denominator was enthusiasm for the poetry exercise videos. In the pandemic's exceptional circumstances and the upheaval many experienced moving home for the duration, students were happy to have a set task they could do in their own time that reassured them they were still progressing in their degree and their ability writing poetry. Indeed, it was the students' overwhelmingly positive response to the videos that made me realize they might be worth sharing with other instructors, if nothing else to lighten others' workloads.

Exercise 2: The moment of surprise

All poems fall loosely into two categories, lyric and narrative, and I devote one lecture in the freshman poetry seminar to the distinction and what it means for poets' approach to various elements of poetry, particularly imagery and structure. With the first exercise's emphasis on lyric poetry, on an idea of the self and identity, with the second exercise I wanted to move to a clearly narrative focus.

I framed the exercise as the telling of a story that begins with the speaker doing something everyday, something ordinary, and being surprised. I emphasized the importance of visualizing the narrative—the setting and the action—without explaining why the speaker had been surprised, to leave that for the reader to infer. As an example, I read Elizabeth Bishop's "In the Waiting Room," which begins with a six-year-old girl in a dentist's waiting room as her aunt has an appointment. After paging through an issue of *National Geographic* and remarking on the photographs (of one of African women, the speaker comments, "Their breasts were horrifying"), she hears her aunt cry out as though in pain, only to realize that she herself cried out (159) The surprise implicitly arises from the speaker's identification of her femaleness with both her aunt's and the African women's.

In the student responses to the exercise, one freshman wrote about walking home from a friend's when a car crash occurs, and for a moment the victims and the witness hesitate about whom to help and how (do they assist the instigator of the crash as well as the victims of it?). In another, a senior wrote a poem in which the speaker walks home from a pub and abruptly realizes she is smiling. In both poems, the surprise arises naturally from the course of events, and the speaker's reaction to it gives insight to their character.

Exercise 3: How to

In the third video, I based my exercise on a poem from the freshmen's reading for that week, "How to Approach a Foal" by Wendy Videlock. The poem consists entirely of similes, all beginning with like. Here are the poem's first and last stanzas:

> like a lagoon,
> like a canoe,
> like you…

like a pearl,
like you
are new to the world.
   (2015:140, 141)

After reading the poem aloud, I address its structure, first its use of short-lined tercets to allow us to apprehend the similes fairly slowly. Secondly, I address the progression of the poem: the poem begins with one of its most unexpected comparisons (how do you approach a foal like a lagoon?), which creates an initial sense of surprise as well as intrigue, and concludes with its most predictable comparison. The suspension of what we might have anticipated all along until the poem's conclusion is, I claim, what makes the ending so satisfying: Yes, yes, of course, like I am as new to the world as the foal!

In the drafting of a poem using "How to Approach a Foal" as a model, I ask students to come up with their own how to: they could go with something topical, such as how to survive isolation or how to do social distancing, or something else they have experienced, such as how to bake your first cake. The next step is to brainstorm 10, 20, 30 similes—the more the better, and they should feel free to include the most preposterous possibilities to try to find more original comparisons. After composing a long list, students should note the similes that seem most effective with a check or other mark. Lastly, they order the selected list of the best similes from the most surprising to the most expected to complete a draft of the poem. Student poems from this exercise included "How to Survive Quarantine" and "How to Tie Shoelaces." One of my seniors commented:

> I'd say that the video that helped me the most was the exercise 3 'How To' video. The "how to" aspect made it feel less like a writing task and more like an experimentation with something that didn't have to look like a traditional poem (or the idea I had of a traditional poem). It felt more tangible to create a poem that focused on instructions (however ambiguous they might have been) on how to do something. I think the poem that I subsequently produced that week was the best because I could link it to current events. The suggestion of "How to survive quarantine" was one I pursued because I felt like I needed to tell myself how to do it more than anything, and it was definitely something that was already on my mind that week.
>
> Having a concrete layout for the poem helped hugely as well as I could sit down and feel like I was constructing the poem rather than just trying to pull it out of thin air. I also liked the options that arose from the drafting process. By writing down multiple similes and only having to pick the very best ones that I wanted to include gave me a lot of freedom in the drafting process which I sometimes feel daunted by. I also really liked the example poem by Wendy Videlock and have reread it since.

Exercise 4: Make your own myth

The first section of Moniza Alvi's collection *How the Stone Found Its Voice* inspired my fourth exercise. I begin the video by announcing that in this week's exercise, students will invent their own myths, and to give a sense of the possibilities, I read aloud all the titles in the first section of Alvi's book: "How the World Split in Two," "How the Countries Slipped Away," "How the Answers Got Their Questions," "How the City Lost Its Colour," "How the Animals Tried on Our Clothes," "How the Sky Got a Hole in It," "How the Words Feared the Mouth," "How a Long Way Off Rolled Itself Up," "How the Children Were Born," "How Thought Accompanied the Traveller," "How Yesterday Joined Today and Tomorrow," and finally the title poem, "How the Stone Found Its Voice."

I proceed to read "How the Stone Found Its Voice" and show the students its structure by turning the book to the screen: couplets until a single-line stanza at the end, a difference that helps give the ending more force. I ask students to come up with their own myth about how something came to be, taking some time to brainstorm possibilities, drawing from Alvi's examples to show that one might take a whimsical or a more realistic approach. One of the benefits of this exercise is that it reminds students that they can "make stuff up"; some are so used to associating poetry with capital-T truth and direct personal experience that they sometimes forget that they can fictionalize. Seeing how imaginative such "fictional" poems are can prove liberating to students, opening up a much broader range of possibilities for what a poem looks like. Responding to this exercise, one student poet wrote a poem titled "Doppelganger" about how the speaker's doppelganger came to life, and as I read it I kept shaking my head, delighted with the originality of the idea.

Exercise 5: From past to present

In the fifth exercise, I used a poem from the freshmen's reading, Saeed Jones' "Body & Kentucky Bourbon," because it collapses the distinction between lyric and narrative, or to put it another way, conflates them. In this poem in which the speaker remembers their Kentucky, "white trash" former lover, the speaker establishes a point in the present from which to reflect, looking back at the relationship with the lover, and returns to a present informed by that relationship. This exercise follows a few weeks after the initial exercises in distinct lyric and narrative modes, so students try those as differentiated ways of working in a poem before considering how the two might blend.

After reading the poem aloud, I note the use of free-verse couplets that work to pace the poem effectively. I ask the students to take the poem as a model in which they vividly recount a memory of a person or event and relate that to a moment in the present, so the poem suggests how the memory has influenced the person's development in some manner. In this way the students learn to combine elements of narrative poetry, such as setting, character, and action, with those of lyric poetry, such as the idea of how a past experience informs present identity. One senior commented, "I liked the idea of linking a memory to the present day and decided to focus on the beginning of a relationship compared with how I see it today. Writing in couplets was an effective way to slow the pacing down, to allow the reader to take in the details of a memory. I also used a recurring image (the subject's eyes) in order to connect the memory with the present day. I never would have thought of this by myself [...]." While I would still pursue this exercise in the classroom, where I could discuss the poem with the students more before embarking on the exercise, I suspect it proved overly ambitious as an asynchronous video, as I saw less evidence of poems from the exercise in the subsequent online workshops.

Exercise 6: The object prose poem

With the final exercise, I decided to focus on prose poetry, coordinating with the freshmen's lecture that week on the form, and considering the fact that many of the seniors, working on developing their own, thesis-equivalent chapbooks, were struggling to produce new work. As many did not commonly compose prose poems, I hoped they might find prose poetry a potentially different, inspiring avenue. While I had used a prose poem, Jennifer Lee Tsai's "Self-Portrait at Four Years Old," in the first exercise, I had not discussed the poem's form in detail.

After welcoming students, I explain that prose poetry shares with lined poetry the same two essential qualities, in my thinking, of all poems. One, prose poems have the same quality of distillation, concentration, or focus of lined poems, the sense of distilling something down to its essence—what Gwendolyn Brooks spoke of when she said, "Poetry is life distilled." Two, prose poems also have musicality. Of course, they aren't generally in meter (though in some one can discern iambic runs), but they employ some of the same types of repetition of sound found in lined poems, including full and partial rhyme, assonance, alliteration, and consonance. While a lined poem derives some of its musicality from the use of the line (particularly in how it contributes to a poem's pacing with line length), a prose poem uses sentence rhythms.[2]

While prose poems vary greatly (and here I refer students to the library's electronic copy of the anthology *The Penguin Book of the Prose Poem* for a broad range of examples), one type of prose poem useful to consider for those trying the form for the first time is the object prose poem. In the video, I read the opening of Francis Ponge's poem "Rain" and the entirety of his poem "Crate" to illustrate how each poem focuses on and develops the object of the title. I point out that prose poems also have stanza breaks, in the use of white space between paragraphs, and try to read the poems in a way that highlights their specificity of language and their wit, as when "Crate," which has already talked about the object's disposability, concludes, "it remains a likable object on whose fate we will not dwell for long" (2018: 301).

In "Rain" and "Crate," we find the poet elaborating two ordinary objects with such close observation, such specificity of language, that we see them anew and vividly. The exercise I propose to the students is to do the same thing with another everyday object: a fence post, a shopfront, a glove found in the road. Alternatively, if the students are more interested in an extraordinary object, I show my rather fearsome Sumatran mask and talk about it briefly. Whether they choose an ordinary or extraordinary object, they should bring all their senses to bear in evoking it so that we experience it more fully, more distinctly than we had before. Resulting student poems focused on a dress, a journal, even a komodo dragon! Shortly after completing the exercise, one student remarked:

> Without these exercises, I would have nothing written anything near good enough to submit for our poetry collection. My other modules have been very full-on, but these challenges, along with those presented in lectures, were invaluable in keeping me on track and writing. I believe that I've understood more and more of the course and techniques through following these exercises. My poems seem more focused and musical.

Research and results

While the videos began in a moment of necessity, as a practical method for transforming one part of a face-to-face seminar into an online one, research in online pedagogy supports the usefulness of asynchronous, instructor-made videos. As Michael E. Griffiths and Charles R. Graham found in their use in instructing education students at Brigham Young University, such videos can provide a sense of the instructor's immediacy and foster in the students a stronger feeling of connection with the instructor, and these perceptions of immediacy and connection help motivate students (2009: 16, 22).

The creation of a sense of community among students also has benefits. In the face of the pandemic, I was particularly concerned about my students' mental as well as physical well-being, and I expected that continuing the feeling of community online that I strove to create in the classroom could help mitigate feelings of isolation. Alfred P. Rovai (2000) addresses the difficulties of creating a sense of community in asynchronous learning environments, finding that "heightened awareness to social presence" is crucial for nourishing a sense of community among learners (289), and "as social presence goes down so does sense of community" (290). By manifesting a social presence in the videos, I hoped to maintain the sense of community previously fostered in the face-to-face seminars and help students feel less isolated. As one student commented, "I much prefer having video exercises from you as opposed to ones found online because it feels like the closest to replicating an actual in-person poetry class, and having that little bit of familiarity is really soothing actually when we're in a time of such unfamiliarity." Another student remarked that while she "personally wouldn't mind watching poetry exercise videos from a range of people," "Something that I do like about having the instructor in the video, though, is that I feel as though I'm still on the same course now as I was in the start of the year and I think there's a certain trust and familiarity between students and instructors that I find reassuring."

Lastly, and most practically, the videos helped students create new work at a time when they struggled to—everything. As I learned from their emails and the synchronous video sessions I later included, they struggled with living with their families again; they struggled with unwieldy schedules that sometimes seemed to offer endless free time and sometimes none at all; they struggled with new employment as they stocked supermarket shelves and became volunteer carers; and a few struggled with the virus itself, both in their families and in their own bodies. The videos helped them "reach the finish line," as one student remarked: the end of a class for the freshmen, the end of the degree for the seniors, and hopefully for all of them, a life enriched by reading and writing poetry.

Notes

1 In the three-year undergraduate system in the UK, freshman and senior loosely apply to first- and third-year students.
2 I elaborate more fully on my understanding of the prose poem in my essay "The Sense of Distillation: On Prose Poetry" in *The Craft: A Guide to Making Poetry Happen in the 21st Century*, edited by Rishi Dastidar (Nine Arches, 2019).

Works cited

Alvi, Moniza. *How the Stone Found Its Voice*. Bloodaxe, 2005.
Bishop, Elizabeth. "In the Waiting Room." *The Complete Poems 1927–1979*. Farrar, Straus & Giroux, 1984, pp. 159–161.
Crowther, Claire. "Self Portrait as Windscreen." *On Narrowness*. Shearsman, 2015, p. 42.
Etter, Carrie. "The Sense of Distillation: On Prose Poetry." *The Craft: A Guide for Making Poetry Happen in the 21st Century*, edited by Rishi Dastidar. Nine Arches, 2019, pp. 42–47.
Etter, Carrie. "Poetry Exercise 1: Poem as Self-Portrait." YouTube, 13 June 2020, www.youtube.com/watch?v=nF6xkIjAJKU.
Etter, Carrie. "Poetry Exercise 2: The Moment of Surprise." YouTube, 13 June 2020, www.youtube.com/watch?v=sEFm01SwzAU.
Etter, Carrie. "Poetry Exercise 3: How To." YouTube, 13 June 2020, www.youtube.com/watch?v=s_Nv9DlkNTA.
Etter, Carrie. "Poetry Exercise 4: Make Your Own Myth." YouTube, 13 June 2020, www.youtube.com/watch?v=EJeq2cO5zJE.
Etter, Carrie. "Poetry Exercise 5: From Past to Present." YouTube, 13 June 2020, www.youtube.com/watch?v=HEgieDsbGvE.
Etter, Carrie. "Poetry Exercise 6: The Object Prose Poem." YouTube, 13 June 2020, www.youtube.com/watch?v=s8HJTUz373U.
Griffiths, Michael E., and Charles R. Graham. "The Potential of Asynchronous Video in Online Education." *Distance Learning*, vol. 6, no. 2, 2009, pp. 13–22.
Hero, Claire. "On the Pedagogy of Poetics: Methods of Addressing Problems in Poetry by Beginners." *English in Aotearoa*, no. 55, 2005, pp. 3–9.
Levertov, Denise. "On the Function of the Line." *Claims for Poetry*, edited by Donald Hall. University of Michigan Press, 1979, pp. 265–272.

Jones, Saaed. "Body & Kentucky Bourbon." *The Best American Poetry 2015*, edited by Sherman Alexie. Scribner, 2015, pp. 68–69.

Oliver, Mary. *A Poetry Handbook*. Harcourt, 1994.

Ponge, Francis. "Crate." Trans. Joshua Corey and Jean-Luc Garneau. *The Penguin Book of the Prose Poem*, edited by Jeremy Noel-Tod. Penguin, 2018, p. 301.

Ponge, Francis. "Rain." Trans. Beverly Bie Brahic. *The Penguin Book of the Prose Poem*, edited by Jeremy Noel-Tod. Penguin, 2018, pp. 298–299.

Rovai, Alfred P. "Building and Sustaining Community in Asynchronous Learning Networks." *The Internet and Higher Education*, vol. 3, no. 4, 2000, pp. 285–297.

Tsai, Jennifer Lee. "Self Portrait at Four Years Old." *Kismet*. Ignitionpress, 2019, p. 1.

Videlock, Wendy. "How to Approach a Foal." *The Best American Poetry 2015*, edited by Sherman Alexie. Scribner, 2015, pp. 140–141.

Wirtz, Jason. "Poets on Pedagogy." *Creative Writing: Teaching Theory and Practice*, vol. 2, no. 2, 2010, pp. 59–86.

11 A sense of openness
Using individual student blogs in online creative writing courses

Lucy Biederman

At an MFA presidential forum in 2012, Kathleen Fitzpatrick encouraged literature professors "to recognize that the forms of writing that engage so many today *are writing*, and to figure out how to put those forms to work for us, rather than dismissing them as inherently frivolous and degraded." Chief among those forms is the blog, which, Fitzpatrick argues, "provides an arena in which scholars can work through ideas in an ongoing process of engagement with their peers." What can, or should, such expansive visions of writing mean for professors and students of creative writing, particularly in online courses?

One way to think about teaching creative writing online is to consider what students (and instructors) can gain from an online course that would be unavailable or impossible in a face-to-face course. An online creative writing course can offer opportunities to read and write in more expansive, interconnected ways, particularly when instructors recognize forms of web writing *as writing* (to paraphrase Fitzpatrick). In this essay, I describe a semester-long blogging assignment that I use in online creative writing courses. This assignment carries the goal of providing students an expansive vision of the forms of contemporary creative writing, as well as opportunities for deeper metacognition about their own writing and reading both on and offline.

Part one: why to assign blogs in online creative writing courses

Positing a distinction between "closed" and "open" online courses, Laura Gibbs has argued for and modeled an online pedagogy that makes use of "the Internet [as] the most open, interconnected wide-ranging kind of space" ("Teaching in Higher Ed"). In online creative writing courses, creating a fruitfully "open" course can be a particular challenge, because the wide-ranging nature of the Internet undermines the sense of community surrounding writing that can be essential to establishing a course that depends on feedback among student writers. One way to address that challenge is through student-authored individual blogs, which allow each student to establish a "presence" online directly related to the course and its attendant writing community but also quite literally linked to the other sites on the Web. Students use personal blogs to share metacognitive commentary on their writing processes and works in progress, responses to assigned texts, ideas for creative work, and more. Students write directly to an audience of peers via their blogs, an audience that can be a more immediate incentive to write and write well than an instructor's assessment. As students examine course texts and their own writing processes on their blogs, a community is formed, based not on a shared self-perception as writers or assessment-driven necessity, but on writing itself. This assignment is low stakes in terms of assessment, but high purpose, because of its public nature. When combined with discussion forums and other opportunities for both low- and higher-stakes writing, blogs are also effective because they challenge students to think deeply about targeting their discussions, insights, and writing for various rhetorical situations.

My student blogging assignment developed from my reading of the writing scholar Robert Boice, whose admonition to write in "brief, daily sessions," is well known among academic writers, but less so among creative writers—although Boice notes that such a method "works for all kinds of writers, including literary types, scholars, and pulpsters" (*Advice for New Faculty* 138, 141). By studying the working habits of academic faculty, Boice discovered that successful academic writers "devote only moderate amounts of time to writing but they do it regularly ... [and] in brief sessions" (*First Order* 101). I find this method of writing useful in my own work because of the practical way it cuts against stultifying myths of how creative writing is accomplished. In *Bird by Bird*, Anne Lamott labels these myths "the fantasy of the uninitiated," describing an image of writers who "sit down at their desks every morning feeling like a million dollars ... and dive in, typing fully formed passages as fast as a court reporter" (21). Such myths are so persistent that Boice draws on them, even though his work addresses academic, not creative, writing. He calls this style of writing "creative madness": a "romantic" notion of writing accomplished "amid high and sustained passions" (*Advice for New Faculty* 175).

I assign individual student blogs to help creative writing students learn—by doing—that brief, regular bouts of writing add up over time. When, by the end of the course, students have an online record of their writing process and progress consisting of between six and 14 blog entries (depending on the length of the semester), I don't have to convince them that these sessions add up. Their own production stands as proof. Despite entering into the assignment with trepidation, students end the semester scrolling through their blogs with pride and surprise at their output and the variety of that output.

Student blogs also fulfill, in an online context, Boice's advice to write in a "facilitating location" (*Advice for New Faculty* 139). For Boice and the writers he studied, this means establishing a physical location as a writing space. Boice finds that "exemplary writers make their writing spots comfortable and comforting. They display artwork and other decorations and mementos" (*Advice for New Faculty* 139). This practice can be employed effectively in online courses by having students establish their own blogs as an online writing space devoted to regular reflection about the writing life.

But what makes blogging different from participating in a forum or discussion board, or writing in a journal? This is a question I invite students to answer, iteratively, throughout the course. The forum, where course questions are posed and answered, and the discussion board, where workshops are held, each offer unique—and differently directed—discursive contexts. Every student has already navigated this discursive and rhetorical variation in online writing, often without realizing it. Posting a Facebook status is not the same as sending an email, which is different from a tweet. Encountering a variety of online rhetorical situations in a creative writing class presents students with opportunities for deeper metacognition about their writing and reading both online and offline.

Blogging also encourages creative writing students to think about publishing in new ways. Unlike the journal writing exercises I assign in face-to-face creative writing courses, blogs (as long as they are maintained outside a learning management system) are born public—a truth that is emphasized by the "Publish" button one must hit in order to make a post visible. The word publish is loaded, perhaps particularly for creative writers, for whom publication can seem synonymous with success, or like the one and only goal in writing.

Jack Dougherty considers the benefits and pitfalls of assigning student blogs from a privacy standpoint in "Public Writing and Student Privacy," noting that "all students deserve—and are legally entitled under U.S. law—some degree of privacy in our educational institutions and ownership over the words they have authored" (2015: 115). Dougherty points out that the Family Education Rights and Privacy Act of 1974 (FERPA) predates the Internet, meaning that its guidance on online student writing is unclear. After consulting with experts, Dougherty created a "Public writing and student privacy policy," for inclusion in his syllabus. The policy includes copyright information (students hold copyright to their own writing) and privacy information (students have instructor's permission to publish "using only a first name, or initials, or a pseudonym," as well as the ability to change or delete blogs after the course has concluded) (117). Holly Oberle takes another tack in her blogging assignment, deleting all student blogs "permanently" after the course has concluded (2015: 207). Doing so, Oberle notes, "allows students to 'experiment' with public writing before throwing themselves into the multifarious and unpredictable world of the Internet" (207).

Perhaps surprisingly, I have found that although I offer students the opportunity to blog anonymously, nearly all my students choose to blog using their full names. Dougherty leads a class discussion regarding "the pros and cons of listing their full name, first name, or a pseudonym in the byline" (118). Although Dougherty is an education professor, the discussion about whether to publish under one's own name is particularly relevant to creative writers, for whom publication—whether via a Big Five publishing house, a self-publishing company, or a literary journal—is often a goal. In making this determination, students consider whether they want their blogs to be visible in web searches for their name and whether or in what way they want to receive recognition among a reading public for their writing. Additionally, students consider the policy of most literary journals that work must not be previously published in any form; this last consideration is less relevant when creative writing students use their blogs—as I encourage them to do—to reflect on the writing process, rather than to post drafts.

Students tend to use their blogs to focus on common topics such as fruitful investigations and discussions about the nature of publishing, what it means and how it feels to publish one's work, and the vulnerability inherent in doing so. For example, in a post reflecting on her changing attitudes toward blogging in one of my online creative writing courses, Emily wrote that the task of posting on a blog was, at first, "very unappealing. ... The idea of anyone being able to read it made me censor myself in a way I felt I could not control." But something happened as she continued to write.

> Focusing less on what would happen after I posted ... and more about the potential topics I could cover made it so much easier to write something I was proud of. I found myself thinking deeply about the texts I was reading and finding creative ways to spark ideas. Sometimes ideas for blogs come quickly, and I can't type them out fast enough. Other times, the ideas seem locked away, and I have to fish around for them. Sometimes, I play a game I made up when I was little; flipping through the pages of a book and choosing to read one at random. It helps me jumpstart my thoughts on a topic, or lead me in a direction I was having trouble finding.
>
> (Nobbe, 2017)

The challenges, solutions, and growth Emily expresses in this post mirrors many of my creative writing students' experiences publishing their writing on blogs. As Boice advises, Emily sometimes begins blog posts "without inspiration" (2009: 141). And she has found on her own what Boice discovered by studying writers: "Inspiration and motivation come far more reliably in the wake of working than in advance of it" (*ibid.*).

I have experimented with assigning blogs in both online and face-to-face courses, across various courses, from literature to composition to creative writing. Blogging has been most successful and best received among students in my courses that are a) online, b) upper-level undergraduate or graduate-level, and c) creative writing and/or literature-focused. These are students who already have experience with metacognition regarding their writing. Blogs deepen and regularize that metacognitive work, which helps students get more out of and give more to workshops and revisions.

Part two: how to assign blogs in online creative writing courses

Some platforms, the most prominent of which is Edublogs, allow instructors to assign and assess student blogs via a centralized site, through which students establish and maintain their blogs. For example, Edublogs makes all student blogs visible on a single feed, allowing blogs to be assessed with the click of a button. I have had more success, however, with allowing students to choose their own blog platforms, like Blogger, Google Sites, or any other blog hosting service. Giving this decision to students increases their sense of ownership over their blogs, as well as the likeliness that they will continue to blog after the class is over. Sending students out onto the Internet to make a blog however they see fit promotes a sense of what Gibbs calls "openness," as students seek platforms that best suit their voice, intentions, and aesthetic. This enforces the sense of a blog as a regular "place" to write, designed by each student for that purpose. To help students set up their blogs, I provide links to sites that explain the differences among various blogging platforms, and I let students know that most blogging platforms are either intuitive or feature robust help sections. I provide simple blogging requirements, which I post to the course LMS and link to in my introductory email. As an instructor, it is fascinating to see the various ways students use sites like Tumblr, Blogger, and Wix to serve their writing. Since students are able to select their own platform, organization and assessment become concerns for consideration when assigning a blogging project.

Organizing

During the first week of the course, students create their blogs and submit their blog URLs via a Google form, which automatically populates into a spreadsheet. This is useful for grading and keeping track of student blogging. The spreadsheet allows me to easily and quickly grade student blogs weekly, rather than once in a while. The expectation for weekly blogging in addition to the course's creative writing assignments builds into the course metacognition, regular reflection, and ongoing conversation among student writers.

To create the Google form, I use a Blank template and create a "short answer" question like, "What is your blog address?" I also include other questions that will yield information I can use to organize student blogs on the resulting spreadsheet. For example, in addition to the blog address column, my student blog spreadsheet has columns for email address, name, and course number. Once the spreadsheet is up and running, I add a "share?" column that lets me know whether the student has given me permission to share their blog in Monday emails, and an "email" column that helps me keep track of when and whether I have shared each student's blog with the class (more on both these practices below). The spreadsheet becomes its own centralized information source. When I grade student blogs each week, I access them by clicking on the links available under the "blog address" column on the spreadsheet.

Assigning

I introduce the blogging assignment to students in my first communication with them, an introductory email that explains course goals and assessment policies. In my introduction, I emphasize the public nature of blogging, as well as its relevance to writing outside of class. In one such introductory email, for example, I wrote:

> After you've acquainted yourself with the syllabus, check out the Blogging link, and read the Course Blog Assignment Sheet [see box below]. This is where you will find information about the blogging element of the course. If you have blogged before, that's great; if you haven't, that's also great. One of the exciting things about learning online is that it all but forces you to share your writing with others. We are all public writers, whether we like it or not, and blogging is one of those forms that make explicit the public nature of 21-century life and writing. That's one of the many reasons this course relies on blogging; there are others, which I will discuss in coming Monday emails.

I make a point of acknowledging that not all students will necessarily be excited to begin blogging—even as I encourage them to try it out. Boice notes the reluctance many writers have to sharing their work, especially in formative stages, and the blogging assignment asks students to do just that. Blogging, however, is a way of what Boice calls "joining the conversation" (2009: 186). This is a matter, Boice writes, not simply of

> sharing what you write. It also means socializing with other writers working on problems like your own. It means recognizing that when you write in a new area, you will save yourself unnecessary pain by becoming a useful part of an ongoing conversation.
>
> (2009: 186)

Students soon find thisced out on their own.

Course blog assignment sheet: Blog requirements

1. **Establish an aesthetic for your blog,** including a title, relevant images as headers, and something (anything!) other than the default visual settings. This is worth 2 points, and must be accomplished by the end of the first week of the course (5 p.m. on Sunday).
2. **Write 12 entries of at least 400 words each (or 600 words each if you are taking this course at the graduate level).** You will write one entry for each week of the course. Posts that take compositional and formal risks (like lists or multimedia posts) may deviate from the word-length to requirement.
3. **Post your entry to your blog by Sunday of each week at 5 p.m.** You do not need to wait for Sunday. You can post at any time during the week, but 5 p.m. on Sunday is the due date each week; after that, your post will count for the next week.

Students' reluctance to share writing sometimes is accompanied by concerns about what to write about, or finding suitable topics week after week, particularly while they are also producing poems and/or stories. For this reason, I provide students with numerous blogging prompts, in a variety of formats. In each of my "Monday emails," which I think of as loosely equivalent to lectures, I introduce the week's themes, creative writing assignments, and readings. I pepper these emails with suggestions for blog posts (which provides a further incentive for students to read them). Tying these to texts students are reading and discussing is particularly effective. For example, at the beginning of a week in which students began short stories using experimental forms, I offered a prompt based on Joyce Carol Oates's 1978 *Paris Review* interview. That week, several of Oates's experimental stories were assigned as reading, so students were already thinking about Oates's authorial tactics. I wrote,

> In addition to reading the two Oates's stories this week, take a look at the excerpt below from an interview that appeared in *The Paris Review*. Do you agree with Oates that art is "genuinely transcendental"? And, more specifically, have you found the experience of writing to be as Oates describes it—capable of entirely altering one's mental and emotional state, even the state of one's soul? Have you ever had such an experience writing—in this class or in some other context?
>
> INTERVIEWER
> Do you find emotional stability is necessary in order to write? Or can you get to work whatever your state of mind? Is your mood reflected in what you write? How do you describe that perfect state in which you can write from early morning into the afternoon?
>
> OATES
> One must be pitiless about this matter of "mood." In a sense, the writing will *create* the mood. If art is, as I believe it to be, a genuinely transcendental function—a means by which we rise out of limited, parochial states of mind—then it should not matter very much what states of mind or emotion we are in. Generally I've found this to be true: I have forced myself to begin writing when I've been utterly exhausted, when I've felt my soul as thin as a playing card, when nothing has seemed worth enduring for another five minutes ... and somehow the activity of writing changes everything. Or appears to do so ...
>
> (Phillips, 1978)

This prompt is a suggestion, rather than a requirement. As long as students write the required word count each week, the choice for the writing-centric topic is theirs. Because such choice can lead to indecision or writing avoidance, I also equip students with a suggestions page at the beginning of the semester (see box below).

What should I write about?

Your blog will be about the writing life. While you are welcome to post the poems and stories you compose for this class, those posts will not receive credit as blog posts (since you are already receiving credit for them). Here are some suggestions for blog posts (though you're not required to use any of them):

1 **Close reading.** Choose a passage from the week's reading assignment that intrigued you, infuriated you, puzzled you, confused you, jarred you, or otherwise provoked you to think about its meaning. Write a post in which you discuss the passage, its meaning, and your reaction.
2 **POV (for fiction).** Write your blog post for the week in the voice and/or style of a character from the week's reading assignment.
3 **Writing process.** How do you write? When and where? What type of writing is most comfortable for you? How has your writing process changed over time? Examine your composition of a piece. How did you write it?
4 **The favorite.** What's your favorite piece of creative writing you've written? Why?
5 **On creativity.** How do you define creativity? Why do you think it is so important to people to be creative?
6 **Writer's block.** Do you believe in writer's block? Have you ever experienced it?
7 **Revision.** What is your revision process? How important is revision?
8 **Parody.** Write a parody of one of the piece assigned as reading for the week.
9 **New genre.** Rewrite one of the week's readings or a section of the week's reading in another form. Turn a novel into a poem, a paragraph into a one-act play. How does this shift in genre change the meaning of the text?
10 **A current event.** If something we're reading is relevant to the cultural, social, or political scene today, write a post in which you connect the reading with the current phenomenon.
11 **Respond** in depth to some issue that came up on the discussion board, building upon it, disagreeing with it, or re-thinking it.
12 **Do** a dramatic reading of a portion of the text and post it to your blog.

Assessing

When I first began assigning blogs, I graded on a different schedule than I do now: I assessed student blog posts three or four times during the semester, rather than every week. I have altered that original assessment schedule for a variety of reasons. First, reading student blogs a handful of times a semester, rather than once a week, encouraged students to write several posts in the days or hours before each "blog check," rather than doing the kind of regular writing blogging is intended to promote. Second, reading student blogs every week helps me understand students' experiences in the class. It is a way of connecting with students through their own writing. Third, grading more frequently lowers the stakes, allowing students to approach blogging as a process, as opposed to a product-driven assignment. On the course blog assignment sheet, I introduce a simple rubric that I use to assess blog posts each week (Table 11.1).

In addition to receiving points for their weekly posts, students receive other types of feedback on their blogs, including replies in the comments section from me and their classmates. In my first attempts at assigning student blogs, I required students to comment on at least two other student blogs each week. I have since determined that this introduced an artificial element into blogging. Now, I let commenting happen organically—and it does, given that students are writing for their audience of peers. Another form of feedback students receive is recognition in my Monday email, where I point students to particularly strong posts by their peers.

However, as useful as has been to direct students to each other's writing, I have learned that this practice *can* backfire. In a humorous post about blogging and writing anxiety titled "Blogging for Class: A Ten Step Process," Erin, a student in a literature and creative writing course, writes:

> Step Five: Park butt in front of computer with every assigned text arrayed like a rainbow. Today's post will nimbly address each one, resulting in an erudite cohesive argument about the 21st century novel that will show up in Dr. Lucy's Monday email as an exemplar for everyone else in class.
>
> (King, 2017)

Despite, or maybe even because of her anxiety surrounding blogging, Erin's inventive, humorous tone *is* an exemplar for what blogging can provide the online classroom.

Faculty reluctant to teach online frequently note that the nuances of face-to-face in-class interactions are lost in the online environment. Assigning student blogs has shown me that online learning environments can be an opportunity to hear students differently, in ways that are often *more* nuanced than in traditional classroom settings. Blogging is a form that offers students a way assert their

Table 11.1 Grading rubric for course blogs

2 points	Substantial post that engages with any of the weeks' course readings, by the deadline (this is the norm)
1 point	Insubstantial post
0 points	Missing post

voices in front of an audience; to think and write about their writing lives, and to practice tones of writing that we don't often make room for in academic spaces—even in creative writing courses. And one that can offer students and instructors new, more open, ways of reflecting about creative writing.

Works cited

Boice, Robert. *Professors as Writers: A Self-Help Guide to Productive Writing.* New Forum Press, 1990.

Boice, Robert. *First-Order Principles for College Teachers: Ten Basic Ways to Improve the Teaching Process.* Anker Pub. Co., 1996.

Boice, Robert. *Advice for New Faculty Members: Nihil Nimus.* Allyn & Bacon, 2009.

Dougherty, Jack. "Public Writing and Student Privacy." *Web Writing: Why and How for Liberal Arts Teaching and Learning,* edited by Jack Dougherty and Tennyson O'Donnell, University of Michigan Press, 2015, pp. 115–124. JSTOR, www.jstor.org/stable/j.ctv65sxgk.15.

Fitzpatrick, Kathleen. "Networking the Field." Kathleen Fitzpatrick (blog), 10 January 2012. kfitz.info/networking-the-field.

King, Erin. "Blogging for Class: A Ten Step Process." *EEK & The 21st Century Novel* (blog), 30 July 2017. eek21novel.blogspot.com/2017/07/blogging-for-class-ten-step-process.html.

Lamott, Anne. *Bird by Bird: Some Instructions on Writing and Life.* Knopf, 2007.

Nobbe, Emily. "The Benefits of Blogging." The Novelty of the Novel (blog), 30 July 2017. noveltyofthenovel.blogspot.com/2017/07/the-benefits-of-blogging.html.

Oberle, Holly. "Web Writing as Intercultural Dialogue." *Web Writing: Why and How for Liberal Arts Teaching and Learning,* edited by Jack Dougherty and Tennyson O'Donnell, University of Michigan Press, 2015, pp. 201–212. JSTOR, www.jstor.org/stable/j.ctv65sxgk.22.

Phillips, Robert. "Joyce Carol Oates, The Art of Fiction No. 72." *The Paris Review,* Issue 74, 1978. www.theparisreview.org/interviews/3441/joyce-carol-oates-the-art-of-fiction-no-2-joyce-carol-oates.

Stachowiak, Bonni, host. "How to Create Engaging Online Classes with Laura Gibbs." Teaching in Higher Ed, ep. 228, 25 October 2018, teachinginhighered.com/podcast/how-to-create-engaging-online-classes/.

12 Motivate, accommodate, and emulate

The 30-Day Writing Challenge in an online creative writing classroom

Sarah Layden

Before I began writing fiction, I was a newspaper reporter. Motivated by daily deadlines, I cranked out copy, made rapid revisions based on my editor's red marks, and was gratified to see my work in print the next day. I also longed for more time to write longer pieces on my own schedule, since I'd always wanted to write creatively. After going back for my MFA in fiction writing, I was glad to have grad school professors who prioritized deadlines. Once I completed my degree, with an open expanse of time to write and absolutely no one waiting to read my work, I, perhaps predictably, came to miss those deadlines and feedback.

Luckily, I knew that my process would respond well to a schedule and self-imposed deadlines, so I created a calendar with tasks broken down into clear starts and finishes. Sometimes a daily word count was the goal. On other days, I'd block off time—usually one- or two-hour increments, eliminating distractions like the Internet—and see how much I could get done. While I was happy to share my different attempts at process with my college-level creative writing students, I was also aware that what worked for me might not necessarily work for them. They were under different pressures and constraints. That became even clearer once I began teaching creative writing online, when the common factor of stress for my students seemed to be time. Students wanted and intended to make time to write, but they were taking an online course to have flexibility and control around their busy schedules: some worked full time, some were taking classes for degree requirements and/or professional development, some were parents. More than a few fit all of these categories.

Enter the 30-Day Writing Challenge: an ungraded exercise that tasks students with creating and posting new daily writing for a month straight. Students emerge from the challenge with a body of work to draw from: some pieces to develop and revise, others to let marinate in a folder as the ideas sink in, and a handful that move directly to the recycle bin. The idea is to build a habit of mind, which includes being present at the page and the screen. The 30-Day Challenge will be just that: a challenge, and a set schedule and defined list of best practices will guide any teacher who wants to set up this production-heavy activity in their online classroom. Using a discussion board or similar technology, the class builds a visible community practice, turning a solitary activity into a social one, and creating an archive/reference point of both the writing and the responses to it. And if anyone protests or struggles? It's only 30 days, and chances are they'll see the value in the exercise once they've watched their peer collaborators—and perhaps you as well, daring educator?—successfully model it.

To write well takes creating a sustainable writing practice without expectations of perfection. In fact, failure provides moments for learning and growth, as Anna Leahy asserts in the useful edited collection *Can Creative Writing Really Be Taught?* "My students do not always write stellar work; not every exercise leads to brilliance expressed originally and authentically. Whether teaching or writing, failure—obstacles—is part of the creative process; missteps are opportunities" (2017: 47). It's a lesson passed down by bestsellers and practicing novices alike: in drafting, it helps to lower your standards. Pulitzer Prize-winning novelist Jennifer Egan contends that writer's block is due to setting an unrealistically high bar. "You can only write regularly if you're willing to write badly. You can't write regularly and well. One should accept bad writing as a way of priming the pump, a warm-up exercise that allows you to write well" (2013: 35). Low-stakes writing—that which emphasizes process, drafting, and development, and is given a completion grade if it's graded at all—is the perfect way for students to prime the pump, as Egan suggests. Daily writing, no matter its quality, will eventually lead to the habit of turning to the page. And the habit will eventually yield stronger writing as time goes on.

Some may worry that this type of challenge—one that is ungraded, with an emphasis on drafting, and that values production over perfection—can lead to a lack of rigor, or somehow reflects a mindset of cheerleading or unearned self-esteem boosting. Leahy considers how this relates to the self-esteem mindset, noting its utility when it emerges from unmitigated doing.

> Of course, an odd thing about this responsibility of the creative writing instructor is that it must remain mostly hidden in the classroom in order for the students to recognize their accomplishments as their own, even as those accomplishments emerge out of the orchestrated learning environment. Part of the difficulty of teaching creative writing is making the teaching look easy. It's the writing that must look hard, worthy of accomplishing—self-esteem is, then, a by-product of the accomplishment of writing.
>
> (2017: 48)

Keep in mind, too, that a 30-Day Writing Challenge is but one element of a course, and fits particularly well in the online environment, framed as a tool that is low stakes, high accountability, and asynchronously flexible. Students can adapt it to their own lives and schedules, and will create a body of work—short poems, and scenes or starts to essays and stories—as prewriting and inspiration for longer pieces, perhaps to be workshopped later. Many students have been posting their lives online since a very tender age, via the latest social media platform (or all of them). They are highly familiar with the idea of an online self, and quite good at conveying themselves in this way. Posting creatively in an academic context using their preexisting technological expertise lets students be in charge of their own learning and writing process. Not to mention, it can be crucial in an online class to create opportunities for individuality and expression: to put a face on the learner, so to speak, for both teacher and peers. In the online writing challenge, students are self-directed and gain ownership of the process, becoming resourceful agents of their own writing lives.

Additionally, there are benefits for teachers, too. The clear position of the National Writing Project and the Association of Writers and Writing Programs is that the best teachers of writing are practicing writers. To teach at the college level, an MFA or a book (or both) is a standard requirement. Secondary school teachers don't have the same requirements, and in a testing-heavy educational environment, they may find they aren't encouraged or supported to write creatively or teach creative writing units. My online course, Creative Writing for Teachers, attracts grad students and secondary school teachers who may or may not conceive of themselves as writers. Yet they ask the students in their classrooms to engage with the page in ways they may not practice. Active and preservice teachers participating in a writing challenge shows them how to manage exactly what they're asking students to do—and helps them work out kinks or tailor the challenge to better fit their different classrooms and school environment.

When a writing teacher writes, and visibly identifies as a writer, they gain greater authority and authentic credibility in the classroom. They are in the struggle – and the joy – with the students, fostering a greater sense of classroom community that ripples outward. No matter the grade level, the peer-to-peer benefits of making writing visible online is the start of a highly engaged virtual workshop space. In the 30-Day Writing Challenge, students post their short daily writing to a discussion board on the course site: everyone shares, reads, and comments on the work. Prolific writer and teacher Wallace Stegner, who founded the Stanford University creative writing program, extolled the value of the peer experience in a workshop. "In my experience, the best teaching that goes on in a college writing class is done by members of the class, upon one another" (2002: 35). Stegner also famously said, "Talent can't be taught, but it can be awakened." Teachers cannot see what lives in the imaginative wells of students' brains. But we can help students tap into those wells by providing prompts and a framework, and valuable space and time for the work to come into existence.

Part of imaginative work, as Jeff VanderMeer describes it in his idea-sparking *Wonderbook*, is nurturing the imagination and making space for it. In *The Right to Write*, Julia Cameron promotes a similar practice with her "Morning Pages," three pages of daily writing before nearly anything else interrupts your day, that "will train your censor to let you create" (2017: 16). A writing challenge is an excellent way to fool an internal censor, particularly because writers are tasked with showing up and making something, whether they feel inspired or not. Inspiration occasionally may arrive like a lightning bolt; more often, though, we have to train ourselves to be ready for the moment when inspiration does strike. Hopefully more often—and with fewer side effects—than being hit by actual lightning.

Even successful student writers can struggle with the motivation to write creatively. One prolific student of mine, Ashley Williams, made the writing challenge look easy. She used it toward a longer drafting process: in the challenge, she began a short piece of fiction, which she developed into a full story for a class assignment, and submitted it for a department award. She won the award, and later saw the story published in an anthology. Even with this well-earned success, in her final course reflection she described the 30/30 challenge as the toughest part of the class.

> I have read a lot about writing, listened to authors talk, and the common consensus is that writers need to write, and every day so that it becomes a habit. In a high school classroom, I think this could be relatively easy, due to daily attendance. Writing daily in a college level is difficult, because there are other demands on time. I often found myself writing right before bed, not at my best, just so that I could turn something in, or sitting and writing for large blocks of time. Some of the pieces were horrible, others not so bad. However, one advantage was that I did finish a draft of my fiction story, and I completed it early. While it was stressful and a bit demanding, I can definitely see how this exercise helps writers.
>
> (Williams, 2016)

In an online classroom, a 30-Day Writing Challenge offers high accountability for students. They're expected to show up and post based on the parameters you've identified, and because everyone's posts are visible on a class discussion board, it's easy for peers to see who contributes (and who doesn't). Like your running buddy or weightlifting spotter, peers become accountability partners as they anticipate reading one another's work. They also know they'll be missed when they don't show up. A clear set of guidelines, ideally listed in the syllabus and/or a detailed assignment, reinforces the setup for the challenge and provides the repercussions for failing to participate.

The discussion board for my graduate Creative Writing for Teachers class opens with this call to action:

30/30 Project

- Mon–Fri (Weekdays), Weeks 1–6 of the course
- 30 days, 30 poems (or short posts—stories/fiction, creative nonfiction, whatever you choose)
- Deadline: Midnight each night.
- All posts due by Friday, end of Week 6, by 11:59 p.m.

Use material from the day's assignments and drafting or create something new: the idea is to generate new ideas and new writing through the daily practice of writing. As teachers, we might ask our students to complete a writing challenge as a way to compose regularly, to gain discipline, and to keep thoughts flowing. Writing alongside students—in a challenge or in daily exercises/activities—is a way to show them the importance and significance of what you're asking of them.

This is a writing **challenge** and counts toward overall participation. Keep track of your posts on the provided chart (a very simple Word doc made up of a table grid).

20–30 posts = full credit
15–19 posts = high partial credit
14–below = low partial credit

Clarity and transparency are key for online teaching, no matter the subject. *The Online Teaching Survival Guide* by Judith Boettcher and Rita-Marie Conrad emphasizes a set of best practices, listing "Be Present at Your Course" and "Create a Supportive Online Course" at the top of the list. Presence is not just logging in: online teachers excel through a blend of social presence, teaching presence, and cognitive presence.

> Many faculty remain daunted by the shift in learning dynamics and relationships created by these tools, and many are still struggling to adapt. In an environment infused with these tools, the faculty member moves from the center of the class communication pattern, as was common in the traditional transmission mode of learning, to the periphery or, in the stage model, to the wings.
>
> (2016: 41)

Some learning management systems track how much time students have spent in the course site. If you're trying to measure participation activity, these stats may be misleading: people complete the work at different speeds, for one thing, a flaunted advantage of online courses. It's theoretically possible, if unadvisable, for students to "be online" but actually doing something else (gasp!) thus padding the stats, or they may want to fly under the radar, to be enrolled but not really there. I doubt most people get into teaching to be a time cop, and isn't it the quality of participation that matters most? The writing challenge offers a potentially useful solution to the engagement issue in online courses, giving students opportunities for valuable interaction in an environment where they might otherwise appear invisible or purposely disappear. It also allows the teacher to "show up" in a way that encourages participation: for this particular assignment, you're not there to assign a grade or judge the quality of the work. You're there to encourage consistent, active participation. When students know that you're reading the posts (which can be indicated with an occasional comment, "like," or making a brief reference to a post in an eventual draft), they take the challenge more seriously. Similarly, you can track who isn't participating and communicate with them early in the term, offering brainstorming support through optional prompts, or assignments tied to the course reading.

Related, online students have fewer opportunities to get to know one another. Many of my students report that despite wanting the flexibility of online learning, they feel isolated by the experience. A 30-Day Writing Challenge provides a simple way for them to interact and know more about each other's writing, and depending on their subject matter, more about their lives, too. One may be writing creative nonfiction about learning how to make her ancestors' recipes, inspiring another classmate to respond with a book recommendation or to share a story of her own. Another may find poetic inspiration in what's out the window: hummingbirds in summer, a robin returning in spring. And soon another writer is compelled to write about a childhood vacation spent birdwatching on the Gulf of Mexico, where one flock of pelicans resembled planes in formation, scaring him as a child. Speaking of scary, the class film buff suggests a re-watch of Alfred Hitchcock's *The Birds*, which calls up an association that inspires yet another piece of writing from a self-proclaimed allegedly "blocked" writer. (Speaking of associations, readers of a certain age will hear shades of INXS's song "Mediate" in the title of this chapter.) These daily posts accrue into a kind of creative chorus, providing inspiration for one another as they read each other's work and provide encouragement. It benefits them as writers, and it benefits them as readers. In the closed environment of an online class, it's a relatively safe—or at least contained—way for writers to practice putting their work before an audience.

In *Teaching Creative Writing: Practical Approaches*, edited by Elaine Walker, Ian Williams describes creating a 30/30 challenge for the month of April, to coincide with National Poetry Month. An online challenge "combines the intimacy of a traditional poetry class with the feeling of social media and the academic rigour of a science fair project" (2012: 142).

If we are meeting our students where they are, building exercises and posts that resemble a familiar practice in the online world gives them one less new task to focus on: instead of learning the ins and outs of a new technology, they're prioritizing the creation of new work. Williams also encourages teachers to be "present" online as the challenge kicks off. Students need to know that their work isn't merely disappearing into an online void. As a way to organize the work, he also creates a separate discussion post for each day of the challenge. These moves can help writers gain confidence and, yes, self-esteem. This helps foster a sense of responsibility in both student and teacher, as both are active participants in their learning.

I saw that in action when high school English teacher Jennifer Teague took my online course as part of her graduate program. Sitting down daily with an assignment to create something new sparked her creativity. It increased her confidence in her own writing as well as her teaching: if she could successfully complete a writing challenge, then so could her students. Her reflection illustrated a keen understanding of the limitations at the secondary level when trying to implement creative writing in English classes:

> Daily writing practice seems to be critical for writing development as well. The 30/30 project acts as a low-stakes opportunity to practice with creative ideas. Once students make the habit of writing each day, while being exposed to the diverse and plentiful published works, their writing is bound to improve. Students in today's high school English courses do not have many opportunities to write creatively and (in my experience) feel overwhelmed when asked to do so. Through a daily creative writing challenge, they will get past the initial "freak out" moment, and it will be perfectly OK if their writing isn't great. They need the practice, and through that practice, they will improve.
>
> (Teague, 2019)

She delivered this enthusiasm to her students the following term, and reported back that she incorporated a writing challenge into her own classroom with high school seniors. "It has been a wonderful experience," she emailed. "We started on the very first day of school. It helped to normalize the action of writing again. I think my students have been so far removed from that process for so long that the 30/30 helped breathe new life and confidence. They're anxiously awaiting the next round."

In a writing challenge, I emphasize the importance of building a practice, and that participation is the primary measure of evaluation. Some students may not be able to meet the 30 consecutive days; I consider that acceptable. The only penalty is for egregious slacking, based around the point range I devised for transparency's sake. Rebecca Watkins, a student and teacher who went on to an MFA program, reflected that the 30/30 challenge was made worthwhile by virtue of its difficulty, and appreciated that even without completing all 30 posts, she still found the effort worthwhile:

> Another aspect of the class that I really enjoyed was the 30/30 writing challenge. Although I did not get all thirty days, my solid twenty-four were satisfying enough because I was able to challenge myself to make a habit out of writing a little each day. As a teacher, I often have my students write daily in a journal, or by responding to prompts, but instead of writing with them, I'd use the time to grade or do additional prep. Because of this assignment, I was able to coach myself into following the same routine I set out for my own students. When I sat down with them at the desks and began to write in my journal, they seemed more excited about their own writing—we were in it together. This exercise isn't easy. There were days when I felt like no words would come and no ideas were near. To break this slump, I turned to the many writing prompts we were given.
>
> (Watkins, 2019)

So how do you set up a writing challenge in your own online classroom? A discussion board works particularly well, though you can use any course technology that best serves your purposes. The following steps can serve as a guideline:

- Dive in. Set the tone and start immediately, especially if your course is compressed into a shorter time period than a full semester. Invite the first post on the first day.
- Emphasize that this is generative work and drafting, not expected to be publishable or perfect at this stage. These are starts to longer pieces that may come later. If your creative writing class utilizes the workshop, encourage students to develop these starts into longer pieces they can submit for feedback.
- Be flexible. For those who can't be (or don't want to be) online every day, offer an option to post the week's pieces all at once. If some prefer writing in a notebook, they could upload pictures of their writing (as long as it's legible), demonstrating different process stages. Students are learning about what works for them. Allow for room to put preferences into practice.
- Be flexible, II: schedule the challenge for weekdays and take the weekend off. While I understand the appeal of NaNoWriMo, pushing to finish a full novel in an arbitrary period of time is a literal challenge for a set period of time, not a sustainable way to live. My writing process lives for slow rumination. I recognize that NaNo is a No for Me. Still, the emphasis on production 24/7 isn't healthy. That's fine if you want to do it for yourself, but don't drag your students into it. (They do, after all, fill out course evaluations at the end.) A 30-day challenge works perfectly for a six-week class, with posts made five days a week. Adjust your challenge dates around your schedule.
- Be flexible, III: If you set a daily deadline, make it 11:59 p.m. Your students with jobs and families will be grateful.
- Use your course reading for inspiration. Let students be inspired by a wide variety of voices, styles, and writers.
- Imitate the work of others. Writing an imitation of a poem, story, or essay can lead to inspiration when students emulate one aspect—voice, imagery, plot—then diverge into their own unique piece of writing.
    a   Ask students to write an imitation of a flash fiction that uses a single-word title, using a different subject/title of their choosing. Some excellent online models: Kathy Fish's "Prague," from *SmokeLong Quarterly*, Jamaica Kincaid's "Girl" from *The New Yorker*, Rumaan Alam's "Minuet" from *Wigleaf*.
    b   Have students visit the popular website *Verse Daily*, and write a response poem to something that sparks their interest.
- Build in solo field trips where students go in search of imagery, then post their writing to the 30/30 challenge

- a Visit an art museum, either in person or online, and write an ekphrastic poem, or one that draws inspiration from visual art. Possible models: the John Keats poem "Ode on a Grecian Urn," "Photograph from September 11" by Wisława Szymborska, or Anne Sexton's "The Starry Night."
- b Place Field Trip: visit and observe a public place in order to write a sketch of what it's like: the sights, sounds, smells, and feel. Eavesdrop on passerby and use lines of dialogue in the sketch.

- Offer optional prompts. Also, be open to and encourage diverging from the prompts. Creative writing students may or may not need a nudge to get started; options help. A prompt forms a container in which the imagination can run wild. I'd suggest building a list of prompts that they can choose from, or ignore completely as their brains take hold of the images that crop up. Sometimes prompts work in a strange sort of reverse, as they give writers something to reject: *I don't know what I want to write yet, but I know I don't want that.*

  - a Read Katha Pollitt's poem "Archaeology," then write a poem that contains a metaphor for your writing process.
  - b Read Ira Sukrungruang's creative nonfiction piece "Chop Suey," in *Brevity: A Journal of Concise Literary Nonfiction*, then write a brief essay or scene reflecting on a moment of conflict from childhood.
  - c Build a prompt bank. In addition to the many, many resources on the internet (such as *Brevity*'s craft essays, The National Writing Project's "Resources" page, and the *Pleiades* series of revision/craft exercises by Matthew Salesses), books like *The Poet's Companion* by Kim Addonizio and Dorianne Laux, *Writing Fiction* by Janet Burroway, and *The Writer's Field Guide to the Craft of Writing Fiction* by Michael Noll (with companion blog "Read to Write Stories") are diverse treasure troves of creative writing inspiration and prompts.

- Grade for completion. Students take more risks when they aren't being evaluated for a grade. Because this is a demonstrative, visible activity, I assign it as a participation grade. Students receive full credit for completing the challenge (this can be a range that you deem successful, such as 20–25 total posts), and partial credit for partial completion.

I offer a final point that is not so much a tip as my challenge to you, dear teachers: practice the 30-day challenge alongside your students. They will appreciate seeing your early drafts, which may lead to a bigger piece, or may be relegated to your personal "flop" folder, to be mined for later work. I've completed the challenge with my students several times, leading to short pieces that I later developed into poems, essays, and stories. One year, I chipped away at a novel draft for each of the thirty days. As expected, I've also produced pages and pages of other work that remains in a folder. No matter. If the best writing teachers are ones who are practicing writers, then that is visibly demonstrated in an online 30-day writing challenge, where pedagogy meets writing practice as teacher becomes participant.

Works cited

Boettcher, Judith V., and Rita-Marie Conrad. *The Online Teaching Survival Guide: Simple and Practical Pedagogical Tips.* Jossey-Bass, 2016.

Cameron, Julia. *The Right to Write: An Invitation and Initiation into the Writing Life.* Hay House, 2017.

Egan, Jennifer. "Jennifer Egan." *Why We Write: 20 Acclaimed Authors on How and Why They Do What They Do,* edited by Meredith Maran, Plume, 2013, pp. 28–35.

Leahy, Anna. "'It's Such a Good Feeling': Self-Esteem, the Growth Mindset, and Creative Writing." *Can Creative Writing Really Be Taught? Resisting Lore in Creative Writing Pedagogy,* edited by Stephanie Vanderslice and Rebecca Manery, Bloomsbury, 2017, pp. 44–56.

"National Writing Project." About NWP – National Writing Project, archive.nwp.org/cs/public/print/doc/about.csp.

"National Writing Project." Resource Topics – National Writing Project, archive.nwp.org/cs/public/print/doc/resources/topics.csp.

Stegner, Wallace, and Lynn Stegner. *On Teaching and Writing Fiction.* Penguin Books, 2002.

Teague, Jennifer. "Final Portfolio Reflection." Canvas, IUPUI, 2019, canvas.iu.edu.

VanderMeer, Jeff. *Wonderbook: An Illustrated Guide to Creating Imaginative Fiction.* Abrams Image, 2018.

Watkins, Rebecca. "Final Portfolio Reflection." Canvas, IUPUI, 2019, canvas.iu.edu.

Williams, Ashley. "Final Portfolio Reflection." Canvas, IUPUI, 2016, canvas.iu.edu.

Williams, Ian. "30/30 Projects: Developing a Daily Writing Habit." *Teaching Creative Writing: Practical Approaches,* edited by Elaine Walker, CWS, 2012, pp. 140–142.

13 Using flash fiction as a pedagogical tool in teaching creative writing online

Ashley Jae Carranza

Many issues arise when teaching creative writing to students of all levels. Some of the most difficult issues to overcome revolve around the base-level components of a story and how to aid students in mastering them. Some of these base issues include building conflict, characters, voice, convincing dialogue, and paring down content. When working in an online learning environment, the instructor's main goal should be creating activities that pay strong attention to these issues. With little face-to-face interaction in an asynchronous course, instructors must choose strong, self-reliant content to model the ultimate learning benchmarks. The flash-fiction genre provides creative writing students easily accessible examples of foundations they need to become successful writers.

Flash fiction, when used for critique and analysis, is an excellent tool for creative writing students. This type of fiction exists as far back as stories themselves, but became more visible through authors such as Ernest Hemingway, and became mass published and more mainstream in the 1980s (Masterclass). As of February 2020, the organization Poets & Writers lists roughly 400 literary magazines specializing in or accepting flash-fiction submissions. These figures demonstrate that flash's popularity is growing. This increasing growth makes flash easily accessible to the online literary community and provides budding readers a means to apply practical examination of texts. The principles of flash fiction in stories under 1,000 words are prime examples of self-contained pieces of literature that readers/writers can use to learn techniques quickly and utilize those techniques in their own writing.

Utilizing flash fiction as a pedagogical tool is ideal for online or low-residency creative writing professors because it is ample in the online literary community, can be assigned flexibly to a variety of lesson plans ranging from simple narrative tools to literary devices and story elements, and gets the point across to students in a manner that requires little face-to-face communication. Tony Williams discusses the reasoning behind using flash as an educational approach. He states:

> not everyone will enjoy reading and writing flash fiction, but I think every prose writer should try their hand at it. Learning to fit a story into a very

> small space demands tremendous discipline which will serve you well in your longer projects.
>
> (2014: 315)

Using flash as a model of piecing together units of text is a primary goal in utilizing this genre in curriculum, but in addition it can serve as a quick lesson on what *not* to do as well. According to C. S. Lakin, using examples of writing in the realm of education provides writers with a wealth of practical knowledge. Writers need to go beyond reliance on their instructors and need to be able to pull from actual examples to hone in on their crafts:

> What writers need are not more books and instructors telling them what to do and how to do it. They need examples. And not just examples of great fiction writing. They need examples of weak, flawed writing too. What helps writers most is to read passages that demonstrate flawed writing, then be shown revisions that target specific flaws and offer clear, effective solutions to those problems.
>
> (2015: 1)

As flash fiction is in high demand, mass publication means that the quality of stories varies, providing readers/writers with a wide scope of materials from which they can learn both what they wish to include and what they wish to avoid in their own writing.

In an online environment, allowing students to explore numerous publications is ideal and removes pressure from the instructor—students can use objective reasoning to determine elements that cement a piece's validity. Readers who utilize flash fiction are able to identify story markers, have the ability to read numerous works quickly, and then use the skills they pick up within the realm of their own works under loose professorial guidance. In the world of online pedagogy, the instructor acts as a vessel to the information, and it is up to the students to use the information to build their own repertoire of writing tools.

What is flash fiction and why is its popularity growing?

Flash fiction is defined as self-contained stories composed of 1,000 words or fewer. In many cases, flash can be much shorter than this limit, even as brief as one sentence. Although many claim that the shorter a story, the easier it is to write, Ketaki Latkar's *Free Press Journal* article shines light on what it really means to comprise a well-constructed piece of flash:

> The operative words for the genre are short and snappy, and getting it right is no mean job. The writing ... banks entirely on the element of appeal in the shortest span of time and the choice of the most appropriate set of words, of course, without the loss of emotion and essence.
>
> (2018)

While novelists have hundreds of pages in which to build a plot and develop character relationships, flash authors use strict decision-making skills to fit those elements into "the shortest span."

In a world where Twitter is king and your average reader is hit with short bursts of text, both for informational and entertainment purposes, it is no surprise that literature is following suit. Of course, people still read and write novels, but the fact that extremely short stories are gaining prevalence is no coincidence. This is neither positive, nor negative; it just *is*.

What is positive about this movement, however, is that authors specializing in flash master some of the most difficult authorial responsibilities that writers face. Due to the shortened nature of these texts authors must capture brevity, causing them to get to the heart of their story, and stay there. In this genre, there is no room for extraneous language or story elements. Everything a flash writer uses is necessary and serves a purpose. This gives the writing a raw, authentic feeling that people get during real life experiences. Much like other societal trends requiring immediate satisfaction and completion, readers consume these stories within minutes. Whereas longer works may take days or more to complete, a reader can finish a piece of flash, analyze it both for content and literary breakdown, and consider how these elements can be applied in one's own writing, all during one sitting. For an online class, flash fiction is one way to expose students to a variety of authors and concepts quickly.

Evolving approaches and dissection analysis

The aim of the flash-fiction approach is not to encourage authors to specialize in flash, but to help authors identify strong writing techniques. Authors who specialize in longer works have the luxury to write as much or as little as they choose, but can apply flash principles to texts of any page count. The aim of this approach is to allow online students the opportunity to scaffold their own writing through analyzing short texts. The ultimate design of this approach is for students to use very structured close reads to help them be able to create texts that also require close reads.

The approach that I am suggesting, *dissection analysis*, involves close reading with guiding questions that are incredibly flexible and can be suited to any short piece. The way that this is different from other approaches is that it asks students to utilize criteria that can be applied to an array of stories regardless of genre or content. In my experience as both a creative writing graduate student as well as a college instructor, I've found that colleges are apt to provide students with writing on technical issues. These texts discuss *how* to write and *why* certain techniques work, but offer minimal finished products students can deconstruct based on what they've learned about these principles. Educator and social scientist Tom Haymes reflects this sentiment as he states,

> basic textbooks have never been a rich lode of ideas to start with. They rarely contain very rich information and usually sacrifice depth for breadth.

> They suffer from, and mirror, the lecture mentality of education. When you have to exhort faculty "not to teach the textbook," you are exhorting them not to lecture—or worse—read the textbook to their classes.
>
> (2019: 1)

Much as we see in English composition courses, the majority of textbooks used do not cater to the process of promoting stronger writing through example; composition textbooks publish mostly step-by-step guides on composition (with few to no examples of what this actually looks like), and narrative essays meant for comprehension analysis.

Comprehension analysis is a useful tool, but it is only one type of activity that English and writing majors need to become well-rounded scholars. Editors tend to neglect publishing actual student essays that students could analyze as writing samples. Many colleges focus more on giving technical information and less on scaffolding practical application. If students do not apply the principles they learn from technical aspects, then the understanding isn't truly there. Students may be able to tell you what it *means* to write a "good" story and different elements that make a "good" story, but if they do not actually apply these theories and practices to critiquing stories, then that knowledge is moot. Professor Joseph R. Teller states, "In short, the more time a course focuses on 'critical reading' and content, the less time it spends on structure, argument, evidence, logical reasoning, and concise, clear prose—the tools a composition class should give undergraduates" (2016). Although this applies mainly to early composition classes, this is the basis with which writing pupils begin their college experiences. This is also a pattern that professors copy (which is fine in upper-level, concentration-specific seminar courses), but should not be the norm for creative writing foundations. Seeing the techniques utilized in writing samples and detailing the ways in which other authors utilize these skills change the way that early career writers approach their own art.

While comprehension questions for particular stories is one appropriate practice for English majors, creative writing majors need something else. Creative writing majors need to understand the skeletal structure that goes into each and every story a writer creates. Dissection analysis allows students to stop thinking about the overall meaning of the story and start paying attention to smaller details which may be overlooked when the focus of the activity is comprehending content and plotline. This is one way to help students write more well-crafted pieces themselves. Students often get so wrapped up with the idea that they have to present the entire story that they will sometimes miss out on smaller features that really make the story worthwhile; the big picture overshadows construction of smaller pieces. Tony Williams suggests that flash can help with these issues:

> The genre ... helps you to unlock ways of writing that you never suspected were at hand ... Very often, longer texts are made up of lots of short ones, whether these are the scenes or sections of a short story or the chapters of

the novel. It is important to see these component texts as formal units in their own right. Mastering flash will put you in a good position to construct such units, paying attention to the little narrative arcs even while another part of you is eyeing the grand novelistic vista.

(320)

The goal, again, is not to ask students to become flash-fiction experts, but to introduce them to the genre, see what it has to offer, and use some of the principles (as are fit to each writer's style). Flash fiction facilitates new reading opportunities from which writers can sharpen their techniques.

Although many professors stand behind the idea that the best writers are also the best readers, they do not necessarily reinforce this message in their pedagogical practices. In order to meet common objectives such as exploring various techniques and performing editorial duties, professors flock to several overused methods. In many MFA programs, particularly ones online where actual discussion amongst peers is limited, many professors will utilize workshopping and peer-review of each other's writing to help maximize time. Students also purchase numerous textbooks that provide them academic information about the process of creative writing. While these approaches are necessary, this leaves a gaping hole in a student's ability to perform practical analysis on other works that could be beneficial to them. Workshopping specifically may be misconstrued for less experienced writers who may "[confuse] critique ... with personal insult, confusing a workshop with a soapbox from which you can declaim your strongly held views on writing, rather than treating class as an open-ended discussion among equals" (Abramson, 2018: 38–39). In addition to creating an environment in which students may feel judged or personally attacked, workshopping limits the materials from which students can choose and learn from. Much as previously discussed with the pedagogical reasoning in composition courses, we see again guides on what a student should do, but provide few examples of writers who execute these skills in the real world. On the other side of this argument, many professors still require that students read novels. Colleges should not rely solely on the novel requirement and should use it in conjunction with other types of texts; reading novels requires a look at the big picture, a picture that takes hundreds of pages to paint. Close reads on a novel are important because they help students piece together the entire story. Meanwhile, close reads on shorter texts help students piece together precise technical choices. Numerous sources and activities build a balanced repertoire in the student population.

The online classroom environment is a particularly strong ground for presenting sample materials because students are already online. When thinking about presenting materials for student use, one should compare the dynamic between an in-person class and an online class. When preparing materials to provide to an in-person course, instructors are more likely to lean towards handouts and/or packets. A tangible assignment in a physical classroom is appropriate, but it is also limiting. If students are enrolled in an online class and they are logged in already, instructors can disseminate much more material in much less time. Instead of handing out a packet with ten stories, instructors can inform students of websites and databases that multiply their resources endlessly. Given the tools, this simple sharing of information can lead students to find their own materials they may not have known existed previously. Of course, instructors can share this type of information with students in an in-person class, but in order to do it at the same level as in an online environment, all students would need to have a laptop with them or take a class trip to the library and the instructor would need to allot time for students to conduct the searches, etc.

Many professors implement technological assignments for work to be completed outside of class. However, Flower Darby from *The Chronicle of Higher Education* makes several statements that indicate that professors who are accustomed to teaching in-person may not test the waters with online work as much as they could:

> Fundamentally, good teaching requires you to be in the classroom with your students. When you teach in person, you don't leave students to their own devices. You're with them, engaging in any number of teacherly activities: explaining, guiding, asking, illustrating, answering questions.
>
> (2020)

Her article also goes on to state that although the online population is growing, as of 2017, 91 percent of professors taught in-person while only 9 percent worked solely online. Her data and analysis indicate that those in a physical classroom may tend to engage with students more hands-on, meaning that lessons outside of a professor–student interaction may be limited.

Keeping this in mind, it seems detailed Internet searches through literary magazines as discussed is unlikely to occur for traditional, in-person classes. Based on these figures, assigning self-driven lit mag research as homework would (probably) fall on the side of supplementary guidance and not take prevalence over traditional methods on paper. If a majority of class time is spent with instructors as guides on the side through a journey across online literary magazines, a more sensical approach for the classroom setting is online as opposed to in-person. This doorway to unlimited resources may be one reason that many students and instructors report a preference for online education. According to statistics analyzed by the University of the Potomac:

> 77% of educators believe that online learning is just as good as traditional learning, if not better. Nearly 70% of all students claim online instruction to be as good as or better than in a traditional classroom setting. 26% of online students claim to learn better online than in a classroom.
>
> (potomac.edu)

When students are at the reins of their own learning, they can delve deeper into the search in an environment of their own choosing, without the constraints of a traditional classroom that dictates a start and end time. If online education is the most viable method for teaching creative writing, how can flash fiction and dissection analysis work effectively in this platform?

Practical application

To begin with, as with any online course, professors must ensure that the materials are front-loaded, well-planned, and organized in a manner where students can use them independently. There are many ways that professors can integrate flash fiction dissection into the online classroom, ranging from providing texts for students to asking students to post stories that they have found themselves. The end result, however, should ultimately provide and require students to use the class critique criteria, whichever particular criteria applies, and to either reflect on how they can apply these aspects into their own writing, or craft an assignment that utilizes at least one of the principles they discuss.

A simple template for a set of guiding questions for dissection analysis may include, but is not limited to, the following criteria:

Table 13.1

Point of view	Presence/Use of dialogue	Quality/Believability of dialogue	Characterization	Diction
Sentence structure/paring down phrasing	Description- Confusing? Clear? Able to visualize the action or setting?	What makes the story climactic or anticlimactic?	Is there a moment of realization? Is it for the reader or for the character?	Is it relatable? Does it have to be?
Is the writer *showing* or *telling*?	Degree of predictability?	Cliche or overdone?	Allusion?	Implications and Inferences

Although listing out these areas for critique so simplistically may not seem up to par with traditional college or graduate level curriculum, the return to basic literary functions is quintessential for sharpening one's skills. In terms of smaller elements of structure, author and writing instructor James Scott Bell states,

> Once you understand why it works, you are free to use that understanding to fit your artistic purposes. But you will soon come to realize that the further you move from sound structure, the harder it will be to bring your readers along with you.
>
> (2004: 24)

Overlooking a piece's basic structural skeleton can result in subpar writing, regardless of how clever the premise is. In my experience as an editor for three literary magazines, these elements are the elements that make or break a story. When deciding whether to publish a story, the issue usually does not lie in the content, but small parts of the presentation, which is something that early career writers do not always take into consideration. Analysis through close reading allows students to reflect on how all of the individual parts play an essential role in the overall effectiveness of the story.

In addition to the criteria that students can use for critiquing purposes, there are other facets of utmost importance to consider within the genre. Something important to note about flash fiction, especially when analyzing its parts, is its ability to involve the reader. Flash's condensed formula enables, and actually insists, that the reader plays a part in the telling of the story. In order to preserve the genre's shortened nature, the reader inadvertently takes agency in piecing stories together in a process that Frederick Aldama refers to as "gap-filling." Ohio State University professor Aldama uses flash fiction in depth to teach students the foundations of solid writing. He suggests that this form of writing not only functions as a mode of entertainment, but that there is scientific methodology behind the way that a reader processes flash. One aspect of this scientific approach is the notion that:

> Exercises ... which develop student understanding ... present details [and] entail omitted details, [and] reinforce the message that any work of fiction is a selection of components. Rigorous thematic, narratological, and cognitive close reading makes clear that authors provide carefully written cues while leaving substantive gaps for readers to fill. Seeing that [short stories are] riddled with gaps, students nonetheless come to understand the story as a whole, its components—characters, things, actions—and its form. Moreover, they learn that they re-create a rich and complete story via a strict economy of storytelling that instructs them to fill the gaps. Deliberately slow-paced close reading of this kind, moving between ... micro and macro levels of analysis, promises collective discovery. In this way, readers appreciate that how the text is designed, what it conveys, and when it succeeds on its own terms are inexhaustible questions.
>
> (2014:134)

Studying short fiction and utilizing the principles in one's own writing transcends literary niceties; it plays on the reader's psychology, their biology, and draws them in as it asks them to perform a task. Forcing a reader to fill gaps reconnects with human purpose. Human existence requires people to act in order for survival; people are not meant for inactivity. Writing that is too forward, too telling, is usually not a pleasurable experience for a reader. When a writer knows about this visceral connection, and when they practice dissecting and learning from writers who specialize in the art of creating gaps, these writers insert themselves into the practice of creating these types of living, breathing texts themselves.

However, although overtly prevalent in flash, the idea of requiring a reader to fill gaps is not something specific to super-short stories. Stephen King demonstrates how important this trimming down or gap-filling is for all readers as well. King describes the overuse of description and how it takes away from the reader's ability to interact with the text in his book *On Writing*. He provides an example of how detail can engage readers and connect them more thoroughly without telling them everything. King states:

> Look—here's a table covered with red cloth. On it is a cage the size of a small fish aquarium. In the cage is a white rabbit with a pink nose and pink-rimmed eyes.... On its back, clearly marked in blue ink, is the numeral 8.... The most interesting thing here isn't even the carrot-munching rabbit in the cage, but the number on its back. Not a six, not a four, not nineteen-point-five. It's an eight. This is what we're looking at, and we all see it. I didn't tell you. You didn't ask me. I never opened my mouth and you never opened yours. We're not even in the same *year* together, let alone the same room... except we are together. We are close. We're having a meeting of the minds.... We've engaged in an act of telepathy.
>
> (2000: 105)

In terms of professionalism, writers must not write for the sole purpose of writing; they must write to engage their reader and build a relationship with the text. Showing students the methodology that plays into gap-filling provokes motivation to write with reader engagement in mind. Flash is a quick, efficient mode of allowing students to visualize what the process looks like.

Implementing this dissection analysis strategy into an online discussion board or individual posts stimulates extensive student responses. Giving students the guiding questions takes their analytical skills to a higher level and allows the opportunity for students to challenge one another's responses using specific textual examples obtained through the close read. The easiest, most ideal pieces of flash for this specific type of online discussion board are 100- or 101-word stories. Not only are these stories published at a faster rate than longer pieces of fiction, making them more numerous and accessible, but their length makes them quick to read and dissect; all students have the time to read and go over the text, and when they present their opinions on the text, the specific references they mention are easily locatable for classmates who may want to challenge or re-address them.

My classes use dissection analysis on a regular basis, leading to rigorous, meaningful discussion, both tailored to and expanding beyond the critique criteria I provide. One story we use as a precursor to our first workshopping section is a story I wrote specifically to be used in this context called "Friends in Low Places," which receives an array of feedback:

Friends in Low Places

"Mommy, Mommy! I'm not afraid of the potty anymore!" Faith exclaimed.
"I told you there were no snakes in there!" Mommy smiled.

"Oh, yes there was," Faith beamed, "but he was nice. He gave me some chocolate."

Mommy's smile straightened out. "Don't try to trick me, little missy. Nothing can survive in the sewers. You're being silly."

"No, I'm not, come on!" Faith grabbed Mommy's hand and led her to the bathroom.

"See, there's nothing here," Mommy said through a cracked voice, ignoring the thin line of water that streaked the floor and ended at a crumpled ball of foil.

Out of 19 students who wrote responses to this story during a recent semester, there was an array of topics mentioned, while many notated similar reactions to the strengths and weaknesses in their critiques.

Based on the feedback that students give, the instructor can then tailor the corresponding writing assignment to include elements that they discussed most highly. This literary element is fresh and the class has a text to reference, either as a model to follow or a model to avoid. This allows students control over their work, creating a mutually respectful environment in which the instructor demonstrates that he or she values student opinions and in which students use instructor-provided materials to help them shape their own writing. In the above scenario, based on the high number of responses in regard to diction, dialogue, and detail, an appropriate follow-up assignment could include one or more of those devices and asks students to write with a specific focus on dialogue to push the plot forward, etc. This process can be duplicated with any given story, again playing into the benefits of an online community where stories are ample.

Table 13.2

Strengths/Weaknesses addressed in student critiques	Number of students discussing this topic
Character relationship as realistic	4
Dialogue to push the plot forward	3
Dialogue as realistic and advantageous for characterization	4
Reader utilizes gap-filling	2
Authorial use of diction (positive response)	6
Overall sentence structure (positive response)	1
Details/Description (positive response)	5
Reader/Character epiphany (twist)	2
Anticlimactic	1
Trouble visualizing the scenario	4
Lack of description regarding setting	1

Beyond the critique criteria for dissection analysis, flash offers examples of rules that all authors should follow, regardless of genre or specialty. In addition to the breakdown and analysis of given stories, sentence structure is another lesson to be learned from these types of stories. Flash models effective methods to say what you mean, and mean what you say. Oftentimes, writers do not know how to phrase their sentences in a way that appropriately establishes setting, characters, or action in general. Flash-fiction pieces demonstrate ways in which writers can cut right into the core of what they are trying to illustrate. This is a skill that many underestimate; the ability to simplify is just as important as any other skill necessary for writing good fiction.

In this same vein, writers need to recognize that sentence structure is the backbone for the story. Aldama asks his students to analyze deliberate phrasing and the function it serves in the storytelling process. He begins his unit with one-sentence stories ranging from six to ten words and focuses on the semantics of these stories. The diction carries meaning and purpose, particularly because there are so few words. His class analyzes the placement of each word, how the story would change if words were reversed, etc., and they explore the ways that the sentence's layout affects the reader's interpretation of the story itself. Analyzing such seemingly minute details develops a writer's ability to phrase their work accurately. This accurate phrasing transfers exactly what the writer intends for the reader to receive. Understanding semantics gives the writer power to properly convey their message.

In an article entitled "13 Tips for Writing Flash Fiction," Denise Ganley of *Flash Fiction Online* literary magazine gives aspiring flash writers several pieces of information to help them perfect their craft. These rules, however, fit the writing field as a whole. Not all rules specific to flash apply to other genres, but several are applicable regardless. These rules cover both areas of focus—content/purpose, and sentence structure/executive choices on diction. Dissection analysis will help readers/writers gain the tools necessary not only to understand that the following rules improve writing, but afford them experience in recognizing *how* these rules work in practice.

Students see these rules, examine their presence in stories, and make the connection between the rule and the result of following the rule. With the combination of dissection analysis, attention to structural details, and conscious choice in terms of diction/paring down to sharpen meaning, flash becomes the trifecta in terms of modeled writing.

Table 13.3

Take out all unnecessary words	Do not use excessive adjectives and adverbs	Create visceral reaction without manipulating the reader with melodrama
Choose effective titles	Choose subtle themes	Build strong character arcs, at least for the protagonist

Meeting other course objectives

One of the more difficult objectives to reach as an instructor is providing opportunities for students to explore modes of publication. Although many students enter MFAs or creative writing programs already having had their works published, there are those who enter programs with little to no experience in this field. For those who enter programs hoping to leave understanding the submission process, flash mags are flexible teaching/learning options.

Due to the quick turnaround time, frequent publication schedule (some flash sites publish a story each day), and higher publication rates, flash sites effectively familiarize students with the submission process. (Acceptance rates for specific journals can be located in various databases such as Duotrope or The Submission Grinder, sites dedicated to publicizing statistics and other data. This can help guide writers to fitting magazines.) Many flash sites accept simultaneous submissions and even provide detailed feedback to authors when their work is rejected. With larger journals or journals that accept a variety of genres or longer works, staff rarely has enough time to personally address submissions. Constant rejection without reasoning is frustrating for early career writers (which is an unfortunate truth about being a writer), but having a journal give specific feedback on a piece can help writers to workshop their own texts. Specific feedback reveals avenues for improvement that students may not receive from other sources. Students can submit to numerous sources in a short amount of time and work on numerous skills including navigating the ever-popular Submittable site, writing cover letters for stories, meeting expectations for specific journals, researching journals for desired content, and tracking submissions via spreadsheets, etc. These journals also offer higher probability for publication, meaning that while students meet the publication objective, they may also gain publication recognition for their resumes.

Another aspect of creative writing education that often goes untouched is active editing. Practicing dissection analysis on pieces of flash fiction exposes students to thorough editing skills that work in the real world. Expanding beyond editing one's own work or classmates' work is vital for students who wish to enter the workforce as editors. Developing an editorial thinking process and voice prior to actually working as an editor increases the likelihood that a graduate will obtain a job in the first place, which is a consideration that programs sometimes gloss over.

While focusing on creative writing, students rarely have the opportunity to edit unless they choose specifically to take a class that publishes the school's literary journal, etc. MFA programs focus heavily on workshopping, but this roundtable discussion does not effectively mirror the responsibility of working as an editor for a journal or publishing house. If a student does not intend to enter the working world as an editor and forgoes the opportunity to serve in an editing course, then their editorial experience is dwindled to the minimal workshopping they practice with classmate trade and grades. With roughly 5,300 colleges and universities in the United States (Education Unlimited), it seems as though opportunities for students to practice active, professional editing would be ample. However, New Pages informational writing site lists that there are currently 521 undergraduate literary magazines, while Poets & Writers lists only 165 graduate school literary magazines. Another troubling part of these numbers is that while some schools house journals, most colleges and universities do not require students to take courses in editing, publications, or design. They may be encouraged to participate, but students will be hard-pressed to find schools that will *make* them participate in these classes. Once the school doors close, students lose the opportunity to practice the skills they did not address unless they figure out a way to do it themselves.

Many student complaints upon completing a Creative Writing degree or MFA program revolve around this very notion. When searching Google about MFAs, a lot of what pops up will be articles dissuading others from joining these programs. One painfully truthful opinion comes from Caitlin Berve, Creative Writing MFA graduate. Berve warns:

> MFA programs are not publishing programs. They don't have courses on editing, marketing, or anything to do with actually getting your book into the world. In my experience, they also don't have connections in the publishing industry, so they can't make introductions to help you get an internship or entry level job. MFAs in no way prepare you for a career as a writer. They are too focused on the art of writing to help their students figure out how to actually make a living after they graduate.

Although disappointing, this student's experience is not the one that points at these same issues. Whether or not you find this to be a valid claim, this is what she and other students are saying about our programs. It may be time to reevaluate the pedagogical approaches we are taking to ensure that the experiences are practical, realistic, and set students up for success in the real world. Using the avenue of flash fiction to strengthen editorial skills, practice submitting, and give students a taste of what the literary world is actually like means they will have a better chance of turning their dreams into careers.

Active editing should be a requirement to ensure that the student can go into any field related to writing—regardless of what they intend to do after obtaining their degree. Creative writing students need exposure in all regards of the writing world. Many enter a college or graduate program with the wool over their eyes, intending to become famous authors, therefore disregarding studying other available options, including delving into the more likely chance that they could work as an editor. This does not mean that students should be forced to take editing classes, but professors who are aware of this issue should do what they can to incorporate more detailed editing work into their classes. The online platform is an ideal setting to meet these standards. Mock editing duties can be implemented easily through the class discussion board or third-party website meant for specific classes. Integrating assignments that call for rigorous, numerous rounds of dissection analysis on a variety of flash-fiction pieces enforces practices that creative writing graduates need to be familiar with to truly make them into well-rounded, knowledgeable writers who can approach all realms of the writing spectrum.

Conclusion

As writing changes and popular fiction becomes shorter and shorter, colleges need to use the trend as a pedagogical tool for the betterment of their students. The truth is that flash fiction follows strict rules in order to remain effective, and that writers can apply these rules to all writing—regardless of style or form—to create vast improvements in their works. Utilizing flash from online journals is efficient, plentiful, and quick, making it the ultimate resource for an online learning community. Combining the tried, true classic methods of close reading and guiding questions together through the dissection analysis approach provides students with solid critiquing criteria that they can use on any story. Practical application of this criteria makes a connection between writers and their own work. When they can recognize technical aspects in short stories, they can find ways to apply those techniques into their own writing, therefore strengthening their own abilities and works. The mere study of flash outside of the dissection analysis method is pertinent as well, as students can learn the rules of diction and brevity. Using flash-fiction journals to promote working the submission process and editing skills ensures that professors hit all objectives for creative writing courses. Grabbing hold of these resources that are becoming more and more accessible every day makes sense, and when completed in a meaningful way can produce well-rounded graduates who tell stories that matter.

Works cited

Abramson, Seth. *The Insider's Guide to Graduate Degrees in Creative Writing*. London: Bloomsbury, 2018.

Aldama, Frederick. "A Scientific Approach to the Teaching of a Flash Fiction." Research Gate, January 2014. Accessed December 2019.

Bell, James Scott. *Plot & Structure*. Reader's Digest/F+W Publications, 2004.

Berve, Caitlin. "The Truth about an M.F.A. in Creative Writing." Ignited Ink Writing, July 16, 2018. https://www.ignitedinkwriting.com/ignite-your-ink-blog-for-writers/the-truth-about-a-mfa-in-creative-writing/2018. Accessed 9 June 2020.

Darby, Flower. "How to Be a Better Online Teacher: Advice Guide." *The Chronicle for Higher Education*. https://www.chronicle.com/interactives/advice-online-teaching. Accessed February 2020.

Duotrope. duotrope.com. AccessedFebruary 2020.

Education Unlimited. "How Many Universities & Colleges are in the US?", August 2019. https://www.educationunlimited.com/blog/how-many-universities-colleges-are-in-the-us/. Accessed February 2020.

Ganley, Denise. "13 Tips for Writing Flash Fiction." *Flash Fiction Online*, April 2015. http://flashfictiononline.com/main/2015/04/thirteen-tips-for-writing-flash-fiction/. Accessed July 2018.

Haymes, Tom. "Why Do We Still Have Basic Textbooks in Higher Ed?" *eCampus News*, 12 February 2019. https://www.ecampusnews.com/2019/02/12/why-do-we-still-have-basic-textbooks-in-higher-ed/. Accessed 9 June 2020.

King, Stephen. *On Writing: A Memoir of the Craft*. New York: Scribner, 2000.

Lakin, C. S. *5 Editors Tackle the 12 Fatal Flaws of Fiction Writing*. Morgan Hill, CA: Ubiquitous Press., 2015.

Latkar, Ketaki. "Micro Fiction: The New-Age Writing Fad." *Free Press Journal*, May 18, 2017. http://www.freepressjournal.in/featured-blog/micro-fiction-the-new-age- new- age-writing-fad/ 1075708. Accessed July 2018.

MasterClass. "Writing 101: What is Flash Fiction? Learn How to Write Flash Fiction in 7 Steps." MasterClass, August 2019. https://www.masterclass.com/articles/writing-101-what-is-flash-fiction-learn-how-to-write-flash-fiction-in-7-steps#3-characteristics-of-flash-fiction. AccessedFebruary 2020.

New Pages. "New Pages Guide to Student Literary Magazines." https://www.newpages.com/magazines/undergrad-lit-mags. Accessed February 2020.

Poets & Writers. pw.org/literary_magazines. AccessedFebruary 2020.

Teller, Joseph R. "Are We Teaching Composition All Wrong?" *The Chronicle of Higher Education*, October 2016. https://www.chronicle.com/article/Are-We-Teaching-Composition/237969. Accessed February 2020.

The Submission Grinder. thegrinder.diabolicalplots.com. AccessedFebruary 2020.

University of the Potomac. "*Online Learning vs. Traditional Learning.*" https://potomac.edu/learning/online-learning-vs-traditional-learning/. Accessed February 2020.

Williams, Tony. "Flash Fiction." *The Handbook of Creative Writing*, edited by Steven Earnshaw. Edinburgh: Edinburgh University Press, 2014, pp. 315–324.

Index

Adobe Creative Cloud 66
Adobe Creative Suite 62
Affinity Photo 62
Apple iPad Pro 57, 62–64, 66
Apple Keynote 61
Apple Pencil 57
art text 62
assessment 9, 49, 107, 110, 136
Association of Writers and Writing Programs (AWP) 12, 14, 141
asynchronous 31–40, 43, 50, 63, 103–104, 106, 119, 126, 140, 149

Blackboard 10–11, 63–65
blog 105, 129–138

"canned" commentary 36–37
change agent 1, 3
collaboration 7, 47–48, 59, 63, 71, 89, 95, 103
community 8, 9, 31–40, 85, 91, 93, 95, 97, 111, 126
comprehension analysis 152
content warnings 49
creative nonfiction 61, 103, 104, 111

deadlines 53, 55, 58, 64, 66, 106, 139
digital native 10
digital oral histories 89, 96, 99
digital pedagogy 88–89, 95, 98
discussions 12–13, 15, 22, 24, 60, 63, 104
dissection analysis 151–152, 155, 157, 159–162
diversity 70
Dropbox 64, 68

editing 160–162
emails 37, 62, 64, 133–135
exercises 63, 146–147

feedback 36–37, 48, 58, 73, 75–77, 79, 101, 103–111, 136–137, 157–158, 160
flash fiction 146, 149–162

genre 89–91, 93, 95–96, 99
Google Docs 63
Google Forms 133
graduate 57, 59–61
graphic narrative 89, 92–93, 95, 99
graphic novels 89–93

interdisciplinary 22, 88–90, 92–93, 95–96, 98
interpersonal relations 19

language 19–21, 28–29
learning management system 10, 103, 133
low residency 149
luddite 10
lyric poetry 122, 124

macro-editing 57
Master of Fine Arts (MFA) 57, 59–61, 63, 153, 160–161
metacognition 13, 15, 132
microcommunity 105–106
Microsoft OneDrive 63, 64
Microsoft Teams 74
Moodle 74
motivation 4–9

narrative poetry 122, 124
National Writing Project 141, 147
new media 89, 95

Online Learning Consortium (OLC) 10
online writing instruction (OWI) 88, 93, 98
open educational resources (OER) 32

parallel text response 25–26
pedagogy 4, 7–8, 27, 67, 70, 71, 88–90, 92–93, 95–96, 98, 150
persona 17–30
poetry 20, 61, 119–127
Poets & Writers Magazine 149, 161
professional development 8, 13
professional writing 88–90, 92–93, 95, 98
prompts 107–108, 119–127, 135–136, 146–147
prose poetry 121, 125
psychology 2
public writing 131–132, 133–134
publishing 131, 152, 160–161

rapport 102–103
reader response 20
reading 18–21, 24, 63, 69, 119–120, 149–153, 156, 162
reflection 75, 101, 103–104, 111
responding 21, 57, 70, 75, 136–137

self-editing 57, 59–60, 63
social media 38–39, 140
software 57, 59–61
sound writing 91, 95–97

student success 6, 9
synchronous 61

teacher presence 22, 26–27, 31–40, 119–120, 126, 143
teacher writer 57, 59
text expander 62
Think Tank Days 5–6
trauma 67
Twitter 38, 151

undergraduate 60–61

video 65, 71, 119–120, 126–127
word count 106, 108, 134
workshop 57–70, 73–83, 88, 93, 95, 99, 101–111, 153, 157, 160
workshop cover sheet 68–69
writer-based prose 13, 15
Writing Across the Curriculum (WAC) 14
writing samples 35–36

YouTube 61, 65, 74

Zoom 73–87